THE
JOHNNY CASH
DISCOGRAPHY,
1984–1993

Johnny Cash and his wife, June Carter Cash, March 1993.

THE
JOHNNY CASH
DISCOGRAPHY,
1984–1993

Compiled by
John L. Smith

Foreword by Marty Stuart

Discographies, Number 57

Greenwood Press
Westport, Connecticut • London

Library of Congress Cataloging-in-Publication Data

Smith, John L.
    The Johnny Cash discography, 1984–1993 / compiled by John L. Smith
; foreword by Marty Stuart.
       p.   cm.—(Discographies, ISSN 0192–334X ; no. 57)
    Includes bibliographical references (p.   ) and index.
    ISBN 0-313-29167-5
    1. Cash, Johnny—Discography.   I. Title.   II. Series.
ML156.7.C32S58   1994
016.78242′1642′092—dc20   94–6334

British Library Cataloguing in Publication Data is available.

Library of Congress Catalog Card Number: 94–6334
ISBN: 0-313-29167-5
ISSN: 0192-334X

First published in 1994

Greenwood Press, 88 Post Road West, Westport, CT 06881
An imprint of Greenwood Publishing Group, Inc.

Printed in the United States of America

The paper used in this book complies with the
Permanent Paper Standard issued by the National
Information Standards Organization (Z39.48–1984).

10 9 8 7 6 5 4 3 2 1

For Charlene - my partner and best friend. And for Bill Horn Cloud (a.k.a. the "Indian Johnny Cash"), singer and builder of windmills, and Nancy Red Cloud Horn Cloud who are both now one with the spirits. Mitakuye Oyasin.

CONTENTS

FOREWORD
BY MARTY STUART

Wounded Knee, South Dakota

He's like a mountain in the distance that I always keep my eye on. I can see him from anywhere. He never ceases to amaze me. He makes me think. I will always believe in him. Who else could sign a rock and roll record deal when they're 60 years old and then go back to Branson and sing about it? I think a lot of his brilliance lies in these kinds of unpredictable moves that he's famous for. His body, his soul and his works prove that he took a real drink from Life's cup. I'm believing he's got more songs to write and sing and some magic left up his sleeve, all the while drawing his true inspiration from the River of Life that he claims by his own desire. Because he knows Who's waiting on the other side. So, "Sing It Pretty, Sue".

Marty Stuart

PREFACE

As we sat on the back steps of the small log church watching the sun go down and discussing solutions to all the world's problems we certainly were not oblivious to where we were and what had happened here. This was August 1993. Behind us in front of the church lay the long retangular mass grave of Big Foot and some of the members of his Minniconjou Lakota buried here in December 1890. This was Wounded Knee, South Dakota.

We sat there talking of our plans, where we had been and where we wanted to go. My friend recently had his first gold record and seems well on his way to collecting several more in the years ahead. Being somewhat of a history student I was remembering the events of that December in 1890 and thinking how the shadows caused by the setting sun seemed so eerie as we watched them lengthen across the hills. But I also kept thinking of how I needed to meet the deadline of volume two of my Johnny Cash discography. What in the world did this place and this beautiful sunset have to do with the book? Then suddenly I realized it had everything to do with it.

In March 1967 Johnny Cash and I sat in his dressing room backstage at the old KRNT Theater in Des Moines, Iowa. Marshall Grant and Luther Perkins had been there for awhile but soon left to sell pictures to a waiting audience. While John shined his shoes with pieces of newspaper we talked at length about the Native Americans. John's interest was well known to me and he had sung frequently of their plight. In March 1959 he had recorded **OLD APACHE SQUAW** only to have it buried in an album because the record people considered it to be too radical for the public. Then came **IRA HAYES** and the *Bitter Tears* album (CBS/CL-2248/CS-9048). The circumstances surrounding the **IRA HAYES** controversy are well known and despite the initial misunderstanding by some whites, and Natives Americans as well, **IRA HAYES** became a hit for Johnny Cash.

Putting his shoes aside he told me he had just recorded another Indian song that he wanted me to hear. I can still remember John winding and rewinding that reel-to-reel tape machine trying to find the newly recorded **FLINT ARROWHEAD**. He never did find it that day as the time for his second of three shows caused him to head for the stage. As we said our goodbyes we both mentioned how someday soon we would have to find the time to go to South Dakota and visit the Wounded Knee area together.

In 1968 a documentary on Johnny Cash was being filmed by Arthur Barron Productions for the Public Broadcasting System. I received a call saying this would be a great opportunity for our South Dakota adventure and a portion of the trip would be included in the documentary. So December 1968 found us on the Pine Ridge Reservation in southwestern South Dakota. John had done a benefit concert for St. Francis Mission on the Rosebud Reservation the previous evening and the next morning we drove to the Wounded Knee area on Pine Ridge. At this time there was an old trading post/grocery store at the base of what has become known as "Cemetery Hill" at Wounded Knee. This store, a nearby museum and a church which stood on Cemetery Hill were destroyed in 1973 during the American Indian Movement's (AIM) involvement on the Pine Ridge Reservation which would become known as "Wounded Knee II."

But in 1968 the trading post, although small, did a thriving business. Word of our coming had reached the area via the "mocassin telegragh" and we were greeted by a rather sizable crowd. We all crowded into the trading post, film crew included, and John asked if any of them had attended the concert the night before but because of the distance of over a hundred miles nobody from this area had gone. He said that was too bad and if he had brought his guitar he would do a show right there. Suddenly from the back room of the store someone brought out an old black guitar. So there stood Johnny and June Carter Cash in this small historic trading post in the South Dakota outback singing for a crowd of Lakota Indians. A man who had sung for thousands, and before diginitaries, literally the world over, was now putting on probably the smallest "concert" of his career.

After about three or four songs we moved outside where we were met by William Horn Cloud, a direct descendent of a survivor of Wounded Knee in 1890. Also with him were Jesse White Lance and Edgar Red Cloud, a grandson of the famous Red Cloud. As we walked from the trading post up Cemetery Hill, Horn Cloud explained in great detail where Big Foot was camped, how the soldiers were deployed and where the military guns were set up on top of the hill. From the top a grand view of the area could be seen. Horn Cloud pointed out where the women and children and wounded tried to escape into the ravines that snaked their way along in front of us but at a considerable distance. Even though I had been here several times before, I was mesmerized just as John and June were listening to Horn Cloud. I could almost hear the shouts and screams, hear the guns and smell the powder. Then John was shown the mass grave and marble marker on which are carved the names of those buried there. Nobody said a word and the only sound was the blowing of the ever-present South Dakota wind. Then it was time to go.

John and June and I started back for Rapid City and the airport. I purposely took a route through the Badlands that followed, in part, the trail Big Foot took in December 1890. As we drove June soon fell asleep on the back seat. John and I talked for awhile about Wounded Knee and the events leading up to it and the people involved. Then silence. During our trip back to Rapid City we would talk for awhile and then John would take notes for awhile and then put the paper and pencil back in his pocket. This routine was repeated several times during the course of our trip: ask questions and talk, and more writing. Finally, when we reached the airport John told June and me he had written a song about Wounded Knee. With no accompaniment other than tapping his hand on his leg, he sang his newly composed **BIG FOOT**.

The song and footage from our Wounded Knee tour were included in the Barron documentary entitled *"CASH"* which was shown on PBS a few months later. Additional footage was later added to the entire documentary and it was released in commerical theaters as *"Johnny Cash: The Man And His Music."*

In June 1972 John went into his studios at the House of Cash complex and recorded **BIG FOOT** and Columbia Records included it in his *America* album (CBS/KC-31645) later that year.

I have told this story many times over the years to anyone who would listen. And sitting on the church steps on that August evening in 1993 it was all so clear again. William Horn Cloud and his beautiful wife Nancy, who was the great granddaughter of the famous Red Cloud, both passed away in 1992 and with their passing went a part of history. I acted as pall-bearer at William's funeral and John sent a note of condolence.

As I have been preparing this discography and listing the many songs that Johnny Cash has written and/or performed over the span of his almost forty years in the music business, I wonder just how many more stories could be found if one could only have been there.

The following is a brief explanation of the formatting of this volume of the discography. For reference purposes I will refer to the 1985 Johnny Cash discography throughout as volume one and this current listing as volume two.

SESSIONS

The "Sessions" portion of this present volume will differ only slightly from volume one published in 1985. All session dates and recording locations will be underlined. This will be followed by musicians, including producers, if known, who participated in that particular session(s). Master number, song title and composer will be listed along with initial release information. That is: "A" indicates single releases, "B" album releases, and "C" compact discs. All songs throughout the session listing will be given in **bold** print while albums and/or compact discs will be *italicized.* Additional pertinent data will be given in a NOTE within that individual session.

RELEASES

This section will include singles, albums and compact disc releases from 1984 to date. The listings will be given under the label and will include release number and date of release, if known. The albums and compact discs shown here are certainly not considered complete. I do have a separate "catalog" of Cash releases but because of limited space I have tried to include only significant releases with particular emphasis on the current "CD" format. A number of vinyl long-play albums are also included. There have been no major extended-play releases since 1985. However, in their *Sun Records: The Discography* (1987) Colin Escott and Martin Hawkins mention three extended-play albums on the original Sun label assigned numbers of EPA-101, 102, 103 with an advertised release date of October 1957 but never released. No song contents were given and all three apparently were simply titled *Johnny Cash.* (See *The Johnny Cash Discography* [1985] for information pertaining to the six extended-play albums that were released by Sun Records.)

In the very near future I intend to complete work on a manuscript entitled *The Johnny Cash Recording Catalog.* This will be a listing of releases from the United States and several foreign countries.

BILLBOARD CHART LISTINGS

Perhaps the most significant additions to this present volume are the "Billboard Chart Listings" and the following "Sessions Index." I personally checked every issue of *Billboard Magazine* from 1955 through 1991, both the Country charts and Pop charts, for albums and single release entries. In the following I have shown year, month and week-ending dates. Under the dates I have shown the particular placement of a given song and/or album title for that specific week. For example, the first page of chart listings begins with the "Singles: Country Charts" with a date of November 26, 1955 and shows **CRY, CRY, CRY** on the charts at number 14 for one week. In addition to the standard "Country Chart" listings for singles, *Billboard Magazine* also had two supplementary charts which they called "Most Played C&W In Juke Boxes" and "Most Played C&W By Jockeys." The "Juke Boxes" segment ended with the May 27, 1957 issue while the "Jockeys" chart ceased to exist following the October 13, 1958 issue.

APPENDIX A: Pre-1984 Sessions

Some time ago a Johnny Cash fan called me to say he had recently purchased a copy of volume one of the discography and while he was pleased with the overall publication, he was quick to say "But it's wrong!"

Since that first publication in 1985 new information has come to light regarding Sun Records and early CBS material. Through the efforts of Richard Weize at Bear Family Records, Colin Escott and Martin Hawkins, and the Charly Record Company some gaps in the recording career of Johnny Cash have been filled. However, at times the new information also raises new questions. Most of the newly discovered data does not significantly change the existing information. I hope in the future to incorporate volume one and volume two under one cover and at that time make the slight changes in the session material as needed.

I have, however, in this Appendix added material that I feel contributes to the overall integrity of the discography. Some of the data is new but for the most part it is information that simply clarifies already known material. For example, I did mention in volume one Johnny Western's major role in several sessions where he recorded vocal tracks with Cash coming into the studio later and overdubbing his own voice in place of Western's. Now, thanks to Richard Weize we have a better idea of the whole concept of those sessions. The "Million Dollar Quartet" session was purposely omitted the first time around but I explain in this section why I chose to include it now. The August 1974 soundtrack sessions for the railroad documentary were left out of the first volume because I felt, at the time, since they did not appear on a commerical record release, they should not be included. As you will see I have now added them to this present volume because of their significance.

One last comment. It would be naive to think that Johnny Cash, or any artist for that matter, completed every master in one take. And while I have in the past, and continue with this volume, primarily shown only the released master it must be understood each song could require an infinite number of takes. In the Bear Family CD boxed sets *Man In Black, 1954-1958* (BCD-15517) and *Man In Black, 1959-1962* (BCD-15562) Richard Weize has included one entire CD devoted solely to outtakes, along with a sprinkling of alternate takes throughout the remaining CDs.

So to my "But it's wrong!" caller, given the information available to me at the time in the form of recorded and printed data and personal interviews with the individuals involved I can only answer as perhaps Ol' Waylon would have been tempted to do: "I'm just doin' the best I can with what I got, Hoss."

APPENDIX B: Alphabetical "Billboard" Chart Entries

I have also included a cross-reference table listing all songs (s) and albums/CD (a) in alphabetical order following the actual listings. This table gives single release and/or album/CD number, when it first entered the charts, how many weeks it remained on the charts and its peak position. If an entry reached number one and held that position for more than one week then the number of weeks at number one will be given in parenthesis. Those titles followed by (+) indicates "Most Played C&W In Juke Boxes" chart; (++) "Most Played C&W By Jockeys" and (*) indicates a Pop chart entry. Record company abbreviations used in the table include: "A/S" = American/Smash Records; "CBS" = Columbia Records; "CL" = Cachet Records; "M/P" = Mercury/Polygram Records; "Sun" = original Sun Records; "SUN" = Sun International.

SESSIONS INDEX

This section will include not only an index of data from the current discography "Sessions" section but also from the 1985 edition. I have tried to keep the two volumes separate by showing the first volume as (I) and the second volume as (II). I cannot, obviously, go back and change entries as they appear in volume one. But I have tried to simplify certain entries as they appear in volume two and consequently how they read in the index. The prime example is the way I have treated "Carter Family," "New Carter Family" and "Carter Sisters." With a couple of exceptions I have elected to list the individual members of the Carter Family/Sisters and, as a result, Anita and Helen Carter will have separate entries in the index as will June Carter Cash and Carlene Carter. I will, however, also list "June Carter" primarily as the name pertains to composer credits.

Again, the ideal situation would have been to incorporate the 1985 edition with this present volume, thereby including all the changes that have been discovered over the past ten years. Unfortunately, that is not the case at present. But it is hoped that this present volume will be an adequate companion to the 1985 edition and through the use of the "Billboard" and "Sessions Index" sections the two volumes can be made to merge and complement each other.

As always, the final comments should be that I do take full responsibility for the accuracy of the information contained within these pages and would hope that any mistakes discovered by readers would be brought to my attention for correction.

ACKNOWLEDGEMENTS

This is where the discographer becomes humble and thanks all those persons who have assisted him in his compilation. But for those few brave souls who have ever attempted an in-depth discography, the scope of humility is an ever widening circle. From their own families to record companies, musicians, fans and the artists themselves, the discographer needs the support and cooperation of them all. And if you're "lucky" at some point it all starts to make sense and fall into place.

I could have easily duplicated the "Acknowledgements" section of the 1985 publication which I will refer to throughout these pages unofficially as "volume one." For the most part the same people continued their support over the past ten years as helped in the beginning. There have also been some new faces who came to my aid as well and I will attempt to list them here and hope I do not omit anyone.

The people of Greenwood Publishing Group have shown kindness and great patience with me over the past ten years. That cooperation has continued with this present volume thanks to editor, Alicia Merritt. Our many long-distance conversations were very pleasant and enlightening and, on occasion, even pertained to the manuscript.

Lilian Larsson from Sweden has kept me updated with Cash's European releases. She is also responsible for some great additions to my personal record collection.

The Johnny Cash Fan Club, with Curtis and Alma Todd and Ray and Jeanne Witherell as co-presidents, has continued sending me the newsletters and journals whose pages are filled with information and shows the depth of feelings of Johnny Cash fans the world over.

We fans of Johnny Cash certainly owe Richard Weize of Bear Family Records in Germany an enormous debt for the boxed sets he has brought forth in the past few years. In some cases he has shown me the error of my ways by bringing to light additional information concerning Cash's early Sun and Columbia sessions. Unfortunately, because of repetition I cannot go back and revise that material in this volume. Beside Bear Family, Charly Records of England has maintained a steady flow of Sun material. If fans of Sun Records, and Johnny Cash in particular, have the Bear Family and Charly Records in their collection they are to be commended.

To Twylla and Virgil Kerr for opening the windows of Microsoft Word for me and thereby raising my trauma level to new heights--"Thank You" (I think).

Carolyn Austin, of the Nashville Musicians Union, has kept me updated with session information just as her predecessor, Pat Maguire, did for so many years.

Johnny Western, now a DJ for KFDI Radio in Wichita, Kansas, and former member of the Johnny Cash traveling show, knows the admiration for the man that fills these pages. And I feel very fortunate that he allowed me to be part of the production of the Bear Family box set entitled "Johnny Western: Heroes And Cowboys" (BCD-15552). Some of that material involved Cash and the Tennessee Three.

And then, of course, there is the "Mad-Hatter." I first met Marty Stuart in Des Moines, Iowa in February 1980 when he played his first show as a member of the Cash troupe. Since that time we have become friends. I have introduced him to my world and he has allowed me to have as much of a glimpse of his as I care to see. We have traveled some main roads and some back roads together and have discussed Johnny Cash, the man and his music, frequently. Marty is a singer, songwriter, musician, producer, historian and future super-star and soon to become the next "twenty-year" overnight sensation. At this writing he has achieved his first gold record--and I have to believe only the first of many. When it comes time to write the "Marty Stuart Discography," I want to be first in line. Marty wrote the "Foreword" for this volume as we were traveling one of those back roads on our way to the reservation. He read it to me as we sat alone on the back steps of a small log church atop "Cemetery Hill" at Wounded Knee, South Dakota. (Pila, Kola.)

I have to mention my "bevy of blondes" -- my wife, Charlene, and daughters, Jennifer and Jessi. They share in my admiration and adulation for Johnny Cash. They have sacrified valuable time so I could devote to this discographical research but in so doing I think they have come to see John the way I do, more than a performer, more than a public figure.

The House of Cash organization and Hugh Waddell have always been there to answer questions or at the very least point me in the right direction. Hugh and I held many a lengthy conversation in the latter stages of this manuscript preparation, especially as it pertained to the material done under the watchful eye, and ear, of Rick Rubin. Reba Hancock, John's sister and office manager, makes the entire discography process seem easy. I once said that a measure of an organization is a reflection of the performer. I should take that a step further and include band members and road crew as well. Jay Duro and his small group are the ones that do most of the "fetchin' and carryin'" so we can sit and enjoy a Johnny Cash Show. The mere fact that these same individuals had been with John for this long says enough.

Lou Robin deserves special mention for his tireless devotion to the whole Johnny Cash concept. And I believe his frontline interference for the Cash road show, and consequently his battle scars acquired over time, makes him eligible for more than one purple heart.

Over the years a Johnny Cash Show has become more than just good music and entertainment for me and my family. They have become "events." I treasure the visits with John and June in ways they will never know. His letters to me and members of my family have literally been a source of inspiration, especially earlier this year. His dedication to this recording history over the years has taken many forms, but perhaps none as important as his participation in seeing to it that I received precise information pertaining to the Rick Rubin supervised "sessions" as well as those he did in the privacy of his own Cedar Hill Refuge facility.

When that fifth face is carved on Mt. Rushmore I have to believe it will be Johnny Cash.

At this writing John has signed what amounts to a lifetime recording contract with American Records. I can't wait to get started on volume three!

THE
JOHNNY CASH
DISCOGRAPHY,
1984–1993

SESSIONS

February 22, 1984
1111 Sound Studio or Soundshop Studio, Nashville, Tennessee
Ray Charles, vocal; "A" Strings; Pete Bordonall, electric guitar; JOHNNY CASH, vocal; Pete Drake, steel guitar; Kenneth Malone, drums; Terry McMillan, harmonica, percussion; Louis Nunley, vocal harmony; Hargus Robbins, keyboard; Judy Rodman, vocal harmony; Billy Sanford, Dale Sellers, acoustic guitars; Henry Strzelecki, bass; Wendy Suits, vocal harmony; Hershel Wiginton, vocal harmony. Prod. Billy Sherrill.

NCO-135312 **CRAZY OLD SOLDIER** (Paul Kennerley-Troy Seals)
  A - CBS/38-04860 b/w **It Ain't Gonna Worry My Mind** (w/o Cash)
  B - CBS/FC-39415 *Friendship*

NOTE: The exact studio location for this Ray Charles session is unknown. The two locations given above were taken from the album jacket.
==
May 8, 1984 (10a-1p)
1111 Sound Studio, Nashville, Tennessee
Marty Stuart, guitar. Overdub session only. Prod. Billy Sherrill.

NCO-135370 **CHICKEN IN BLACK** (G. Gentry)
  A - CBS/38-04513 b/w **Battle Of Nashville**
  B - CBS/NE-1278 *Four Star Country*

NOTE: See also note for session dated April 12, 1984 - 1st session in volume one. A music video was made using the soundtrack of this song. I originally showed this master as released from the first session on April 12, 1984 in volume one. However, information since that publication has revealed this additional overdub session.
==
May 17, 1984 (2p-5:15p)
1111 Sound Studio, Nashville, Tennessee
Johnny Cash, vocal, guitar; Pete Drake, steel guitar; Jerry Kennedy, guitar; Kenneth Malone, drums; Terry McMillan, harmonica; Hargus Robbins, piano; Billy Sanford, electric guitar; Dale Sellers, rhythm guitar; Marty Stuart, guitar; John Williams, electric

bass; Bobby Wood, piano. Prod. Billy Sherrill.

NCO-135462 **I KNOW YOU LOVE ME** (Joe Chambers-Larry Jenkins)

NCO-135465 **IF I TOLD YOU WHO IT WAS** (Bobby Braddock-Curly Putnam)

NCO-135468 **YOU GIVE ME MUSIC** (John R. Cash)
   (see overdub session: June 1, 1984)

MOVIN' ON
(see overdub session: May 18, 1984 - 1st session)

NOTE: The Musicians Union gives this date for **I KNOW YOU LOVE ME** while CBS
Records shows May 18, 1984.
==
May 18, 1984 - 1st session (10a-1:30p)
1111 Sound Studio, Nashville, Tennessee
Marty Stuart, guitar. Overdub session only. Prod. Billy Sherrill.

NCO-135468 **YOU GIVE ME MUSIC** (John R. Cash)
   (see overdub session: June 1, 1984)

MOVIN' ON

NOTE: Musicians Union files list this first master as **I GIVE YOU LOVE** for this
session.
==
May 18, 1984 - 2nd session (2p-5p)
1111 Sound Studio, Nashville, Tennessee
Johnny Cash, vocal, guitar; June Carter Cash, vocal; Pete Drake, steel guitar; Jerry
Kennedy, guitar; Kenneth Malone, drums; Terry McMillan, harmonica; Hargus Robbins,
piano; Billy Sanford, electric guitar; Dale Sellers, rhythm guitar; Marty Stuart, guitar;
Bobby Wood, piano; Robert Wray, guitar. Prod. Billy Sherrill.

NCO-135463 **MY ELUSIVE DREAMS** (Curly Putnam-Billy Sherrill)
   (see overdub session: June 1, 1984)

NCO-135464 **BABY RIDE EAST** (Richard Dobson)

==
June 1, 1984 (2p-5p)
1111 Sound Studio, Nashville, Tennessee
John Catchings, cello; Mark Feldman, violin; Richard Grosjean, Victoria Haltom,
Theodore Madsen, Robert Mason, Phyllis Mazza, Conni McCollister, unknown
instruments; William McElhiney, trumpet; Laura Molyneaux, William Puett, unknown
instruments; Samuel Terranova, violin; Alan Umstead, unknown instrument; Kristin
Wilkinson, viola. Overdub session only. Prod. Billy Sherrill.

NCO-135463 **MY ELUSIVE DREAMS** (Curly Putnam-Billy Sherrill)

I STILL MISS SOMEONE (John R. Cash-R. Cash Jr)

NCO-135468 **YOU GIVE ME MUSIC** (John R. Cash)

NCO-135373 **I CAME TO BELIEVE** (John R. Cash)

NOTE: This is the first listing of **I STILL MISS SOMEONE** and the original session date for this master is unknown at this time.

==

June 14, 1984 (10a-1p)
1111 Sound Studio, Nashville, Tennessee
Johnny Cash, vocal, guitar; Pete Drake, steel guitar; Jerry Kennedy, guitar; Kenneth Malone, drums; Terry McMillan, harmonica; Hargus Robbins, piano; Billy Sanford, Dale Sellers, electric guitar; Marty Stuart, Robert Wray, guitar. Prod. Billy Sherrill.

NCO-135466 **SHE USED TO LOVE ME** (K. Fleming-D. Morgan-C. Quillen)

NCO-135467 **CALL YOUR MOTHER** (John R. Cash)

==

October 2, 1984 - 3 sessions (10a-1p;2p-5p;6p-9p)
Woodland Studio, Nashville, Tennessee
Johnny Cash, vocal, guitar; Joe Barry Bailey, guitar; Gene Chrisman, drums; James Cobb, guitar; Bob Emmons, keyboard; Mike Leech, bass; Marty Stuart, guitar, mandolin; Bobby Wood, keyboards. Prod. Chips Moman.

NCO-135611 **THEY KILLED HIM** (Kris Kristofferson)
    (see overdub/release session: October 8, 1984)

NCO-135612 **AGAINST THE WIND** (Bob Seger)
    (see session: Late 1984)

NCO-135613 **EASY STREET** (Chips Moman-Bobby Emmons)
    A - CBS/38-05672 b/w **I'm Leaving Now**
    B - CBS/FC-39951 *Rainbow*

NOTE: When **AGAINST THE WIND** was released on the *Highwayman* album (FC-40056) Waylon and Willie were included. However, no mention is made of either of them at this session. This could have been either re-made or overdubbed at a later session. When this master of **EASY STREET** was released it included strings and vocal harmony. No session(s) show strings but the album jacket does show vocal harmony as: June Carter Cash, James Cobb, Paul Davis, Chips Moman, Marty Stuart, Toni Wine and Bobby Wood. Waylon is also mentioned but he is not on any of these masters.

==

October 3, 1984 (10a-1p)
Woodland Studio, Nashville, Tennessee
Johnny Cash, vocal, guitar; Joe Barry Bailey, guitar; Gene Chrisman, drums; James Cobb, guitar; Bob Emmons, keyboard; Mike Leech, bass; Marty Stuart, guitar, mandolin; Bobby Wood, keyboards. Prod. Chips Moman.

EVERYTHING YOU WANTED TO KNOW ABOUT DRINKING

NOTE: See session dated September 3, 1986 - 3rd session for a probable re-make of this master.

==

October 8, 1984 (6p-9p)
Moman Studio, Nashville, Tennessee
Joe Barry Bailey, guitar; Bob Emmons, keyboard; Reggie Young, guitar. Overdub session only. Prod. Chips Moman.

NCO-135611 **THEY KILLED HIM** (Kris Kristofferson)
   A - CBS/38-04740 b/w **Three Bells**

==

December 4, 1984 - 2 sessions (2p-5p;6p-9p)
Moman Studio, Nashville, Tennessee
Johnny Cash, vocal, guitar; Gene Chrisman, drums; James Cobb, guitar; Bob Emmons, keyboard; Jack Hale, Wayne Jackson, brass -1; Mike Leech, bass; Marty Stuart, guitar, mandolin -2; Bobby Wood, keyboard; Reggie Young, guitar. Prod. Chips Moman.

LOVE IS THE WAY (Kris Kristofferson)

NCO-135670 **HAVE YOU EVER SEEN THE RAIN** (John Fogerty)
   B - CBS/FC-39951 *Rainbow*

NCO-135673 **LOVE ME LIKE YOU USED TO** (Bobby Emmons)
   B - CBS/FC-39951 *Rainbow*

NCO-136010 **THEY'RE ALL THE SAME** -1,2 (Willie Nelson)
   B - CBS/FC-39951 *Rainbow*

NOTE: All three of these released masters used vocal harmony which could have included: June Carter Cash, James Cobb, Paul Davis, Chips Moman, Marty Stuart, Toni Wine and Bobby Wood. Both **THEY'RE ALL THE SAME** and **LOVE ME LIKE YOU USED TO** include strings on the released versions but no mention is made in any session information. No horns were mentioned for this session either but **THEY'RE ALL THE SAME** does use them and so Hale and Jackson have been added to this session. The strings and horns were probably added at some overdub session.

==

December 5, 1984 - 2 sessions (2p-5p;6p-9p)
Moman Studio, Nashville, Tennessee
Johnny Cash, vocal, guitar; Gene Chrisman, drums; James Cobb, guitar; Bob Emmons, keyboard; Mike Leech, bass; Marty Stuart, guitar, mandolin -1; Bobby Wood, keyboard; Reggie Young, guitar. Prod. Chips Moman.

AMERICAN BY BIRTH (R.A. Wade)

NCO-135668 **UNWED MOTHERS (FATHERS)** -1 (Bobby Braddock-John Prine)
   B - CBS/FC-39951 *Rainbow*

NCO-135669 **HERE COMES THAT RAINBOW** (Kris Kristofferson)
  B - CBS/FC-39951 *Rainbow*

MAYBE YOU SHOULD HAVE BEEN LISTENING

NOTE: The released master of **HERE COMES THAT RAINBOW** included strings and vocal harmony; **UNWED MOTHERS (FATHERS)** included vocal harmony. The vocal harmony probably consisted of: June Carter Cash, James Cobb, Paul Davis, Chips Moman, Marty Stuart, Toni Wine and Bobby Wood. No overdub session is given for either the vocals or strings. **AMERICAN BY BIRTH** was re-made on December 5, 1985 and retitled **DIXIE**.

December 6, 1984 - 2 sessions (2p-5p;6p-9p)
Moman Studio, Nashville, Tennessee
Johnny Cash, vocal, guitar; Earl Ball, piano-second session only; Gene Chrisman, drums; James Cobb, guitar; Bobby Emmons, keyboard; Mike Leech, bass; Marty Stuart, guitar, mandolin; Bobby Wood, piano-first session only; Reggie Young, guitar. Prod. Chips Moman.

I STILL MISS SOMEONE (John R. Cash-Roy Cash Jr)

HIGHWAYMAN (Jimmy Webb)

NOTE: When **HIGHWAYMAN** was released on the album of the same name (CBS/FC-40056) it included Willie, Waylon and Kristofferson with vocals. Since none of these individuals are mentioned at this session this master was either re-made or overdubbed at a later session. See session dated "Late 1984".

Late 1984
Moman Studio/Woodland Sound Studio, Nashville, Tennessee
Johnny Cash, vocal, guitar; Gene Chrisman, drums; James Cobb, guitar; Paul Davis, keyboard, vocal harmony; Bobby Emmons, keyboard; Waylon Jennings, vocal, electric guitar -1; Kris Kristofferson, vocal -2; Mike Leech, electric bass; Chips Moman, guitar, vocal harmony; Willie Nelson, vocal, guitar; Mickey Raphael, harmonica; Johnny Rodriguez, vocal -3; Marty Stuart, guitar, mandolin; Jimmy Tittle, electric bass; Bobby Wood, keyboards; Reggie Young, guitar. Prod. Chips Moman.

NCO-135612 **AGAINST THE WIND** -1 (Bob Seger)
  B - CBS/FC-40056 *Highwayman*

NCO-135671 **HIGHWAYMAN** -1,2 (Jimmy Webb)
  A - CBS/38-04881 b/w **The Human Condition** (w/Willie Nelson)
  B - CBS/FC-40056 *Highwayman*

NCO-135746 **LAST COWBOY SONG** -1,2 (E. Bruce-R. Peterson)
  B - CBS/FC-40056 *Highwayman*

NCO-135747 **TWENTIETH CENTURY IS ALMOST OVER** (S. Goodman-J. Prine)
   A - CBS/38-05594 b/w **Desperados Waiting For A Train** (w/Waylon, Willie, Kris)
   B - CBS/FC-40056 *Highwayman*

NCO-135748 **DEPORTEE** -3 (W. Guthrie-M. Hoffman)
   B - CBS/FC-40056 *Highwayman*

NCO-135750 **BIG RIVER** -1,2 (John R. Cash)
   B - CBS/FC-40056 *Highwayman*

NCO-135751 **COMMITTED TO PARKVIEW** (John R. Cash)
   B - CBS/FC-40056 *Highwayman*

NCO-135758 **JIM, I WORE A TIE TODAY** (C. Walker)
   B - CBS/FC-40056 *Highwayman*

NCO-135759 **DESPERADOS WAITING FOR A TRAIN** -1,2 (Guy Clark)
   A - CBS/38-05594 b/w **Twentieth Century Is Almost Over** (w/Willie Nelson)
   B - CBS/FC-40056 *Highwayman*

NCO-135760 **WELFARE LINE** -1,2 (Paul Kennerley)
   B - CBS/FC-40056 *Highwayman*

NOTE: See note for session dated October 2, 1984 for **AGAINST THE WIND**; see note for session dated December 6, 1984 for **HIGHWAYMAN**. The above master of **BIG RIVER** includes the verse Cash had to omit when he originally recorded it for Sun Records - see session dated November 12, 1957. A music video was made using the soundtrack of **HIGHWAYMAN**. Cash originally recorded **JIM, I WORE A TIE TODAY** on March 27, 1979 - 2nd session and was overdubbed on May 19, 1979 - 3rd session but never released. Willie Nelson was not on the 1979 master.
==

Unknown 1984 Sessions
Moman Studio, Nashville, Tennessee
Johnny Cash, vocal, guitar; Anita, Helen Carter, June Carter Cash, vocal harmony -1; Willie Nelson, vocal -2; remaining musicians unknown. Prod. Chips Moman.

   HUMAN CONDITION -2 (J. Cobb)
   A - CBS/38-04881 b/w **Highwayman** (w/Kris, Waylon, Willie)

NCO-135749 **BORDERLINE (A MUSICIAL WHODUNIT)**
            (Chips Moman-Bobby Emmons)
   B - CBS/FC-39951 *Rainbow*

   THREE BELLS -1 (B. Reisfeld-J. Villard)
   A - CBS/38-04740 b/w **They Killed Him**

NOTE: The album jacket for the *Rainbow* album (CBS/FC-39951) lists musicians but it is not known which of them appeared only on this master of **BORDERLINE**. This master also includes vocal harmony and horns which included: June Carter Cash, James

Cobb, Paul Davis, Chips Moman, Marty Stuart, Toni Wine and Bobby Wood, vocal harmony; Jack Hale and Wayne Jackson, brass.

===

Possibly Early 1985
Music Mill Studio, Nashville, Tennessee
Karen Brooks, vocal; Eddie Bayers, drums; Barry Beckett, keyboard, synthesizers; JOHNNY CASH, vocal; Mark Casstevens, guitar; Sonny Garrish, steel guitar; Dan Kirkpatrick, guitar; Mac McAnally, vocal harmony; Terry McMillan, percussion, harmonica; Bill Payne, keyboard; Michael Rhodes, bass; Randy Sharp, synthesizer, vocal harmony; Wendy Waldman, vocal harmony, Paul Worley, guitar. Prod. Barry Beckett.

DTN-2401   **I WILL DANCE WITH YOU** (Jack W. Routh)
  A - WARNER BROTHERS/7-28979 b/w **Too Bad For Love** (w/o Cash)
  B - WARNER BROTHERS/1-25277 *I Will Dance With You*

NOTE: The exact date of this session is unknown. It is placed here because the Warner Brothers single by Karen Brooks, **I WILL DANCE WITH YOU** (WARNER BROTHERS/7-28979), was released in July 1985. It is not known which of the above personnel appeared on this session.

===

February 4, 1985
Cartee 3 Studio, Nashville, Tennessee
Waylon Jennings, vocal, guitar; Jerry Bridges, bass; JOHNNY CASH, vocal; Sonny Curtis, guitar; Jim Haber, piano; Patti Leatherwood, vocal harmony; Ralph Mooney, steel guitar; Dan Mustoe, drums; Earl Scruggs, banjo; Gary Scruggs, Randy Scruggs, guitar; Tony Joe White, guitar, vocal harmony. Prod. Jerry Bridges-Gary Scruggs.

FWA5-2857   **BE CAREFUL WHO YOU LOVE (ARTHUR'S SONG)**
       (Harlan Howard)
  B - RCA/AHL1-7184 *Sweet Mother Texas* (Waylon Jennings)

===

May 21, 1985 - 2 sessions (2p-5p;6p-9p)
Moman Studio, Nashville, Tennessee
Johnny Cash, vocal, guitar; Waylon Jennings, vocal, guitar; Gene Chrisman, drums; Bobby Emmons, keyboard; Mike Leech, bass; Jerry Shook, guitar; Marty Stuart, guitar, mandolin -1; Jimmy Tittle, bass; Bobby Wood, piano; Reggie Young, guitar. Prod. Chips Moman.

NCO-136208 **FOLKS OUT ON THE ROAD** (E. Raven-F. Myers-D. Powelson)
  (see overdub/release session: December 7, 1985)

NCO-136206 **BALLAD OF FORTY DOLLARS** (Tom T. Hall)
  A - CBS/38-06287 b/w **Field Of Diamonds** (w/Waylon Jennings)
  B - CBS/FC-40347 *Heroes*

NCO-136209 **I'M NEVER GONNA ROAM AGAIN** -1 (Rodney Crowell)
  (see overdub/release session: December 7, 1985)

NOTE: Possible steel guitar on **BALLAD OF FORTY DOLLARS**.

===

May 22, 1985 - 2 sessions (10a-1p;2p-5p)
Moman Studio, Nashville, Tennessee
Johnny Cash, vocal, guitar; Waylon Jennings, vocal, guitar; Gene Chrisman, drums; Bobby Emmons, keyboard; Mike Leech, bass; Jerry Shook, guitar; Marty Stuart, guitar; Jimmy Tittle, bass; Bobby Wood, piano; Reggie Young, guitar. Prod. Chips Moman.

NCO-136203 **HEROES** (J. Kimball-T. Kimmel)
(see overdub/release session: December 7, 1985)

NCO-136207 **ONE TOO MANY MORNINGS** (Bob Dylan)
(see overdub/release session: December 7, 1985)

NCO-136204 **EVEN COWGIRLS GET THE BLUES** (Rodney Crowell)
A - CBS/38-05896 b/w **American By Birth** (w/Waylon Jennings)
B - CBS/FC-40347 *Heroes*

NOTE: **HEROES** includes strings and vocal harmony on released take.

===

May 23, 1985 - 2 sessions (2p-5p;6p-9p)
Moman Studio, Nashville, Tennessee
Johnny Cash, vocal, guitar; Waylon Jennings, vocal, guitar; Gene Chrisman, drums; Bobby Emmons, keyboard; Mike Leech, bass; Jerry Shook, guitar; Marty Stuart, guitar; Jimmy Tittle, bass; Bobby Wood, piano; Reggie Young, guitar. Prod. Chips Moman.

NCO-136205 **I WILL ALWAYS LOVE YOU (IN MY OWN CRAZY WAY)**
(T. Seals-E. Setser-F. Miller)
(see overdub/release session: December 7, 1985)

NCO-136210 **FIELD OF DIAMONDS** (John R. Cash-Jack W. Routh)
(see overdub/release session: December 7, 1985)

NOTE: Musician Union information shows **FIELD OF DIAMONDS** listed as **FEEL THE DIAMONDS IN THE SKY**.

===

July 11, 1985 - 2 sessions (2p-5p;6p-9p)
Moman Studio, Nashville, Tennessee
Johnny Cash, vocal, guitar; Waylon Jennings, vocal, guitar; Gene Chrisman, drums; Bobby Emmons, keyboard; Mike Leech, bass; Jerry Shook, guitar; Marty Stuart, guitar; Jimmy Tittle, bass; Bobby Wood, piano; Reggie Young, guitar. Prod. Chips Moman.

NCO-135994 **I'M LEAVING NOW** (John R. Cash)
(see overdub/release session: July 31, 1985)

NCO-135992 **CASEY'S LAST RIDE** (Kris Kristofferson)
B - CBS/FC-39951 *Rainbow*

NCO-135995 **OLD LONESOME**

NOTE: **CASEY'S LAST RIDE** includes horns and vocal harmony. The horns were provided by Jack Hale and Wayne Jackson while the harmony included: June Carter Cash, James Cobb, Paul Davis, Chips Moman, Marty Stuart, Toni Wine and Bobby Wood. No overdub session was given.

==

July 23, 1985 (6p-9p)
Moman Studio, Nashville, Tennessee
Johnny Cash, vocal, guitar; Gene Chrisman, drums; Bobby Emmons, keyboard; Mike Leech, bass; Jerry Shook, guitar; Marty Stuart, guitar; Jimmy Tittle, bass; Bobby Wood, piano; Reggie Young, guitar. Possible overdub session only. Prod. Chips Moman.

NCO-135994 **I'M LEAVING NOW** (John R. Cash)
    (see overdub/release session: July 31, 1985)

NOTE: It is not clear from session information from the Musicians Union whether this was a re-make or an overdub session.

==

July 31, 1985 (2p-5p)
Moman Studio, Nashville, Tennessee
Jack Hale, brass; Marty Stuart, guitar; Wayne Jackson, brass. Overdub session only. Prod. Chips Moman.

NCO-135994 **I'M LEAVING NOW** (John R. Cash)
    A - CBS/38-05672 b/w **Easy Street**
    B - CBS/FC-39951 *Rainbow*

NOTE: See note for session dated July 23, 1985. This song was reissued in 1989 b/w **RAGGED OLD FLAG**. (See note for session dated January 28, 1974 in volume one.)
==

August 15, 1985 - 2 sessions (2p-5p;6p-9p)
Moman Studio, Nashville, Tennessee
Johnny Cash, vocal, guitar; Jerry Carrigan, guitar; Bobby Emmons, keyboard; Mike Leech, bass; Bobby Wood, piano; Reggie Young, guitar. Prod. Chips Moman.

NCO-135993 **YOU BEAT ALL I EVER SAW** (John R. Cash)
    B - CBS/FC-39951 *Rainbow*

NOTE: The released master included strings and vocal harmony. The harmony was probably provided by: June Carter Cash, Waylon Jennings, Chips Moman, Toni Wine and Bobby Wood. Information from CBS Records indicates this master was done on January 3, 1984 but information from the Musicians Union gives this date.
==

September 1985
Sun Recording Studio/American Studio, Memphis, Tennessee
Johnny Cash, guitar, vocal; Ace Cannon, horn -1; June Carter Cash, vocal -2; Gene Chrisman, drums; Jack Clement, guitar, vocal harmony -3; James Cobb, guitar; Paul Davis, vocal harmony -4; Dave Edmunds, vocal harmony -5; Bobby Emmons, keyboards,

synclavier -6; Rebecca Evans, vocal harmony -7; John Fogerty, vocal harmony -8; Jack Hale, Jr., horn -9; Buddy Harmon, drums; W.S. Holland, drums; Wayne Jackson, horn - 10; The Judds - Wynonna, Naomi, vocal harmony -11; Mike Leech, bass; Bob Lewin, horn -12; Jerry Lee Lewis, keyboard, vocal -13; Kenneth Lovelace, guitar; Memphis Strings -14; Chips Moman, vocal harmony -15; Bob Moore, bass; Rick Nelson, vocal harmony -16; Roy Orbison, vocal -17; Dan Penn, vocal harmony -18; Carl Perkins, guitar, vocal -19; Sam Phillips, vocal harmony -20; Marty Stuart, guitar, vocal harmony -21; Toni Wine, vocal harmony -22; Bobby Wood, keyboards, vocal harmony -23; Bob Wootton, guitar; Reggie Young, guitar. Prod. Chips Moman.

2-58327   **CLASS OF '55** -13,17,19 (Chips Moman-Bobby Emmons)
A - M/P-888-142-7 b/w **We Remember The King** (w/Lewis, Orbison, Perkins)
B - M/P-830-002-1 *Class Of '55*

2-58328   **WAYMORE'S BLUES** -13,17,19 (Waylon Jennings-Curtis Buck)
B - M/P-830-002-1 *Class Of '55*

2-58329   **WE REMEMBER THE KING** -1,3,4,9,10,12,14,17,18,21,22,23
(Paul Kennerley)
A - M/P-888-142-7 b/w **Class Of '55** (w/Lewis, Orbison, Perkins)
B - M/P-830-002-1 *Class Of '55*

2-58331   **ROCK AND ROLL (FAIS DO DO)** -1,6,9,10,12,13,14,17,19
(Michael Smotherman)
A - M/P-884-760-7 b/w **Birth Of Rock And Roll** (Perkins only)
B - M/P-830-002-1 *Class Of '55*

2-58332   **I WILL ROCK AND ROLL WITH YOU** -1,9,10,12 (John R. Cash)
B - M/P-830-002-1 *Class Of '55*

2-58334   **BIG TRAIN** -2,3,5,7,8,11,13,15,16,17,19,20,21,22 (John C. Fogerty)
B - M/P-830-002-1 *Class Of '55*

NOTE: These six masters appear in the album entitled *Class of '55* (830-002-1) released in commerical record outlets on the America/Smash label (Mercury/Polygram) in June 1986. It is not known which of the above musicians played on which masters unless indicated by a number. This same album was offered through a television promotion and included a 28-page booklet entitled *"Sun Record Reunion: Together Again In Memphis"* written by Jim Dickerson with pictures and other insights into the recording sessions. However, the label on the television offering was different than the album available through commerical outlets. The television album was numbered AR/LP-1001 (America Records). It also included in the same album jacket a second record of interviews with several of the participants involved in the sessions, including Cash.

The format for the credits given on the back of the album jackets varies somewhat as well. The above mentioned booklet indicates Cash did **HOME OF THE BLUES** at these sessions but was not included on the album. While the booklet gives a day-to-day summary of the sessions it does not mention all the titles and where they were recorded. It does say that **HOME OF THE BLUES** and **WAYMORE'S BLUES** were done at the Sun Studios while **WE REMEMBER THE KING** and **BIG TRAIN (FROM**

MEMPHIS) were done at American Sound Studios.

===

December 5, 1985 - 1st/2nd sessions (10a-1p;2p-5p)
Moman Studio, Nashville, Tennessee
Johnny Cash, vocal, guitar; Waylon Jennings, vocal, guitar; David Davidson, Richard Grosjean, Connie Heard, Anthony LaMarchina, unknown instruments-probably strings; Mike Leech, bass; Theodore Madsen, Robert Mason, Phyllis Mazza, Conni McCollister, Laura Molyneaux, Kathryn Plummer, Alan Umstead, Catherine Umstead, unknown instruments-probably strings; Kristin Wilkinson, viola. Prod. Chips Moman.

NCO-136205 **I WILL ALWAYS LOVE YOU (IN MY OWN CRAZY WAY)**
            (T. Seals-E. Setser-F. Miller)
       (see overdub/release session: December 7, 1985)

NCO-136207 **ONE TOO MANY MORNINGS** (Bob Dylan)
       (see overdub/release session: December 7, 1985)

NCO-136210 **FIELD OF DIAMONDS** (John R. Cash-Jack W. Routh)
       (see overdub/release session: December 7, 1985)

NCO-136209 **I'M NEVER GONNA ROAM AGAIN** (Rodney Crowell)
       (see overdub/release session: December 7, 1985)

NCO-136208 **FOLKS OUT ON THE ROAD** (E. Raven-F. Myers-D. Powelson)
       (see overdub/release session: December 7, 1985)

NCO-136211 **LOVE IS THE WAY** (Kris Kristofferson)
       (see overdub/release session: December 7, 1985)

NOTE: This could be an overdub session. **FIELD OF DIAMONDS** (May 23, 1985), **I'M NEVER GONNA ROAM AGAIN** (May 21, 1985), **FOLKS OUT ON THE ROAD** (May 21, 1985) have appeared before. **LOVE IS THE WAY** appears here for the first time. It was given on Musician Union information as **LOVE IS THE ANSWER** and **ONE TOO MANY MORNINGS** was given as **A THOUSAND MILES BEHIND**. Cash does not appear as vocalist on **I WILL ALWAYS LOVE YOU** unless he is involved instrumentally.

===

December 5, 1985 - 3rd session (6p-9:30p)
Moman Studio, Nashville, Tennessee
Johnny Cash, vocal, guitar; Waylon Jennings, vocal, guitar; John Cannon, Dennis Good, Wayne Jackson, horns; Mike Leech, bass; Ralph Mooney, steel guitar; Mickey Raphael, harmonica. Prod. Chips Moman.

NCO-136207 **ONE TOO MANY MORNINGS** (Bob Dylan)
       (see overdub/release session: December 7, 1985)

NCO-136212 **AMERICAN BY BIRTH** (R.A. Wade)
       A - CBS/38-05896 b/w **Even Cowgirls Get The Blues** (w/Waylon Jennings)
       B - CBS/FC-40347 *Heroes*

NCO-136210 **FIELD OF DIAMONDS** (John R. Cash-Jack W. Routh)
(see overdub/release session: December 7, 1985)

NOTE: Musicians Union information lists **AMERICAN BY BIRTH** as **DIXIE**. The released take of this title also includes vocal harmony; **FIELD OF DIAMONDS** includes vocal harmony with Waylon playing electric guitar but no vocal. This is probably the last session Cash did for CBS Records prior to his move to the Mercury/Polygram label. The following session for December 7, 1985 was an overdub and Cash was not present.

December 7, 1985
Probably Georgetown Masters, Nashville, Tennessee
Joe Layne; Mike Leech, bass. Overdub and/or mastering session only. Prod. Chips Moman.

NCO-136205 **I WILL ALWAYS LOVE YOU (IN MY OWN CRAZY WAY)**
(T. Seals-E. Setser-F. Miller)
B - CBS/FC-40347 *Heroes*

NCO-136207 **ONE TOO MANY MORNINGS** (Bob Dylan)
B - CBS/FC-40347 *Heroes*

NCO-136210 **FIELD OF DIAMONDS** (John R. Cash-Jack W. Routh)
A - CBS/38-06287 b/w **Ballad Of Forty Dollars** (w/Waylon Jennings)
B - CBS/FC-40347 *Heroes*

NCO-136203 **HEROES** (J. Kimball-T. Kimmell)
B - CBS/FC-40347 *Heroes*

NCO-136209 **I'M NEVER GONNA ROAM AGAIN** (Rodney Crowell)
B - CBS/FC-40347 *Heroes*

NCO-136208 **FOLKS OUT ON THE ROAD** (E. Raven-F. Myers-D. Powelson)
B - CBS/FC-40347 *Heroes*

NCO-136211 **LOVE IS THE WAY** (Kris Kristofferson)
B - CBS/FC-40347 *Heroes*

NOTE: This was actually a "mastering" session as mentioned on the album jacket.

Late 1985
Probably Woodland Sound Studio, Nashville, Tennessee
Glen Campbell, vocal, guitar; "A" Strings, exact personal unknown; Mike Brignardello, bass; JOHNNY CASH, vocal, guitar; Kim Darlingan, bass; Craig Thomas Fall, guitar; Dave Huntsinger, Shane Keister, keyboard, synthesizer; T.J. Kuenster, piano; Brent Rowan, guitar; W. Steven Turner, drums. Prod. Glen Campbell-Ken Harding.

SUFFER LITTLE CHILDREN (Michael Smotherman)
B - WORD/WR-8293 *No More Night*

==

1985
Cartee 3 Studio, Nashville, Tennessee
Jimmy Tittle, vocal, acoustic guitar, bass; JOHNNY CASH, vocal; the remaining musicians include all or part of the following: Earl Ball, piano; Keith Christopher, bass; O.B. Dix, drums; Durwood Edwards, harmonica; Danny Flowers, harmonica; Greg Galbraith, guitar; David Jones, guitar; Mike Joyce, bass; John Norris, electric guitar; Bryan O'Hanlon, drums; Dan Potter, acoustic guitar, vocal harmony; Michael Rhodes, bass; Jim Soldi, guitar; Marty Stuart, acoustic guitar; Duncan Wayne, piano. Prod. Ted Barton.

WAITIN' FOR A SOUTHERN TRAIN (Sonny Throckmorton)
B - DIXIE FROG/DFG-8412 *Jimmy Tittle*

NOTE: This album entitled *Jimmy Tittle* was released only in France on the "Dixie Frog" label. Session information was provided by Jimmy Tittle (personal communication September 15, 1988) and from the liner notes of the album.

==

Early 1986
CBS Studio, Nashville, Tennessee
David Allan Coe, vocal, guitar; JOHNNY CASH, vocal; remaining musicians unknown. Prod. Billy Sherrill.

TEN COMMANDMENTS OF LOVE (M. Paul)
A - CBS/38-07129 b/w **Tanya Montana** (w/o Cash)
B - CBS/FC-40571 *A Matter Of Life And Death*

==

Early 1986
Recording Location Unknown
Will Campbell, narration; JOHNNY CASH, vocal; Jessi Colter, vocal; Waylon Jennings, vocal; Willie Nelson, vocal; remaining vocals and musicians unknown. Prod. Sheldon Curry-Dan Johnson.

LET AMERICA BE AMERICA AGAIN (W. Campbell-S. Curry)
B - WORD/WR-98334 *They Came To America*

NOTE: This is an album release on the Word Record label and distributed by A&M Records. It is entitled *They Came To America* (WR-98334) and released in July 1986 in association with the The Statue of Liberty-Ellis Island Foundation.

==

April 8, 1986
Sound Stage Studio, Nashville, Tennessee
John Schneider, vocal, guitar; Matt Betton, drums; Larry Byrom, slide guitar, steel guitar; JOHNNY CASH, vocal; Emory Gordy, Jr., bass; John Jarvis, piano, synthesizer; Waylon Jennings, vocal, possibly guitar; Mike Lawler, synthesizer; Lisa Silver, fiddle; Billy Joe Walker, Jr., acoustic guitar; Reggie Young, electric guitar. Prod. Jimmy Bowen-John Schneider.

MC-20814   **BETTER CLASS OF LOSER** (Ron Peterson-Harlan Howard)
  A - MCA-52989 b/w **Take The Long Way Home** (Schneider only)
  B - MCA-5789 *Take The Long Way Home*

NOTE: This is a John Schneider session with this master being used on his MCA album entitled *Take The Long Way Home* (MCA-5789). The album was released in October 1986 and the single in December 1986. The exact session personnel for this master are unknown. The musicians listed above were taken from the album jacket.

===

June 23, 1986 (11a-2p)
JMI Recording Studio, Nashville, Tennessee
Anita, Carlene, Helen Carter, June Carter Cash, vocals, guitars; JOHNNY CASH, vocal harmony -1; Mark Howard, mandolin; Roy Huskey, bass; Kenneth Malone, percussion; Richard Scrivenor, autoharp. Prod. Jack Clement.

2-59697   **SAVIOUR OF MY NATURAL LIFE** (Dave Loggins)
  B - HOUSE OF CASH/CS-1001 *Wildwood Flower*
  (see also overdub/release session: February 11, 1988)

       YOU ARE MY FLOWER (A.P. Carter)

       I MADE A STEP

       GOLD WATCH AND CHAIN -1 (A.P. Carter)
  (possible overdub session: August 7, 1986)

       WAVES ON THE SEA (A.P. Carter)
  (possible overdub session: August 7, 1986)

NOTE: Cash indicated his participation in this and the following Carter sessions during a conversation in July 1986 and gave more precise session data when shown these titles in April 1987. See also overdub/release session dated February 11, 1988. The master numbers, where given for the Carter Family material, were assigned by Polygram Records at the time they acquired the masters in 1988. Both the HOC and Polygram releases were available in the United States only on cassette tape. However, when the Polygram material was released in European it was on a vinyl 33 1/3 album.

===

June 24, 1986 (11a-2p)
JMI Recording Studio, Nashville, Tennessee
Anita, Carlene, Helen Carter, June Carter Cash, vocals, guitars; JOHNNY CASH, vocal harmony -1; Mark Howard, mandolin; Roy Huskey, bass; Kenneth Malone, percussion. Prod. Jack Clement.

       I'M GOIN' AWAY TO LEAVE YOU

       I'LL BE ALL SMILES TONIGHT (A.P. Carter)
  (possible overdub session: August 7, 1986)

2-59696   **STORMS ARE ON THE OCEAN** -1
(A.P. Carter-Maybelle Carter-Sarah Carter)
B - HOUSE OF CASH/CS-1001 *Wildwood Flower*

LITTLE DARLIN' PAL OF MINE (A.P. Carter)

2-59699   **FIFTY MILES OF ELBOW ROOM** (Sarah Carter)
B - HOUSE OF CASH/CS-1001 *Wildwood Flower*

===

June 25, 1986 (11a-2p)
JMI Recording Studio, Nashville, Tennessee
Anita, Carlene, Helen Carter, June Carter Cash, vocals, guitars; JOHNNY CASH, vocal harmony -1; Mark Howard, mandolin; Roy Huskey, bass; Kenneth Malone, percussion. Prod. Jack Clement.

2-59701   **CHURCH IN THE WILDWOOD** -1
(A.P. Carter-Maybelle Carter-Sarah Carter)
B - HOUSE OF CASH/CS-1001 *Wildwood Flower*

LONESOME VALLEY -1 (A.P. Carter)
(possible overdub session: August 7, 1986)

BRAZIL
(possible overdub session: August 7, 1986)

WINDING STREAM

SAY THAT YOU LOVE ME AGAIN

===

June 26, 1986 (11a-2p)
JMI Recording Studio, Nashville, Tennessee
Anita, Carlene, Helen Carter, June Carter Cash, vocals, guitars; JOHNNY CASH, vocal harmony -1; Mark Howard, mandolin; Roy Huskey, bass; Kenneth Malone, percussion; Richard Scrivenor, autoharp. Prod. Jack Clement.

WILDWOOD FLOWER (A.P. Carter)
(possible overdub/release session: August 7, 1986)

2-59698   **AIN'T GONNA WORK TOMORROW**
(A.P. Carter-E. Scruggs-L.Flatt)
B - HOUSE OF CASH/CS-1001 *Wildwood Flower*

KEEP ON THE SUNNY SIDE -1 (A.P. Carter)

LOW AND LONESOME SEA

BANKS OF THE OHIO (Maybelle Carter)
(see overdub/release session: August 7, 1986)

===

June 27, 1986 (11a-2p)
JMI Recording Studio, Nashville, Tennessee
Anita, Carlene, Helen Carter, June Carter Cash, vocals, guitars; JOHNNY CASH, vocal harmony -1; Mark Howard, mandolin; Kenneth Malone, percussion; Richard Scrivenor, autoharp. Prod. Jack Clement.

WABASH CANNONBALL -1 (A.P. Carter)

(I'M) THINKING TONIGHT OF MY BLUE EYES (A.P. Carter)

2-59695   **WORRIED MAN BLUES** -1 (A.P. Carter)
B - HOUSE OF CASH/CS-1001 *Wildwood Flower*

GOSPEL SHIP (A.P. Carter)
(possible overdub session: August 7, 1986)

ON THE WALL -1

NOTE: The Mercury/Polygram musician listing shows: Jack Clement, dobro, which is only apparent on **WORRIED MAN BLUES**. And since this is the only title released from this session it is not known if dobro was on the four remaining masters

===

August 7, 1986 - 3 sessions (10a-1p;2p-5p;6p-9p)
JMI Recording Studio, Nashville, Tennessee
Anita, Carlene, Helen Carter, June Carter Cash, vocals, guitars; Charles Cochran, piano; Mark Howard, mandolin; Roy Huskey, bass; Kenneth Malone, percussion.   Possible overdub session only. Prod. Jack Clement.

2-59692   **WILDWOOD FLOWER** (A.P. Carter)
B - HOUSE OF CASH/CS-1001 *Wildwood Flower*
(see also overdub/release session: February 11, 1988)

2-59694   **BANKS OF THE OHIO** (A.P. Carter)
B - HOUSE OF CASH/CS-1001 *Wildwood Flower*
(see also overdub/release session: February 11, 1988)

BRAZIL

LONESOME VALLEY (A.P. Carter)

WAVES ON THE SEA (A.P. Carter)

GOLD WATCH AND CHAIN (A.P. Carter)

I'LL BE ALL SMILES TONIGHT (A.P. Carter)

GOSPEL SHIP (A.P. Carter)

NOTE: These are probably overdub sessions. At this time it is not known if the "Carter Sisters" were present during any of the three sessions. The material from the above Carter Sisters sessions was released on the "House Of Cash" label (HOC-CS-1001) in September 1987 and titled *Wildwood Flower*. Included on the release were two additional songs, **DIXIE DARLING** (2-59693) (A.P. Carter) and **SEVEN BRIDGES ROAD** (2-59700) (Steve Young). Their exact recording date(s) is unknown. **DIXIE DARLING** includes a prominent accordion, probably Joseph Miskulin, on the Mercury/Polygram release but not on the House Of Cash issue. The Mercury/Polygram label information also credits Jim Varney with dulcimer on **DIXIE DARLING**. The following musicians are also listed on the label of the Mercury/Polygram tape release (M/P-834-491-4): Rosie Carter, vocal harmony; Jack Clement, guitar, vocal harmony; Walter T. Forbes, Jr., 5-string banjo, vocal harmony; Mark Howard, guitar, mandolin, vocal harmony; David Carter Jones, guitar; Jody Maphis, vocal harmony; Joseph Miskulin, 4-string banjo, vocal harmony; Mark O'Connor, fiddle, mandola; Tom Skinker, vocal harmony; Marty Stuart, mandolin.

==

September 3, 1986 - 1st session (10a-1p)
JMI Recording Studio, Nashville, Tennessee
Johnny Cash, vocal, guitar; Earl Ball, keyboard; Jack Hale, brass; W.S. Holland, drums; Robert Lewin, brass; Joseph Miskulin, guitar or bass; Jim Soldi, Marty Stuart, guitar; Jimmy Tittle, bass; Bob Wootton, electric guitar. Prod. Jack Clement.

BEANS FOR BREAKFAST (John R. Cash)
(see overdub/release session: September 15, 1986 - 1st session)

STEEL GUITAR RAG
(see possibly overdub session: January 15, 1987 - 2nd session)

NOTE: This is Cash's first session for his new label Mercury/Polygram aside from the Carter Family sessions that would first appear on the House Of Cash (HOC) label before being reissued by Mercury/Polygram.

==

September 3, 1986 - 2nd session (2p-5p)
JMI Recording Studio, Nashville, Tennessee
Johnny Cash, vocal, guitar; Earl Ball, keyboard; Jack Hale, brass; W.S. Holland, drums; Robert Lewin, brass; Joseph Miskulin, guitar or bass; Jim Soldi, Marty Stuart, guitar; Jimmy Tittle, bass; Bob Wootton, electric guitar. Prod. Jack Clement.

OLD McDONALD
(see overdub session: September 12, 1986)

2-59021   **LET HIM ROLL** (Guy Clark)
(see overdub/release session: October 21, 1986 - 2nd session)

==

September 3, 1986 - 3rd session (6p-9p)
JMI Recording Studio, Nashville, Tennessee

Johnny Cash, vocal, guitar; Earl Ball, keyboard; Jack Hale, brass; W.S. Holland, drums; Robert Lewin, brass; Jim Soldi, Marty Stuart, guitar; Jimmy Tittle, bass; Bob Wootton, electric guitar. Prod. Jack Clement.

EVERYTHING YOU WANTED TO KNOW ABOUT DRINKING
(see possible overdub session: October 24, 1986 - 2nd session)

2-59019   **THE BIG LIGHT** (Elvis Costello)
(see overdub/release session: January 13, 1987)

===

September 4, 1986 - 1st session (10a-1p)
JMI Recording Studio, Nashville, Tennessee
Johnny Cash, vocal, guitar; Earl Ball, keyboard; Charlie Cochran, keyboard; Jack Hale, brass; W.S. Holland, drums; Roy Huskey; bass; Robert Lewin, brass; Jim Soldi, Marty Stuart, guitar; Jimmy Tittle, bass. Prod. Jack Clement.

MYSTERY OF LIFE (Joe Nixon)
(see overdub session: January 15, 1987 - 2nd session)

===

September 4, 1986 - 2nd session (2p-5p)
JMI Recording Studio, Nashville, Tennessee
Johnny Cash, vocal, guitar; Earl Ball, keyboard; Charlie Cochran, keyboard; Jack Hale, brass; W.S. Holland, drums; Roy Huskey, bass; Robert Lewin, brass; Jim Soldi, Marty Stuart, guitar; Jimmy Tittle, bass. Prod. Jack Clement.

2-59020   **BALLAD OF BARBARA** (John R. Cash)
(see overdub/release session: January 16, 1987 - 1st session)

STEEL GUITAR RAG
(see possible overdub session: January 15, 1987 - 2nd session)

NOTE: It is not certain whether **STEEL GUITAR RAG** was overdubbed here or if this is a new master. See session dated: September 3, 1986 - 1st session.
===
September 4, 1986 - 3rd session (6p-9p)
JMI Recording Studio, Nashville, Tennessee
Johnny Cash, vocal, guitar; Earl Ball, keyboard; Charlie Cochran, keyboard; Jack Hale, brass; W.S. Holland, drums; Roy Huskey, bass; Robert Lewin, brass; Jim Soldi, Marty Stuart, guitar; Jimmy Tittle, bass. Prod. Jack Clement.

WANTED MAN (Bob Dylan-John R. Cash)
(see overdub session: February 17, 1987)

===

September 12, 1986 (2p-5p)
JMI Recording Studio, Nashville, Tennessee
Mark O'Conner, fiddle. Overdub session only. Prod. Jack Clement.

MYSTERY OF LIFE (Joe Nixon)
(see overdub session: January 15, 1987 - 2nd session)

2-59021   **LET HIM ROLL** (Guy Clark)
(see overdub/release session: October 21, 1986 - 2nd session)

OLD McDONALD

===

September 15, 1986 - 1st session (10a-1p)
JMI Recording Studio, Nashville, Tennessee
Jim Soldi, Marty Stuart, guitar. Overdub session only. Prod. Jack Clement.

90-2404   **BEANS FOR BREAKFAST** (John R. Cash)
A - M/P-878-292-7 b/w **Goin' By The Book**
B - M/P-848-051-2 *The Mystery Of Life*

2-59019   **THE BIG LIGHT** (Elvis Costello)
(see overdub/release session: January 13, 1987)

===

September 15, 1986 - 2nd session (2p-5p)
JMI Recording Studio, Nashville, Tennessee
Jim Soldi, Marty Stuart, guitar. Overdub session only. Prod. Jack Clement.

WANTED MAN (Bob Dylan-John R. Cash)
(see overdub session: February 17, 1987)

STEEL GUITAR RAG
(see overdub session: January 15, 1987 - 2nd session)

===

September 30, 1986 - 1st session (10a-1p)
JMI Recording Studio, Nashville, Tennessee
Johnny Cash, vocal, guitar; Earl Ball, keyboard; Jack Clement; W.S. Holland, drums; Roy
Huskey, bass; Jim Soldi, Marty Stuart, guitar; Jimmy Tittle, bass. Prod. Jack Clement.

HOBO SONG (John Prine)
(see overdub session: September 30, 1986 - 3rd session)

SAM STONE
(see overdub session: January 14, 1987 - 2nd session)

===

September 30, 1986 - 2nd session (2p-5p)
JMI Recording Studio, Nashville, Tennessee
Johnny Cash, vocal, guitar; Earl Ball, keyboard; Jack Clement, jews harp, kazoo; W.S.
Holland, drums; Roy Huskey, bass; Jim Soldi, Marty Stuart, guitar; Jimmy Tittle, bass.

Prod. Jack Clement.

2-59018   **I'D RATHER HAVE YOU** (John R. Cash)
(see overdub/release session: January 16, 1987 - 1st session)

SAM STONE
(see overdub session: January 14, 1987 - 2nd session)

NOTE: It is not known if this master of **SAM STONE** is a re-make or an overdub of the master done at the first session on this date.
==
September 30, 1986 - 3rd session (6p-9p)
JMI Recording Studio, Nashville, Tennessee
Johnny Cash, vocal, guitar; Earl Ball, keyboard; Jack Clement, jews harp, kazoo; W.S. Holland, drums; Roy Huskey, bass; Jim Soldi, Marty Stuart, guitar; Jimmy Tittle, bass. Prod. Jack Clement.

HOBO SONG (John Prine)
B - M/P-848-051-2 *The Mystery Of Life*

2-59018   **I'D RATHER HAVE YOU** (John R. Cash)
(see overdub/release session: January 16, 1987 - 1st session)

NOTE: It is not known whether or not this is an overdub session or re-makes.
==
October 1, 1986 - 1st session (10a-1p)
JMI Recording Studio, Nashville, Tennessee
Johnny Cash, vocal, guitar; Earl Ball, keyboard; Jack Clement; W.S. Holland, drums; Roy Huskey, bass; Jim Soldi, Marty Stuart, guitar; Jimmy Tittle, bass. Prod. Jack Clement.

DIRTY BLACK BOOTS
(see probable overdub session: January 14, 1987 - 2nd session)

==
October 1, 1986 - 2nd session (2p-5p)
JMI Recording Studio, Nashville, Tennessee
Johnny Cash, vocal, guitar; Earl Ball, keyboard; Jack Clement; W.S. Holland, drums; Roy Huskey, bass; Jim Soldi, Marty Stuart, guitar; Jimmy Tittle, bass.   Prod. Jack Clement.

2-59024   **W. LEE O'DANIEL (AND THE LIGHTCRUST DOUGHBOYS)**
(James Talley)
(see overdub/release session: October 21, 1986 - 2nd session)

==
October 1, 1986 - 3rd session (6p-9p)
JMI Recording Studio, Nashville, Tennessee

Johnny Cash, vocal, guitar; Earl Ball, keyboard; Anita, Carlene, Helen Carter, June Carter Cash, vocal harmony; Cindi Cash, vocal harmony; Jack Clement, vocal harmony; Jessi Colter, vocal harmony; W.S. Holland, drums; Roy Huskey, bass; Waylon Jennings, vocal; Bernard Peyton, vocal harmony; Jim Soldi, Marty Stuart, guitar; Jimmy Tittle, bass; Charlie Williams, show announcer. Prod. Jack Clement.

2-59017   **THE NIGHT HANK WILLIAMS CAME TO TOWN**
(Bobby Braddock-Charles Williams)
(see overdub/release session: January 16, 1987 - 2nd session)

==

October 2, 1986 - 1st session (10a-1p)
JMI Recording Studio, Nashville, Tennessee
Johnny Cash, vocal, guitar; Earl Ball, keyboard; Roberto Bianco; Jack Clement; W.S. Holland, drums; Roy Huskey, bass; Jim Soldi, Marty Stuart, guitar; Jimmy Tittle, bass. Prod. Jack Clement.

2-59019   **THE BIG LIGHT** (Elvis Costello)
(see overdub/release session: January 13, 1987)

NOTE: It is not known whether this is a re-make or an overdub of the original done on September 3, 1986 - 3rd session. Roberto Bianco (aka: Robert Biles) does not appear on the album jacket but was given in the information received from the Musicians Union.
==

October 2, 1986 - 2nd session (2p-5p)
JMI Recording Studio, Nashville, Tennessee
Johnny Cash, vocal, guitar; Earl Ball, keyboard; Roberto Bianco; Jack Clement; W.S. Holland, drums; Roy Huskey, bass; Jim Soldi, Marty Stuart, guitar; Jimmy Tittle, bass. Prod. Jack Clement.

2-59023   **LETTER FROM HOME** (Jack W. Routh-John Charles Crowley)
A - M/P-870-010-7 b/w **W. Lee O'Daniel (And The Lightcrust Doughboys)**
B - M/P-832-031-1 *Johnny Cash Is Coming To Town*

==

October 2, 1986 - 3rd session (6p-9p)
JMI Recording Studio, Nashville, Tennessee
Johnny Cash, vocal, guitar; Earl Ball, keyboard; Roberto Bianco; Jack Clement; W.S. Holland, drums; Roy Huskey, bass; Jim Soldi, Marty Stuart, guitar; Jimmy Tittle, bass. Prod. Jack Clement.

2-59025   **HEAVY METAL (DON'T MEAN ROCK AND ROLL TO ME)**
(Guy Clark-Jim McBride)
(see overdub/release session: February 17, 1987)

AN AMERICAN CHRISTMAS

NOTE: See also session dated October 6, 1986 for **AN AMERICAN CHRISTMAS**.
==

October 3, 1986 (10a-1p)
JMI Recording Studio, Nashville, Tennessee
Earl Ball, keyboard; Jim Soldi, Marty Stuart, guitar. Overdub session only. Prod. Jack
Clement.

2-59025   **HEAVY METAL (DON'T MEAN ROCK AND ROLL TO ME)**
            (Guy Clark-Jim McBride)
       (see overdub/release session: February 17, 1987)

2-59019   **THE BIG LIGHT** (Elvis Costello)
       (see overdub/release session: January 13, 1987)

October 6, 1986 (10a-1p)
JMI Recording Studios, Nashville, Tennessee
Johnny Cash, vocal, guitar; Earl Ball, keyboard; Jack Clement; W.S. Holland, drums; Roy
Huskey, bass; Jim Soldi, Marty Stuart, guitar; Jimmy Tittle, bass. Prod. Jack Clement.

AN AMERICAN CHRISTMAS

NOTE: It is not known if this is a re-make or an overdub session for the original master
from session dated October 2, 1986 - 3rd session.

October 21, 1986 - 1st session (10a-1p)
JMI Recording Studio, Nashville, Tennessee
Jim Soldi, Marty Stuart, guitar. Overdub session only. Prod. Jack Clement.

2-59021   **LET HIM ROLL** (Guy Clark)
       (see overdub/release session: October 21, 1986 - 2nd session)

2-59019   **THE BIG LIGHT** (Elvis Costello)
       (see overdub/release session: January 13, 1987)

2-59024   **W. LEE O'DANIEL (AND THE LIGHTCRUST DOUGHBOYS)**
            (James Talley)
       (see overdub/release session: October 21, 1986 - 2nd session)

            WANTED MAN (Bob Dylan-John R. Cash)
       (see overdub session: February 17, 1987)

2-59020   **BALLAD OF BARBARA** (John R. Cash)
       (see overdub/release session: January 16, 1987 - 1st session)

            MYSTERY OF LIFE (Joe Nixon)
       (see overdub session: January 15, 1987 - 2nd session)

October 21, 1986 - 2nd session (2p-5p)
JMI Recording Studio, Nashville, Tennessee
John Prine, possible vocal, guitar; Jim Soldi, Marty Stuart, guitar. Overdub session only.
Prod. Jack Clement.

2-59021   **LET HIM ROLL** (Guy Clark)
    A - M/P-888-838-7 b/w **My Ship Will Sail**
    B - M/P-832-031-1 *Johnny Cash Is Coming To Town*

2-59019   **THE BIG LIGHT** (Elvis Costello)
    (see overdub/release session: January 13, 1987)

2-59024   **W. LEE O'DANIEL (AND THE LIGHTCRUST DOUGHBOYS)**
             (James Talley)
    A - M/P-870-010-7 b/w **Letters From Home**
    B - M/P-832-031-1 *Johnny Cash Is Coming To Town*

NOTE: John Prine is shown on information received from the Musicians Union but is not
credited on the album jacket. A music video was made using the soundtrack of **LET
HIM ROLL** with Waylon Jennings in an acting role.
===

October 22, 1986 (10a-1p)
JMI Recording Studio, Nashville, Tennessee
Jim Soldi, Marty Stuart, guitar. Overdub session only. Prod. Jack Clement.

             WANTED MAN (Bob Dylan-John R. Cash)
    (see overdub session: February 17, 1987)

2-59020   **BALLAD OF BARBARA** (John R. Cash)
    (see overdub/release session: January 16, 1987 - 1st session)

             MYSTERY OF LIFE (Joe Nixon)
    (see overdub session: January 15, 1987 - 2nd session)

===

October 23, 1986 (10a-1p)
JMI Recording Studio, Nashville, Tennessee
Jack Hale, Bob Lewin, brass. Overdub session only. Prod. Jack Clement.

             MYSTERY OF LIFE (Joe Nixon)
    (see overdub session: January 15, 1987 - 2nd session)

2-59019   **THE BIG LIGHT** (Elvis Costello)
    (see overdub/release session: January 13, 1987)

===

October 24, 1986 - 1st session (10a-1p)
JMI Recording Studio, Nashville, Tennessee
Johnny Cash, vocal, guitar; Earl Ball, keyboard; Vassar Clement, fiddle; Jim Soldi,

Marty Stuart, guitar. Prod. Jack Clement.

I'LL GO SOMEWHERE AND SING MY SONGS AGAIN
(Tom T. Hall)
(see possible overdub session: October 24, 1986 - 2nd session)

WHACKOS AND WEIRDOS
(see possible overdub session: October 24, 1986 - 2nd session)

EVERYTHING YOU WANTED TO KNOW ABOUT DRINKING
(see possible overdub session: October 24, 1986 - 2nd session)

NOTE: It is not known if this is a re-make of **EVERYTHING YOU WANTED TO KNOW ABOUT DRINKING** or an overdub of the original master from session dated September 3, 1986 - 3rd session. **WHACKOS AND WEIRDOS** could possibly have been re-recorded in 1989 and retitled **A BACKSTAGE PASS**.

==
October 24, 1986 - 2nd session (2p-5p)
JMI Recording Studio, Nashville, Tennessee
Jim Soldi, Marty Stuart, guitar. Overdub session only. Prod. Jack Clement.

I'LL GO SOMEWHERE AND SING MY SONGS AGAIN
(Tom T. Hall)
B - M/P-848-051-2 *The Mystery Of Life*

WHACKOS AND WEIRDOS

EVERYTHING YOU WANTED TO KNOW ABOUT DRINKING

==
November 21, 1986 - 1st session (2p-5p)
JMI Recording Studio, Nashville, Tennessee
Johnny Cash, vocal, guitar; Joe Allen, bass; Charlie Cochran; W.S. Holland, drums; Jim Soldi, Pete Wade, guitar. Prod. Jack Clement.

2-59026   **MY SHIP WILL SAIL** (Allen Reynolds)
(see overdub/release session: December 10, 1986)

GOIN' BY THE BOOK (Chester Lester)
(see overdub/release session: December 10, 1986)

==
November 21, 1986 - 2nd session (6p-9p)
JMI Recording Studio, Nashville, Tennessee
Johnny Cash, vocal, guitar; Joe Allen, bass; Charlie Cochran, keyboard; W.S. Holland, drums; Jim Soldi, Pete Wade, guitar. Prod. Jack Clement.

SOLID GONE
(see overdub session: December 18, 1986)

==

November 21, 1986 - 3rd session (9p-12m)
JMI Recording Studio, Nashville, Tennessee
Johnny Cash, vocal, guitar; Joe Allen, bass; Charlie Cochran, keyboard; W.S. Holland, drums; Jim Soldi, Pete Wade, guitar. Prod. Jack Clement.

2-59019   **THE BIG LIGHT** (Elvis Costello)
    (see overdub/release session: January 13, 1987)

NOTE: It is unknown if this is a re-make or an overdub of the original master. See sessions dated September 3, 1986 - 3rd session and September 15, 1986 - 1st session; October 2, 1986 - 1st session, October 3, 1986, October 21, 1986 - 1st/2nd sessions and October 23, 1986.

==

December 10, 1986 (2p-5p)
JMI Recording Studio, Nashville, Tennessee
Charles Cochran, keyboard; Roy Huskey, bass; Jim Soldi, guitar. Overdub session only. Prod. Jack Clement.

2-59026   **MY SHIP WILL SAIL** (Allen Reynolds)
    A - M/P-888-838-7 b/w **Let Him Roll**
    B - M/P-832-031-1 *Johnny Cash Is Coming To Town*

             GOIN' BY THE BOOK (Chester Lester)
    A - M/P-878-292-7 b/w **Beans For Breakfast**
    B - M/P-848-051-2 *The Mystery Of Life*

NOTE: **GOIN' BY THE BOOK** was not released until September 1990 prompted, in part, by the Iraqi happenings in the Middle East. A music video was made using **GOIN' BY THE BOOK**.

==

December 18, 1986 (2p-5p)
JMI Recording Studio, Nashville, Tennessee
Charles Cochran, keyboard; Jack Hale, Bob Lewin, Jay Patten, horns. Overdub session only. Prod. Jack Clement.

             SOLID GONE

2-59019   **THE BIG LIGHT** (Elvis Costello)
    (see overdub/release session: January 13, 1987)

==

Late 1986
Gospel Country Network Studio, Nashville, Tennessee
Johnny Cash, vocal, guitar; Earl Ball, piano; Anita, Helen Carter, June Carter Cash, vocal harmony; Jack Hale, horns; W.S. Holland, drums; Bob Lewin, horns; Jim Soldi, guitar; Jimmy Tittle, electric bass; Bob Wootton, electric guitar. Prod. Jack Hale.

U-16394   **MAN IN WHITE** (John R. Cash)
  A - Ezra-227 b/w **Man In White**

NOTE: This song was written after Cash wrote his book of the same name. A music video was made using this master. This single actually had the same song on both sides-- one in stereo and one in monaural.

==

January 12, 1987 (2p-5p)
JMI Recording Studio, Nashville, Tennessee
Johnny Cash, vocal, guitar; Joe Allen, bass; Earl Ball, piano; June Carter Cash, vocal -1; Charles Cochran, keyboard; Jack Hale, brass; W.S. Holland, drums; Bob Lewin, brass; Jerry McEwen; Jim Soldi, guitar; Bob Wootton, electric guitar. Prod. Jack Clement.

WHERE DID WE GO RIGHT -1 (Dave Loggins-Don Schlitz)
(see overdub session: January 19, 1987)

ANTHEM '84 (Kris Kristofferson)
(see overdub session: February 2, 1987)

==

January 13, 1987 (2p-5p)
JMI Recording Studio, Nashville, Tennessee
Johnny Cash, vocal, guitar; Joe Allen, bass; Earl Ball, piano; Charles Cochran, keyboard; Jack Hale, brass; W.S. Holland, drums; Bob Lewin, brass; Jerry McEwen; Jim Soldi, guitar; Bob Wootton, electric guitar. Prod. Jack Clement.

2-59019   **THE BIG LIGHT** (Elvis Costello)
  B - M/P-832-031-1 *Johnny Cash Is Coming To Town*

2-59022   **SIXTEEN TONS** (Merle Travis)
  (see overdub/release session: February 2, 1987)

NOTE: This is possibly a re-make or an overdub session for **THE BIG LIGHT**.

==

January 14, 1987 - 1st session (10a-1p)
JMI Recording Studio, Nashville, Tennessee
Roy Huskey, bass; Joseph Miskulin; Marty Stuart, guitar. Overdub session only. Prod. Jack Clement.

SAM STONE
(see overdub sesssion: January 14, 1987 - 2nd session)

DIRTY BLACK BOOTS
(see probable overdub session: January 14, 1987 - 2nd session)

==

January 14, 1987 - 2nd session (2p-5p)
JMI Recording Studio, Nashville, Tennessee
Joseph Miskulin. Overdub session only. Prod. Jack Clement.

SAM STONE

DIRTY BLACK BOOTS

==

January 15, 1987 - 1st session (10a-1p)
JMI Recording Studio, Nashville, Tennessee
Charles Cochran, keyboard; Roy Huskey, bass; Kenneth Malone, percussion; Joseph Miskulin. Overdub session only. Prod. Jack Clement.

STEEL GUITAR RAG
(see overdub session: January 15, 1987 - 2nd session)

MYSTERY OF LIFE (Joe Nixon)
(see overdub session: January 15, 1987 - 2nd session)

==

January 15, 1987 - 2nd session (2p-5p)
JMI Recording Studio, Nashville, Tennessee
Joseph Miskulin. Overdub session only. Prod. Jack Clement.

STEEL GUITAR RAG

MYSTERY OF LIFE (Joe Nixon)
B - M/P-848-051-2 *The Mystery Of Life*

==

January 16, 1987 - 1st session
JMI Recording Studio, Nashville, Tennessee
Charles Cochran, keyboard; Roy Huskey, bass; Kenneth Malone, percussion; Joseph Miskulin, guitar or bass. Overdub session only. Prod. Jack Clement.

2-59018   **I'D RATHER HAVE YOU** (John R. Cash)
    A - M/P-888-459-7 b/w **The Night Hank Williams Came To Town** (w/Waylon)
    B - M/P-832-031-1 *Johnny Cash Is Coming To Town*

2-59020   **BALLAD OF BARBARA** (John R. Cash)
    A - M/P-888-719-7 b/w **Sixteen Tons**
    B - M/P-832-031-1 *Johnny Cash Is Coming To Town*

==

January 16, 1987 - 2nd session (6p-9p)
JMI Recording Studio, Nashville, Tennessee
Lloyd Green, steel guitar. Overdub session only. Prod. Jack Clement.

2-59017   **THE NIGHT HANK WILLIAMS CAME TO TOWN**
           (Bobby Braddock-Charles Williams)
    A - M/P-888-459-7 b/w **I'd Rather Have You**
    B - M/P-832-031-1 *Johnny Cash Is Coming To Town*

===

January 19, 1987 (2p-5p)
JMI Recording Studio, Nashville, Tennessee
Lloyd Green, steel guitar. Overdub session only. Prod. Jack Clement.

2-59022   **SIXTEEN TONS** (Merle Travis)
   (see overdub/release session: February 2, 1987)

WHERE DID WE GO RIGHT (Dave Loggins-Don Schlitz)

NOTE: **WHERE DID WE GO RIGHT** was probably re-done starting with the first session on December 10, 1987.

===

January 20, 1987 (2p-5p)
JMI Recording Studio, Nashville, Tennessee
Jerry McEwen. Overdub session only. Prod. Jack Clement.

THE HEART
   (see overdub session: January 22, 1987)

ANTHEM '84 (Kris Kristofferson)
   (see overdub session: February 2, 1987)

NOTE: This is the first appearance of **THE HEART** but this has to be an overdub session.

===

January 21, 1987 (2p-5p)
JMI Recording Studio, Nashville, Tennessee
Bob Wootton, electric guitar. Overdub session only. Prod. Jack Clement.

2-59022   **SIXTEEN TONS** (Merle Travis)
   (see overdub/release session: February 2, 1987)

ANTHEM '84 (Kris Kristofferson)
   (see overdub session: February 2, 1987)

===

January 22, 1987 (10a-1p)
JMI Recording Studio, Nashville, Tennessee
Charles Cochran, keyboard; Stuart Duncan, fiddle; Kenneth Malone, percussion; Joseph Miskulin, guitar or bass. Overdub session only. Prod. Jack Clement.

THE HEART

2-59022   **SIXTEEN TONS** (Merle Travis)
   (see overdub/release session: February 2, 1987)

===

February 2, 1987 (2p-5p)
JMI Recording Studio, Nashville, Tennessee
Mike Elliott, acoustic guitar; Kenneth Malone, percussion. Overdub session only. Prod.
Jack Clement.

ANTHEM '84 (Kris Kristofferson)

2-59022   **SIXTEEN TONS** (Merle Travis)
A - M/P-888-719-7 b/w **Ballad Of Barbara**
B - M/P-832-031-1 *Johnny Cash Is Coming To Town*

NOTE: A music video was made using the soundtrack of **SIXTEEN TONS**.
===

February 17, 1987 (10a-1p)
JMI Recording Studio, Nashville, Tennessee
Joe Allen, bass; Kenneth Malone, percussion; Joseph Miskulin; Bernard Peyton; Michael
Rhodes; Daniel Shipp, harmonica. Overdub session only. Prod. Jack Clement.

2-59025   **HEAVY METAL (DON'T MEAN ROCK AND ROLL TO ME)**
(Guy Clark-Jim McBride)
B - M/P-832-031-1 *Johnny Cash Is Coming To Town*

WANTED MAN (Bob Dylan-John R. Cash)
B - M/P-848-051-2 *The Mystery Of Life*

===

April/May 1987 (soundtrack)
Unknown California Studio
Johnny Cash, vocal, guitar; remaining musicians unknown.

LADY OF LOVE (Earl Ball-Peter Bagdonovich)

ONE WISH (Earl Ball-Peter Bagdonovich)

LOVE IS A GAMBLER (Earl Ball-Peter Bagdonovich)

NOTE: These three masters were used in the Peter Bagdonovich film *"Illegally Yours"*
starring Rob Lowe. The film was never released in theaters but only on video cassette.
Information provided by Earl Ball-March 22, 1989.
===

September 1987
Gospel Country Network Studio, Nashville, Tennessee
JoAnne Cash Yates, vocal; JOHNNY CASH, vocal; remaining studio musicians unknown.
Prod. Bill Anderson Jr.

AMAZING GRACE (traditional)
B - JANA 8709-01 *Amazing Grace* (JoAnne Cash Yates)

NOTE: JoAnne Yates is John's sister. This was only released as a cassette and was entitled *Amazing Grace*.

==

October 12, 1987 (10a-1p)
Gospel Country Network Studio, Nashville, Tennessee
Johnny Cash, vocal, guitar; Earl Ball, piano; Jack Hale, brass; W.S. Holland, drums; Bob
Lewin, brass; Jim Soldi, guitar, vocal harmony -1; Jimmy Tittle, bass, vocal harmony -2;
Bob Wootton, electric guitar. Prod. Jimmy Tittle-Johnny Cash.

2-59709   **BLUE TRAIN** (Billy Smith)
    (see overdub/release session: December 2, 1987)

2-59711   **FIVE FEET HIGH AND RISING** (John R. Cash)
    (see overdub/release session: December 2, 1987)

2-59716   **I GOT STRIPES** -1,2 (John R. Cash-C. Williams)
    (see overdub/release session: October 14, 1987)

            GET RHYTHM (John R. Cash)
    (see overdub session: October 14, 1987)

NOTE: Information for this session and those through December 10, 1987 was provided
by Jimmy Tittle, the Nashville Musicians Union and Claudia Mize at Mercury/Polygram
Records.   Musician Union files show **BLUE TRAIN**; **I GOT STRIPES**; **GET
RHYTHM**; **FIVE FEET HIGH AND RISING**; **PEACE IN THE VALLEY**; **RING
OF FIRE** and **LONG BLACK VEIL** done at this session.

==

October 13, 1987 - 2 sessions (11a-2p;3p-6p)
Gospel Country Network Studio, Nashville, Tennessee
Johnny Cash, vocal, guitar; Earl Ball, piano; Jack Hale, brass, harmonica -1; W.S.
Holland, drums; Bob Lewin, brass; Jim Soldi, guitar, vocal harmony -2; Jimmy Tittle,
bass, vocal harmony -3; Bob Wootton, electric guitar. Prod. Jimmy Tittle-Johnny Cash.

2-59721   **FOLSOM PRISON BLUES** -1 (John R. Cash)
    (see overdub/release session: December 10, 1987 - 3rd session)

2-59706   **LONG BLACK VEIL** (Marijohn Wilken-Danny Dill)
    (see overdub/release session: December 10, 1987 - 2nd session)

            RING OF FIRE (June Carter-Merle Kilgore)
    (see overdub session: October 14, 1987)

2-59717   **I WALK THE LINE** (John R. Cash)
    (see overdub/release session: December 9, 1987 - 1st session)

2-59708   **I STILL MISS SOMEONE** (John R. Cash-Roy Cash Jr)
    (see overdub/release session: October 14, 1987)

2-59712   **PEACE IN THE VALLEY** (T.A. Dorsey)
    (see overdub/release session: December 9, 1987 - 1st session)

2-59710   **SUNDAY MORNING COMING DOWN** -2,3 (Kris Kristofferson)
(see overdub/release session: December 10, 1987 - 3rd session)

GET RHYTHM (John R. Cash)
(see overdub session: October 14, 1987)

NOTE: The above master of **GET RHYTHM** was overdubbed during one of the sessions on this date. Musician Union files indicate **BLUE TRAIN**; **I GOT STRIPES**; **GET RHYTHM**; **FIVE FEET HIGH AND RISING**; **PEACE IN THE VALLEY**; **RING OF FIRE** and **LONG BLACK VEIL** were done during these two sessions.
===

October 14, 1987 - 2 sessions (11a-2:30p;3p-7:30p)
Gospel Country Network Studio, Nashville, Tennessee
Jack Hale, Bob Lewin, brass-1st session only; Jim Soldi, guitar-2nd session only. Overdub session only. Prod. Jimmy Tittle-Johnny Cash.

2-59709   **BLUE TRAIN** (Billy Smith)
(see overdub/release session: December 2, 1987)

2-59711   **FIVE FEET HIGH AND RISING** (John R. Cash)
(see overdub/release session: December 2, 1987)

2-59716   **I GOT STRIPES** (John R. Cash-C. Williams)
B - M/P-834-526-1 *Classic Cash*

GET RHYTHM (John R. Cash)

2-59721   **FOLSOM PRISON BLUES** (John R. Cash)
(see overdub/release session: December 10, 1987 - 3rd session)

2-59706   **LONG BLACK VEIL** (Marijohn Wilken-Danny Dill)
(see overdub/release session: December 10, 1987 - 2nd session)

RING OF FIRE (June Carter-Merle Kilgore)

2-59717   **I WALK THE LINE** (John R. Cash)
(see overdub/release session: December 9, 1987 - 1st session)

2-59708   **I STILL MISS SOMEONE** (John R. Cash-Roy Cash Jr.)
B - M/P-834-526-1 *Classic Cash*

2-59712   **PEACE IN THE VALLEY** (T.A. Dorsey)
(see overdub/release session: December 9, 1987 - 1st session)

2-59710   **SUNDAY MORNING COMING DOWN** (Kris Kristofferson)
(see overdub/release session: December 10, 1987 - 3rd session)

NOTE: The above titles were provided by Jimmy Tittle. However, Musician Union files indicate that **RING OF FIRE**; **PEACE IN THE VALLEY** and **LONG BLACK VEIL** were overdubbed with horns at first session while **RING OF FIRE**; **I GOT STRIPES** and **BLUE TRAIN** were overdubbed with guitar at the second session.

==

October 15, 1987 (11a-1p)
Gospel Country Network Studio, Nashville, Tennessee
Jim Soldi, dobro. Overdub session only. Prod. Jimmy Tittle-Johnny Cash.

2-59709   **BLUE TRAIN** (Billy Smith)
    (see overdub/release session: December 2, 1987)

NOTE: Musician Union files also indicate **RING OF FIRE** and **I GOT STRIPES** were overdubbed on this session in addition to **BLUE TRAIN**.

==

December 2, 1987 (12n-2p)
Gospel Country Network Studio, Nashville, Tennessee
Earl Ball, piano. Overdub session only. Prod. Jimmy Tittle-Johnny Cash.

2-59709   **BLUE TRAIN** (Billy Smith)
    B - M/P-834-526-1 *Classic Cash*

2-59711   **FIVE FEET HIGH AND RISING** (John R. Cash)
    B - M/P-834-526-1 *Classic Cash*

==

December 3, 1987 (1p-4p)
Gospel Country Network Studio, Nashville, Tennessee
Johnny Cash, vocal, guitar; Jack Hale, Bob Lewin, brass -1; Jim Soldi, guitar, vocal harmony -2; Jimmy Tittle, bass, vocal harmony -3. Prod. Jimmy Tittle-Johnny Cash.

2-59718   **RING OF FIRE** (remake) -1 (June Carter-Merle Kilgore)
    (see overdub/release session: December 10, 1987)

2-59705   **TENNESSEE FLAT-TOP BOX** (John R. Cash)
    (see overdub/release session: December 10, 1987)

2-59707   **A THING CALLED LOVE** -1 (J.R. Hubbard)
    (see overdub/release session: December 10, 1987)

2-59720   **WAYS OF A WOMAN IN LOVE** (Charlie Rich-Bill Justis)
    (see overdub/release session: December 10, 1987)

2-59719   **BALLAD OF IRA HAYES** (Peter LaFarge)
    (see overdub/release session: December 10, 1987)

2-59714   **HOME OF THE BLUES** (John R. Cash-G. Douglas-L. McAlpin)
    (see overdub/release session: December 10, 1987)

2-59713   **DON'T TAKE YOUR GUNS TO TOWN** (John R. Cash)
    (see overdub/release session: December 10, 1987)

2-59571   **CRY, CRY, CRY** -2,3 (John R. Cash)
(see overdub/release session: December 10, 1987)

2-59715   **GUESS THINGS HAPPEN THAT WAY** (Jack Clement)
(see overdub/release session: December 10, 1987)

2-59722   **SUPPERTIME** (Stamphill)
(see overdub/release session: December 10, 1987)

2-59570   **GET RHYTHM** (remake) -2,3 (John R. Cash)
(see overdub/release session: December 10, 1987)

NOTE: Musician Union files lists the above personnel but indicates only **GET RHYTHM** and **A THING CALLED LOVE** for this session.
==

December 8, 1987 (2p-5p)
JMI Recording Studio, Nashville, Tennessee
Mark Howard, guitar and/or mandolin. Possible overdub session. Prod. Jack Clement.

I'M GONNA WRITE YOU A LETTER

2-59928   **CALL ME THE BREEZE** (J.J. Cale)
(see overdub/release session: May 20, 1988)

NOTE: **CALL ME THE BREEZE** is a duet with John Carter Cash. This would appear to be an overdub session with the original recording date unknown. See sessions dated December 11, 1987 for possible remake.
==

December 9, 1987 - 1st session (10a-1p)
Possibly Berry Hill Sound Studio, Nashville, Tennessee
Matt Rollins, organ -1; Jim Soldi, acoustic guitar -2, electric guitar -3. Overdub session only. Prod. Jimmy Tittle-Johnny Cash.

2-59712   **PEACE IN THE VALLEY** -1 (T.A. Dorsey)
B - M/P-834-526-1 *Classic Cash*

2-59722   **SUPPERTIME** -1 (Stamphill)
(see overdub/release session: December 10, 1987)

2-59710   **SUNDAY MORNING COMING DOWN** -2 (Kris Kristofferson)
(see overdub/release session: December 10, 1987 - 3rd session)

2-59706   **LONG BLACK VEIL** -2 (Marijohn Wilken-Danny Dill)
(see overdub/release session: December 10, 1987 - 2nd session)

2-59705   **TENNESSEE FLAT-TOP BOX** -2 (John R. Cash)
(see overdub/release session: December 10, 1987)

2-59717   **I WALK THE LINE** -2 (John R. Cash)
B - M/P-834-526-1 *Classic Cash*

2-59713   **DON'T TAKE YOUR GUNS TO TOWN** -3 (John R. Cash)
(see overdub/release session: December 10, 1987)

===

December 9, 1987 - 2nd session (5p-6p)
Possibly Berry Hill Sound Studio, Nashville, Tennessee
Jim Soldi, Jimmy Tittle, vocals. Overdub session only. Prod. Jimmy Tittle-Johnny Cash.

2-59571   **CRY, CRY, CRY** (John R. Cash)
(see overdub/release session: December 10, 1987)

===

December 10, 1987 - 1st session (10a-1p)
JMI Recording Studio, Nashville, Tennessee
Johnny Cash, vocal, guitar; possibly John Carter Cash, vocal -1; June Carter Cash, vocal -2; Charles Cochran, piano; W.S. Holland, drums; Mark Howard, guitar; Roy Huskey, bass; Kenneth Malone, percussion; Joseph Miskulin. Prod. Jack Clement.

2-59933   **WATER FROM THE WELLS OF HOME** -1
(John R. Cash-John C. Cash)
(see overdub/release session: June 20, 1988)

I'M GONNA WRITE YOU A LETTER
(see overdub session: January 8, 1988 - 1st session)

2-59927   **WHERE DID WE GO RIGHT** -2 (Dave Loggins-Don Schlitz)
(see overdub/release session: June 22, 1988)

NOTE: **I'M GONNA WRITE YOU A LETTER** and **WHERE DID WE GO RIGHT**
were probably remade at this session.
===

December 10, 1987 - 2nd session (2p-5p)
JMI Recording Studio, Nashville, Tennessee
Johnny Cash, vocal, guitar; possibly John Carter Cash, vocal -1; possibly June Carter Cash, vocal -2; Charles Cochran, piano; W.S. Holland, drums; Mark Howard, guitar; Roy Huskey, bass; Kenneth Malone, percussion; Joseph Miskulin. Prod. Jack Clement.

2-59933   **WATER FROM THE WELLS OF HOME** -1
(John R. Cash-John C. Cash)
(see overdub/release session: June 20, 1988)

I'M GONNA WRITE YOU A LETTER
(see overdub session: January 8, 1988 - 1st session)

2-59927   **WHERE DID WE GO RIGHT** -2 (Dave Loggins-Don Schlitz)
(see overdub/release session: June 22, 1988)

NOTE: This is either an overdub session or a continuation of the first session on this date.
===

December 10, 1987 - 1st session (10a-1p)
Berry Hill Sound Studio, Nashville, Tennessee
Terry McMillan, possible harmonica. Overdub session only. Prod. Jimmy Tittle-Johnny
Cash.

2-59570   **GET RHYTHM** (John R. Cash)
(see overdub/release session: December 10, 1987)

2-59571   **CRY, CRY, CRY** (John R. Cash)
(see overdub/release session: December 10, 1987)

===

December 10, 1987 - 2nd session
Possibly Berry Hill Sound Studio, Nashville, Tennessee
Bryan O'Hanlon, tamborine. Overdub session only. Prod. Jimmy Tittle-Johnny Cash.

2-59706   **LONG BLACK VEIL** (Marijohn Wilken-Danny Dill)
B - M/P-834-526-1 *Classic Cash*

===

December 10, 1987 - 3rd session
Berry Hill Sound Studio, Nashville, Tennessee
Johnny Cash, vocal -1; Jack Hale, Bob Lewin, brass -2; Jim Soldi, synthizer -3, electric
and acoustic guitars -4, dobro -5. Overdub session only. Prod. Jimmy Tittle-Johnny
Cash.

2-59710   **SUNDAY MORNING COMING DOWN** -1 (Kris Kristofferson)
B - M/P-834-526-1 *Classic Cash*

2-59718   **RING OF FIRE** -2 (June Carter-Merle Kilgore)
(see overdub/release session: December 10, 1987)

2-59707   **A THING CALLED LOVE** -3 (J.R. Hubbard)
(see overdub/release session: December 10, 1987)

2-59721   **FOLSOM PRISON BLUES** -4 (John R. Cash)
B - M/P-834-526-1 *Classic Cash*

2-59719   **BALLAD OF IRA HAYES** -5 (Peter LaFarge)
(see overdub/release session: December 10, 1987)

NOTE: Musician Union files reflect only **SUNDAY MORNING COMING DOWN** and
CRY, CRY, CRY being overdubbed at this session.
===

December 10, 1987 - 2 sessions (5p-8p;9p-12m)
Gospel Country Network Studio, Nashville, Tennessee
Johnny Cash, vocal, guitar; Earl Ball, piano; Jack Hale, horns; W.S. Holland, drums; Bob Lewin, horns; Jim Soldi, guitar; Jimmy Tittle, bass; Bob Wootton, electric guitar. This is a possible overdub session. Prod. Jimmy Tittle-Johnny Cash.

2-59718   **RING OF FIRE** (June Carter-Merle Kilgore)
  B - M/P-834-526-1 *Classic Cash*

2-59719   **BALLAD OF IRA HAYES** (Peter LaFarge)
  B - M/P-834-526-1 *Classic Cash*

2-59722   **SUPPERTIME** (Stamphill)
  B - M/P-834-526-1 *Classic Cash*

2-59713   **DON'T TAKE YOUR GUNS TO TOWN** (John R. Cash)
  B - M/P-834-526-1 *Classic Cash*

2-59715   **GUESS THINGS HAPPEN THAT WAY** (Jack Clement)
  B - M/P-834-526-1 *Classic Cash*

2-59705   **TENNESSEE FLAT-TOP BOX** (John R. Cash)
  A - M/P-870-688-7 b/w **That Old Wheel** (w/Hank Williams Jr.)
  B - M/P-834-526-1 *Classic Cash*

2-59570   **GET RHYTHM** (John R. Cash)
  A - M/P-870-237-7 b/w **Cry, Cry, Cry**
  B - M/P-834-526-1 *Classic Cash*

2-59571   **CRY, CRY, CRY** (John R. Cash)
  A - M/P-870-237-7 b/w **Get Rhythm**
  B - M/P-834-526-1 *Classic Cash*

2-59707   **A THING CALLED LOVE** (J.R. Hubbard)
  B - M/P-834-526-1 *Classic Cash*

2-59720   **WAYS OF A WOMAN IN LOVE** (Charlie Rich-Bill Justis)
  B - M/P-834-526-1 *Classic Cash*

2-59714   **HOME OF THE BLUES** (John R. Cash-G. Douglas-L. McAlpin)
  B - M/P-834-526-1 *Classic Cash*

NOTE: Information for these two sessions taken from Musician Union files. It does not necessarily agree with the information furnished above by Jimmy Tittle. The single release of **TENNESSEE FLAT-TOP BOX** (870-688-7) was given a "current" master number of 2-59975.

December 11, 1987 - 1st session (10a-1p)
JMI Recording Studio, Nashville, Tennessee
Johnny Cash, vocal, guitar; Mark Howard, guitar; Roy Huskey, bass; Kenneth Malone, percussion; Joseph Miskulin. Prod. Jack Clement.

ANGEL AND THE BADMAN (John R. Cash)
(see overdub/release session: January 8, 1988 - 3rd session)

LOVE'S FROM THE HEART
(see overdub session: January 8, 1988 - 3rd session)

2-59928   **CALL ME THE BREEZE** (J.J. Cale)
(see overdub/release session: May 20, 1988)

NOTE: **LOVE'S FROM THE HEART** could possibly be same title given as **THE HEART** from January 20, 1987 session.

===

December 11, 1987 - 2nd session (2p-5p)
JMI Recording Studio, Nashville, Tennessee
Johnny Cash, vocal, guitar; Mark Howard; Roy Huskey, bass; Kenneth Malone, percussion; Joseph Miskulin. Prod. Jack Clement.

ANGEL AND THE BADMAN (John R. Cash)
(see overdub/release session: January 8, 1988 - 3rd session)

LOVE'S FROM THE HEART
(see overdub session: January 8, 1988 - 3rd session)

2-59928 ·   **CALL ME THE BREEZE** (J.J. Cale)
(see overdub/release session: May 20, 1988)

NOTE: Possibly a continuation of the first session and not necessarily an overdub session.

===

1987
JMI Recording Studio, Nashville, Tennessee
Johnny Cash, narration.

WE THE PEOPLE
C - FOLK ERA/FE2055CD *We The People*

NOTE: This narration was used on the compact disc release *We The People* on the "Folk Era" label (FE-2055CD).

===

January 8, 1988 - 1st session (12p-3p)
JMI Recording Studio, Nashville, Tennessee
Earl Ball, piano; Joseph Miskulin. Overdub session only. Prod. Jack Clement.

2-59933   **WATER FROM THE WELLS OF HOME**
(John R. Cash-John C. Cash)
(see overdub/release session: June 20, 1988)

I'M GONNA WRITE YOU A LETTER

2-59927   **WHERE DID WE GO RIGHT** (Dave Loggins-Don Schlitz)
(see overdub/release session: June 22, 1988)

===

January 8, 1988 - 2nd session (4p-7p)
JMI Recording Studio, Nashville, Tennessee
Earl Ball, piano; Joseph Miskulin. Overdub session only. Prod. Jack Clement.

ANGEL AND THE BADMAN (John R. Cash)
(see overdub/release session: January 8, 1988 - 3rd session)

2-59928   **CALL ME THE BREEZE** (J.J. Cale)
(see overdub/release session: May 20, 1988)

===

January 8, 1988 - 3rd session (8p-11p)
JMI Recording Studio, Nashville, Tennessee
Earl Ball, piano; Joseph Miskulin. Overdub session only. Prod. Jack Clement.

LOVE'S FROM THE HEART

2-59928   **CALL ME THE BREEZE** (J.J. Cale)
(see overdub/release session: May 20, 1988)

ANGEL AND THE BADMAN (John R. Cash)
B - M/P-848-051-2 *The Mystery Of Life*

===

February 10, 1988 - 1st session (2p-5p)
JMI Recording Studio, Nashville, Tennessee
Johnny Cash, vocal, guitar; Waylon Jennings, vocal, guitar; Charles Cochran, keyboard;
Jessi Colter, vocal harmony -1; Emmylou Harris, vocal harmony -2; Mark Howard, guitar;
Roy Huskey, bass; Kenneth Malone, percussion; Joseph Miskulin, accordion. Prod. Jack
Clement.

I WISH I WAS CRAZY AGAIN (Bob McDill)

2-59930   **SWEETER THAN THE FLOWERS** -1,2
(L. Mann-E. Rouse-M. Burns)
(see overdub/release session: June 21, 1988)

NOTE: It is not known if Colter and Harris are on **I WISH I WAS CRAZY AGAIN** nor
has it been established whether they were on this session or the overdub session of June

21, 1988.

===

February 10, 1988 - 2nd session (6p-9p)
JMI Recording Studio, Nashville, Tennessee
Johnny Cash, vocal, guitar; Charles Cochran, keyboard; Mark Howard; Roy Huskey, bass;
Kenneth Malone, percussion; Joseph Miskulin. Prod. Jack Clement.

KISS THE LADIES GOODNIGHT

I'LL GO SOMEWHERE AND SING MY SONGS AGAIN
(Tom T. Hall)
B - M/P-848-051-2 *The Mystery Of Life*

===

February 11, 1988 (2p-5p)
JMI Recording Studio, Nashville, Tennessee
Mark Howard, mandolin and/or guitar; Joseph Miskulin, piano and/or banjo.   Overdub
session only. Prod. Jack Clement.

2-59692   **WILDWOOD FLOWER** (A.P. Carter)
B - M/P-834-491-4 *Wildwood Flower*

2-59697   **SAVIOUR OF MY NATURAL LIFE** (A.P. Carter)
B - M/P-834-491-4 *Wildwood Flower*

2-59694   **BANKS OF THE OHIO** (A.P. Carter)
B - M/P-834-491-4 *Wildwood Flower*

NOTE: Overdub for material original done in June 1986 and released on the "House of
Cash" label. As mentioned in note for June 23, 1986 no master numbers were given until
Polygram Records assigned them in 1988. Musician credits on the Mercury/Polygram tape
shows James Eller, bass and Bobby Irwin, drums on **SAVIOUR OF MY NATURAL
LIFE**. They are not listed on Musician Union information for either this session or the
one on June 23, 1986. There is a male background vocal on **BANKS OF THE OHIO** --
possibly Joseph Miskulin. The Polygram release was only in cassette form as designated
by "-4" following the release number.

===

February 23, 1988 (2p-5p)
JMI Recording Studio, Nashville, Tennessee
Joseph Miskulin. Overdub session only. Prod. Jack Clement.

2-59925   **LAST OF THE DRIFTERS** (Tom T. Hall)
(see overdub/release session: February 26, 1988 - 2nd session)

2-59928   **CALL ME THE BREEZE** (J.J. Cale)
(see overdub/release session: May 20, 1988)

GOOD MORNING JOHN (Kris Kristofferson)
(see overdub session: February 26, 1988 - 2nd session)

NOTE: I am assuming this is an overdub session eventhough **LAST OF THE DRIFTERS** and this master of **GOOD MORNING JOHN** appear here for the first time. Tom T. Hall duets with Cash on **LAST OF THE DRIFTERS** at the initial recording session.

===

February 24, 1988 (2p-5p)
JMI Recording Studio, Nashville, Tennessee
Joseph Miskulin. Overdub session only. Prod. Jack Clement.

2-59925   **LAST OF THE DRIFTERS** (Tom T. Hall)
    (see overdub/release session: February 26, 1988 - 2nd session)

2-59928   **CALL ME THE BREEZE** (J.J. Cale)
    (see overdub/release session: May 20, 1988)

    GOOD MORNING JOHN (Kris Kristofferson)
    (see overdub session: February 26, 1988 - 2nd session)

===

February 25, 1988 (2p-5p)
JMI Recording Studio, Nashville, Tennessee
Joseph Miskulin. Overdub session only. Prod. Jack Clement.

2-59925   **LAST OF THE DRIFTERS** (Tom T. Hall)
    (see overdub/release session: February 26, 1988 - 2nd session)

2-59928   **CALL ME THE BREEZE** (J.J. Cale)
    (see overdub/release session: May 20, 1988)

    GOOD MORNING JOHN (Kris Kristofferson)
    (see overdub session: February 26, 1988 - 2nd session)

===

February 26, 1988 - 1st session (10a-1p)
JMI Recording Studio, Nashville, Tennessee
Joseph Miskulin. Overdub session only. Prod. Jack Clement.

2-59925   **LAST OF THE DRIFTERS** (Tom T. Hall)
    (see overdub/release session: February 26, 1988 - 2nd session)

2-59928   **CALL ME THE BREEZE** (J.J. Cale)
    (see overdub/release session: May 20, 1988)

    GOOD MORNING JOHN (Kris Kristofferson)
    (see overdub session: February 26, 1988 - 2nd session)

===

February 26, 1988 - 2nd session (2p-5p)
JMI Recording Studio, Nashville, Tennessee

Jack Clement or Lloyd Green, dobro; Lloyd Green, steel guitar; Mark Howard, guitar; Roy Huskey, bass; Waylon Jennings, electric guitar-1; Kenneth Malone, percussion; Joseph Miskulin. Overdub session only. Prod. Jack Clement.

2-59925   **LAST OF THE DRIFTERS** -1 (Tom T. Hall)
A - M/P-874-562-7 b/w **Water From The Wells Of Home**
B - M/P-834-778-1 *Water From The Wells Of Home*

2-59928   **CALL ME THE BREEZE** (J.J. Cale)
(see overdub/release session: May 20, 1988)

GOOD MORNING JOHN (Kris Kristofferson)

NOTE: Although Waylon Jennings' name is not listed for this master his guitar work is unmistakable and Johnny Cash verified Waylon's work in conversation March 22, 1989.
===

March 2, 1988 (3p-6p)
JMI Recording Studio, Nashville, Tennessee
Johnny Cash, vocal, guitar; Charles Cochran, keyboard; Mark Howard, guitar; Roy Huskey, bass; Kenneth Malone, percussion, possibly tamborine; Joseph Miskulin; Hank Williams, Jr., vocal; Bobby Wood, keyboard. Prod. Jack Clement.

2-59929   **THAT OLD WHEEL** (Jennifer Pierce)
(see overdub/release session: June 22, 1988)

===

March 4, 1988 (6p-9p)
JMI Recording Studio, Nashville, Tennessee
Ralph Mooney, steel guitar. Overdub session only. Prod. Jack Clement.

2-59929   **THAT OLD WHEEL** (Jennifer Pierce)
(see overdub/release session: June 22, 1988)

===

March 7, 1988 - 1st session (10a-1p)
JMI Recording Studio, Nashville, Tennessee
Johnny Cash, vocal, guitar; Roy Acuff, vocal harmony; Charles Cochran, keyboard; Jessi Colter, Emmylou Harris, vocal harmony; Mark Howard, guitar; Roy Huskey, bass; Waylon Jennings, vocal harmony; Kenneth Malone, percussion; Joseph Miskulin. Prod. Jack Clement.

2-59926   **AS LONG AS I LIVE** (Roy Acuff)
(see overdub/release session: June 21, 1988)

NOTE: Besides the aforementioned, additional vocal harmony for this title was provided by all or part of the following: Roberto Bianco, Cindi Cash, Allison Clement, Bob Clement, Debra deKelaita, Mark Durham, Claude Hill, Sandy Mason, Joseph Miskulin, Bernard Peyton and Tom Skinker. It is not known which, if any, of the vocal harmonies were done at this initial session or the overdub session. Jack Clement possibly plays ukulele on this master.

==

March 7, 1988 - 2nd session (2p-5p)
JMI Recording Studio, Nashville, Tennessee
Johnny Cash, vocal, guitar; Rosanne Cash, vocal; Charles Cochran, keyboard; Don and Phil Everly, vocals; Mark Howard, guitar; Roy Huskey, bass; Kenneth Malone, percussion, tamborine; Joseph Miskulin. Prod. Jack Clement.

2-59924   **BALLAD OF A TEENAGE QUEEN** (Jack Clement)
(see overdub/release session: June 22, 1988)

==

April 1988
McCartney Recording Studio, England
Johnny Cash, vocal; June Carter Cash, vocal harmony; Linda McCartney, vocal harmony; Paul McCartney, vocal, bass; Stuart Hamish, guitar; Chris Whitten, drums. Prod. Paul McCartney.

2-59932   **NEW MOON OVER JAMAICA**
(Tom T. Hall-John R. Cash-Paul McCartney)
(see overdub/release session: June 20, 1988)

NOTE: Cash recut his vocal in Nashville at the above noted overdub session.

==

May 18, 1988 - 1st session (10a-1p)
JMI Recording Studio, Nashville, Tennessee
Johnny Cash, vocal, guitar; Glen Campbell, vocal; James Dant, drums; Mark Howard, guitar; Roy Huskey, bass; Joseph Miskulin, accordion; Marty Stuart, guitar and/or mandolin; Bobby Wood, keyboard. Prod. Jack Clement.

DIDN'T HE SHINE
(see possible overdub session: May 20, 1988)

2-59931   **A CROFT IN CLACHAN (BALLAD OF ROBB MAC DUNN)**
(John R. Cash)
(see overdub/release session: May 20, 1988)

==

May 18, 1988 - 2nd session (6p-9p)
JMI Recording Studio, Nashville, Tennessee
Ace Cannon, saxophone; Kenneth Malone, percussion; Joseph Miskulin; Marty Stuart, guitar and/or mandolin. Overdub session only. Prod. Jack Clement.

2-59928   **CALL ME THE BREEZE** (J.J. Cale)
(see overdub/release session: May 20, 1988)

==

May 20, 1988 (6p-9p)
JMI Recording Studio, Nashville, Tennessee

Kenneth Malone, percussion; Jody Maphis, vocal harmony -1; Joseph Miskulin, accordion -2; Marty Stuart; Cynthia Wyatt, harp or flute.   Overdub session only.   Prod.   Jack Clement.

2-59928   **CALL ME THE BREEZE** (J.J. Cale)
B - M/P-834-778-1 *Water From The Wells Of Home*

2-59931   **A CROFT IN CLACHAN (BALLAD OF ROBB MAC DUNN)** -2,3
(John R. Cash)
B - M/P-834-778-1 *Water From The Wells Of Home*

DIDN'T HE SHINE

2-59924   **BALLAD OF A TEENAGE QUEEN** -1 (Jack Clement)
(see overdub/release session: June 22, 1988)

===

June 20, 1988 (10a-1p)
JMI Recording Studio, Nashville, Tennessee
Jack Clement, dobro-1; W.S. Holland, drums; Mark Howard, guitar; Roy Huskey, bass; Kenneth Malone, percussion, tambourine.   Overdub session.   Prod. Jack Clement.

2-59933   **WATER FROM THE WELLS OF HOME**
(John R. Cash-John C. Cash)
A - M/P-874-562-7 b/w **Last Of The Drifters** (w/Tom T. Hall)
B - M/P-834-778-1 *Water From The Wells Of Home*

2-59932   **NEW MOON OVER JAMAICA** -1
(Tom T. Hall-John R. Cash-Paul McCartney)
B - M/P-834-778-1 *Water From The Wells Of Home*

2-59924   **BALLAD OF A TEENAGE QUEEN** (Jack Clement)
(see overdub/release session: June 22, 1988)

NOTE: This master of **NEW MOON OVER JAMAICA** was remixed and additional musicians added during this session (see initial session: April 1988).   Tom T. Hall and June Carter Cash provided additional vocal harmony. **WATER FROM THE WELLS OF HOME** includes strings but no mention is made of an overdub session.   Additional vocal harmony on **NEW MOON OVER JAMAICA** and **BALLAD OF A TEENAGE QUEEN** probably includes all or part of the following: Roberto Bianco, Cindi Cash, Allison Clement, Bob Clement, Debra deKelaita, Mark Durham, Claude Hill, Sandy Mason, Joseph Miskulin, Bernard Peyton and Tom Skinker.

===

June 21, 1988 (2p-5p)
JMI Recording Studio, Nashville, Tennessee
Lloyd Green, steel guitar, dobro; Roy Huskey, bass; Kenneth Malone, percussion; Marty Stuart, mandolin; Bobby Wood, keyboard.   Overdub session only.   Prod. Jack Clement.

2-59926   **AS LONG AS I LIVE** (Roy Acuff)
B - M/P-834-778-1 *Water From The Wells Of Home*

2-59929   **THAT OLD WHEEL** (Jennifer Pierce)
(see overdub/release session: June 22, 1988)

2-59930   **SWEETER THAN THE FLOWERS** (L. Mann-E. Rouse-M. Burns)
B - M/P-834-778-1 *Water From The Wells Of Home*

2-59927   **WHERE DID WE GO RIGHT** (Dave Loggins-Don Schlitz)
(see overdub/release session: June 22, 1988)

===

June 22, 1988 (9p-12m)
JMI Recording Studio, Nashville, Tennessee
W.S. Holland, drums; Kenneth Malone, percussion; Gove Scrivenor, vocal harmony -1;
Marty Stuart, mandolin -2; Bobby Wood, keyboard. Overdub session only. Prod. Jack
Clement.

2-59929   **THAT OLD WHEEL** (Jennifer Pierce)
A - M/P-870-688-7 b/w **Tennessee Flat-Top Box**
B - M/P-834-778-1 *Water From The Wells Of Home*

2-59924   **BALLAD OF A TEENAGE QUEEN** -1 (Jack Clement)
A - M/P-872-420-7 b/w **Get Rhythm**
B - M/P-834-778-1 *Water From The Wells Of Home*

2-59927   **WHERE DID WE GO RIGHT** -2 (Dave Loggins-Don Schlitz)
B - M/P-834-778-1 *Water From The Wells Of Home*

NOTE: The released master of **WHERE DID WE GO RIGHT** includes Anita, Helen
and Carlene Carter with vocal harmony. They were probably on the initial session on
December 10, 1987 - 1st session. The single release of **BALLAD OF A TEENAGE
QUEEN** was given a "current" master number of (2-60278).

===

August 22, 1988 - 1st session (10a-1p) (soundtrack)
Digital Recorders, Nashville, Tennessee
Johnny Cash, vocal, guitar; Earl Ball, piano; Jerry Carrigan, guitar; Mark Casstevens,
guitar; Steve Gibson, guitar; Mark Howard, guitar; William McElhiney, trumpet; Terry
McMillan, possible percussion; Robert Wray, guitar.

JUST THE OTHER SIDE OF NOWHERE
(see overdub session: August 23, 1988)

NOTE: This title was recorded for inclusion in the motion picture *Tennessee Waltz*. This
is referred to as a "rehearsal" session in my data.

===

August 22, 1988 - 2nd session (7p-10p) (soundtrack)
Digital Recorders, Nashville, Tennessee

David Davidson, Conni Ellisor, probably strings; Carl Gorodetsky, violin; Robert Green, Richard Grosjean, Michael Hayes, Theodore Madsen, Robert Mason, probably strings; William McElhiney, trumpet; Laura Molyneaux, Elisabeth Small, probably strings; Denis Solee, probably saxophone and/or flute; George Tidwell, trumpet; Kristin Wilkinson, viola. Overdub session only.

JUST THE OTHER SIDE OF NOWHERE
(see overdub session: August 23, 1988)

NOTE: This is referred to as a "recording" session in my data. It is not known if Cash attended this session. See also note for session dated August 22, 1988-1st session.

==

August 23, 1988 (9a-5p) (soundtrack)
Digital Recorders, Nashville, Tennessee
Earl Ball, piano; Dale Burton; Stephen Kennedy; John Pell; Joe Pointer; Kenneth Smith. Overdub session only.

JUST THE OTHER SIDE OF NOWHERE

NOTE: This is shown as a "sideline" session in my data. It is not known if Cash attended this session. See also note for session dated August 22, 1988-1st session.

==

September 13, 1988
Archer Productions Studio, Nashville, Tennessee
Johnny Cash, narration. Prod. Dyann Rivkin.

Gospel Of John
B - 7488CA *The Spoken Word New Testament*

NOTE: With this session Cash started a "spoken word" project for the Thomas Nelson Organization during which he recorded the entire New King James version of the New Testament for release in an audio cassette format. Information for this project was provided by Reba Hancock (personal correspondence: May 18, 1989) and Dyann Rivkin (telephone conversation: May 23, 1989).

==

September 15, 1988
Archer Productions Studio, Nashville, Tennessee
Johnny Cash, narration. Prod. Dyann Rivkin.

Gospel of John (continued)
B - 7488CA *The Spoken Word New Testament*

==

October 25, 1988 (soundtrack) (live)
Faith Assembly of God Church, Kernsville, North Carolina
JoAnne Cash Yates, vocals; JOHNNY CASH, vocals; Faith Assembly of God Choir. Prod. Bill Anderson Jr.

JESUS IS LORD
B - JANA-8901 *JoAnne Cash Yates Live*

GOSPEL MEDLEY
B - JANA-8901 *JoAnne Cash Yates Live*

HOW BEAUTIFUL HEAVEN MUST BE
B - JANA-8901 *JoAnne Cash Yates Live*

LORD I'M COMING HOME
B - JANA-8901 *JoAnne Cash Yates Live*

NOTE: These selections were recorded live at the Faith Assembly of God Church. They were included in an audio cassette (JANA-8901) and a video cassette. JoAnne Cash Yates is Cash's older sister.

==

December 6, 1988
Archer Productions Studio, Nashville, Tennessee
Johnny Cash, narration. Prod. Dyann Rivkin.

Gospel of Matthew
B - 7488CA *The Spoken Word New Testament*

==

December 6, 1988 (2p-5p)
Scruggs Recording Studio, Nashville, Tennessee
Roy Acuff, lead vocal-second verse, vocal harmony; Cynthia Biederman, Sam Bush, Paulette Carlson, vocal harmony; Robert Carpenter, lead vocal-fifth verse, piano; Gretchen Carpenter, vocal harmony; Anita, Helen Carter, June Carter Cash, vocal harmony-first chorus; Cindi Cash, vocal harmony; JOHNNY CASH, lead vocal-first verse, vocal harmony; John Cowan, Steve Dahl, John Denver, vocal harmony; Jerry Douglas, dobro; Jimmie Fadden, drums, vocal harmony; Bela Fleck, Pat Flynn, Radney Foster, Vince Gill, vocal harmony; Jeffrey Hanna, lead vocal-fifth verse, guitar, vocal harmony; Melody Hanna, vocal harmony; Emmylou Harris, Levon Helm, lead vocal-fourth verse; John Hiatt, Chris Hillman, Bruce Hornsby, vocal harmony; Roy Huskey, Jr, upright bass; Jimmy Ibbotson, lead vocal-fifth verse, vocal harmony; David Jones, Pete "Oswald" Kirby, Bill Lloyd, Jimmy Martin, Roger McGuinn, Michael Martin Murphy, Tracy Nelson, vocal harmony; Mark O'Conner, fiddle; Robert Oermann, Brad Parker, Don Schlitz, vocal harmony; Earl Scruggs, banjo, vocal harmony; Gary Scruggs, vocal harmony; Randy Scruggs, lead guitar, vocal harmony; Steve Scruggs, Lynn Shults, vocal harmony; Ricky Skaggs, lead vocal- third verse; Marty Stuart, Wendy Waldman, Steve Wariner, Bobbie White, Buck White, Cheryl White, Sharon White, vocal harmony. Prod. Randy Scruggs-Nitty Gritty Dirt Band.

MC-28627   **WILL THE CIRCLE BE UNBROKEN**
           (A.P. Carter/additional verse: J. Ibbotson)
B - UNIVERSAL/UVL2-12500 *Will The Circle Be Unbroken, Volume Two*

NOTE: This session belongs to the Nitty Gritty Dirt Band (Robert Carpenter, Jimmie

Fadden, Jeffrey Hanna, Jimmy Ibbotson) and was part of their *Will The Circle Be Unbroken, Volume Two* release on the Universal label (UVL2-12500).

December 8, 1988 (10a-1p)
Scruggs Recording Studio, Nashville, Tennessee
Johnny Cash, vocal, guitar; Robert Carpenter, accordion, vocal harmony; Anita, Helen Carter, June Carter Cash, vocal harmony; Jerry Douglas, dobro; Jimmie Fadden, drums; Jeffrey Hanna, guitar, vocal harmony; Roy Huskey, Jr, upright bass; Jimmy Ibbotson, mandolin, vocal harmony; Mark O'Connor, fiddle; Earl Scruggs, banjo; Randy Scruggs, Mother Maybelle's L-5 guitar. Prod. Randy Scruggs-Nitty Gritty Dirt Band.

MC-28609   **LIFE'S RAILWAY TO HEAVEN** (Arr: John R. Cash)
  B - UNIVERSAL/UVL2-12500 *Will The Circle Be Unbroken, Volume Two*

NOTE: See note for session dated December 6, 1988.

1988 (soundtrack)
Studio Location Unknown
Johnny Cash, vocal, guitar; Earl Ball, piano; W.S. Holland, drums; Jim Soldi, guitar; Jimmy Tittle, bass; Bob Wootton, electric guitar.

BALLAD OF DAVY CROCKETT

NOTE: This was done for the season opener of the "Wonderful World Of Disney" in the fall of 1988 on the NBC TV network.

March 6, 1989 - 2 sessions (2p-5p;6p-9p)
Emerald Sound Studio, Nashville, Tennessee
Johnny Cash, vocal, guitar; Waylon Jennings, vocal, guitar; Kris Kristofferson, vocal, guitar; Willie Nelson, vocal, guitar; Glen Campbell, vocal, guitar-2nd session only -1; Gene Chrisman, drums; John Christopher, guitar; Bob Emmons, keyboard; William Lane, keyboard; Mike Leech, bass; Mickey Raphael, harmonica; Bobby Wood, piano; Reggie Young, guitar. Prod. Chips Moman.

NCO-140110 **AMERICAN REMAINS** (R. Rutherford)
  A - CBS/38-73233 b/w **Silver Stallion**
  B - CBS/C-45240 *Highwayman 2*

NCO-14011 **COWBOY HALL OF FAME** -1

NOTE: These March 6 through March 9 sessions were for basic tracks with additional overdubbing of musicians and/or vocals done later. (Conversation with Johnny Cash: March 22, 1989.) At least one overdub session for this project was done in Memphis, Tennessee. **AMERICAN REMAINS** includes vocal backgrounds overdubbed at a later session and probably included: Johnny Barringer, David Edney, Bobby Emmons, Chips Moman, Jack Powell, Rivers Rutherford and Robbie Turner.

March 7, 1989 - 2 sessions (2p-5p;6p-9p)
Emerald Sound Studio, Nashville, Tennessee

Johnny Cash, vocal, guitar; Waylon Jennings, vocal, guitar; Kris Kristofferson, vocal, guitar; Willie Nelson, vocal, guitar; Gene Chrisman, drums; John Christopher, guitar; Bob Emmons, keyboard; William Lane, keyboard; Mike Leech, bass; Mickey Raphael, harmonica; Robbie Turner, steel guitar -1; Bobby Wood, piano; Reggie Young, guitar. Prod. Chips Moman.

NCO-140112 **TEXAS** -1 (Willie Nelson)
    A - CBS/38-73381 b/w **Born And Raised In Black And White**
    B - CBS/C-45240 *Highwayman 2*

NCO-140113 **BORN AND RAISED IN BLACK AND WHITE** -1
        (Don Cook-John Jarvis)
    A - CBS/38-73381 b/w **Texas** (Willie only)
    B - CBS/C-45240 *Highwayman 2*

NCO-140114 **SILVER STALLION** (L. Clayton)
    A - CBS/38-73233 b/w **American Remains**
    B - CBS/C-45240 *Highwayman 2*

NCO-140115 **ANGELS LOVE BAD MEN** (Waylon Jennings-Roger Murrah)
    B - CBS/C-45240 *Highwayman 2*

NOTE: **TEXAS** was probably only the basic track and then either redone or overdubbed later at Nelson's Pedernales Recording Studio, Spiceland, Texas. **BORN AND RAISED IN BLACK AND WHITE** and **SILVER STALLION** include vocal background-see note for session dated March 6, 1989. It is possible that Robbie Turner overdubbed steel guitar on **TEXAS** and **BORN AND RAISED IN BLACK AND WHITE** at a later date as he is not listed by the Musicians Union as being on this session. A music video was made using **SILVER STALLION**.

===

March 8, 1989 - 3 sessions (2p-5p;6p-9p;9p-12m)
Emerald Sound Studio, Nashville, Tennessee
Johnny Cash, vocal, guitar; Waylon Jennings, vocal, guitar; Kris Kristofferson, vocal, guitar; Willie Nelson, vocal, guitar; Gene Chrisman, drums; John Christopher, guitar; Bob Emmons, keyboard; William Lane, keyboard; Mike Leech, bass; Mickey Raphael, harmonica; Robbie Turner, steel guitar -1; Bobby Wood, piano; Reggie Young, guitar. Prod. Chips Moman.

NCO-140116 **YABBA DABBA DOO**

NCO-140117 **ANTHEM '84** (Kris Kristofferson)
    B - CBS/C-45240 *Highwayman 2*

NCO-140118 **SONGS THAT MAKE A DIFFERENCE** (John R. Cash)
    B - CBS/C-45240 *Highwayman 2*

NCO-140119 **WE'RE ALL IN YOUR CORNER TONIGHT** -1
        (Troy Seals-Bobby Emmons)
    B - CBS/C-45240 *Highwayman 2*

NOTE: It is possible Robbie Turner overdubbed steel guitar on **WE'RE ALL IN YOUR CORNER TONIGHT** at a later session as he is not listed by the Musicians Union as having been at this session.

==

March 9, 1989 - 2 sessions (2p-5p;6p-9p)
Emerald Sound Studio, Nashville, Tennessee
Johnny Cash, vocal, guitar; Waylon Jennings, vocal, guitar; Kris Kristofferson, vocal, guitar; Willie Nelson, vocal, guitar; Gene Chrisman, drums; John Christopher, guitar; Bob Emmons, keyboard; William Lane, keyboard; Mike Leech, bass; Mickey Raphael, harmonica; Robbie Turner, steel guitar-1; Bobby Wood, piano; Reggie Young, guitar. Prod. Chips Moman.

NCO-140120 **MODERN GLADIATOR**

NCO-140121 **TWO STORIES WIDE** -1 (Willie Nelson)
   B - CBS/C-45240 *Highwayman 2*

NCO-140122 **LIVING LEGEND** (Kris Kristofferson)
   B - CBS/C-45240 *Highwayman 2*

NOTE: Cash says **MODERN GLADIATOR** was considered at this session but it was decided not to use it (conversation with Johnny Cash - March 22, 1989). It is possible Robbie Turner was not present at this session but overdubbed steel guitar on **TWO STORIES WIDE** later. Two additional sessions were held, September 8, 1989 at Moman Studio, Nashville and October 1989 at Three Alarm Studio, Memphis, to finish the *Highwayman 2* project. According to information from Hugh Waddell of the House of Cash, Cash was present.

==

March 16, 1989
Archer Productions Studio, Nashville, Tennessee
Johnny Cash, narration. Prod. Dyann Rivkin.

      Gospel of Matthew (continued)
   B - 7488CA *The Spoken Word New Testament*

==

April 11, 1989
Archer Productions Studio, Nashville, Tennessee
Johnny Cash, narration. Prod. Dyann Rivkin.

      Gospel of Mark
   B - 7488CA *The Spoken Word New Testament*

==

May 31, 1989
Archer Productions Studio, Nashville, Tennessee
Johnny Cash, narration. Prod. Dyann Rivkin.

Gospel of Luke (Chapters 1-7)
B - 7488CA *The Spoken Word New Testament*

==

June 13, 1989
Archer Productions Studio, Nashville, Tennessee
Johnny Cash, narration. Prod. Dyann Rivkin.

Gospel of Luke (Chapters 8-15)
B - 7488CA *The Spoken Word New Testament*

==

June 15, 1989
Archer Productions Studio, Nashville, Tennessee
Johnny Cash, narration. Prod. Dyann Rivkin.

Gospel of Luke (Chapters 16-24)
B - 7488CA *The Spoken Word New Testament*

==

June 16, 1989
Archer Productions Studio, Nashville, Tennessee
Johnny Cash, narration. Prod. Dyann Rivkin.

Acts (Chapters 1-14)
B - 7488CA *The Spoken Word New Testament*

==

June 26, 1989
Archer Productions Studio, Nashville, Tennessee
Johnny Cash, narration. Prod. Dyann Rivkin.

Acts (Chapters 15-28)
B - 7488CA *The Spoken Word New Testament*

==

June 27, 1989 - 1st session (10a-1p)
Stargem Recording Studio, Nashville, Tennessee
Johnny Cash, vocal, guitar; Earl Ball, piano; W.S. Holland, drums; Roy Huskey, bass;
Billy Sanford, guitar; Jim Soldi, guitar. Prod. Bob Moore.

89-1307   **I DRAW THE LINE**

==

June 27, 1989 - 2nd session (1p-4p)
Stargem Recording Studio, Nashville, Tennessee
Johnny Cash, vocal, guitar; Earl Ball, piano; Carrie Cash, vocal -1; W.S. Holland, drums;
Roy Huskey, bass; Jordanaires, background vocals -2; Billy Sanford, guitar; Jim Soldi,

guitar; Jimmy Tittle, bass. Prod. Bob Moore.

89-1304   **FARMER'S ALMANAC** (John R. Cash)
A - M/P-876-428-7 b/w **I Shall Be Free**
B - M/P-842-155-2 *Boom Chicka Boom*

89-1306   **FAMILY BIBLE** -1,2 (Paul Buskirk-Walter Breeland-Claude Gray)
B - M/P-842-155-2 *Boom Chicka Boom*

NOTE: The Jordanaires' appearance on the following *Boom Chicka Boom* project was done as overdub session(s).
==
June 29, 1989 - 1st session (10a-1p)
Stargem Recording Studio, Nashville, Tennessee
Johnny Cash, vocal, guitar; Earl Ball, piano; W.S. Holland, drums; Roy Huskey, bass; Jordanaires, background vocals; Billy Sanford, guitar; Reggie Young, guitar. Prod. Bob Moore.

89-1303   **CAT'S IN THE CRADLE** (Harry Chapin-Sandy Campbell Chapin)
A - M/P-875-626-7 b/w **I Love You, Love You**
B - M/P-842-155-2 *Boom Chicka Boom*

89-1308   **I LOVE YOU, LOVE YOU** (John R. Cash)
A - M/P-875-626-7 b/w **Cat's In The Cradle**
B - M/P-842-155-2 *Boom Chicka Boom*

NOTE: Session information from Musicians Union indicates Reggie Young worked an extra hour at this session.
==
June 29, 1989 - 2nd session (2p-5p)
Stargem Recording Studio, Nashville, Tennessee
Johnny Cash, vocal, guitar; Earl Ball, piano; W.S. Holland, drums; Billy Sanford, guitar; Jimmy Tittle, bass; Reggie Young, guitar. Prod. Bob Moore.

OLD RED

==
June 30, 1989 - 1st session (10a-1p)
Stargem Recording Studio, Nashville, Tennessee
Johnny Cash, vocal, guitar; Earl Ball, piano; W.S. Holland, drums; Roy Huskey, bass; Billy Sanford, guitar; Reggie Young, guitar. Prod. Bob Moore.

HALLELUJAH JOE

NOTE: Session information from Musicians Union shows Huskey worked an extra hour at this session.
==
June 30, 1989 - 2nd session (2p-5p)
Stargem Recording Studio, Nashville, Tennessee

Johnny Cash, vocal, guitar; Earl Ball, piano; W.S. Holland, drums; Roy Huskey, bass; Billy Sanford, guitar; Reggie Young, guitar. Prod. Bob Moore.

THE STRANGEST DREAM

===

July 2, 1989
Archer Productions Studio, Nashville, Tennessee
Johnny Cash, narration. Prod. Dyann Rivkin.

Romans
B - 7488CA *The Spoken Word New Testament*

===

July 12, 1989
Archer Productions Studio, Nashville, Tennessee
Johnny Cash, narration. Prod. Dyann Rivkin.

First Corinthians
B - 7488CA *The Spoken Word New Testament*

===

July 13, 1989
Archer Productions Studio, Nashville, Tennessee
Johnny Cash, narration. Prod. Dyann Rivkin.

Second Corinthians
B - 7488CA *The Spoken Word New Testament*

Galatians
B - 7488CA *The Spoken Word New Testament*

===

July 14, 1989
Archer Productions Studio, Nashville, Tennessee
Johnny Cash, narration. Prod. Dyann Rivkin.

Ephesians
B - 7488CA *The Spoken Word New Testament*

Philippians
B - 7488CA *The Spoken Word New Testament*

Colossians
B - 7488CA *The Spoken Word New Testament*

===

July 31, 1989
Archer Productions Studio, Nashville, Tennessee
Johnny Cash, narration. Prod. Dyann Rivkin.

First Thessalonians
B - 7488CA *The Spoken Word New Testament*

Second Thessalonians
B - 7488CA *The Spoken Word New Testament*

First Timothy
B - 7488CA *The Spoken Word New Testament*

Second Timothy
B - 7488CA *The Spoken Word New Testament*

Titus
B - 7488CA *The Spoken Word New Testament*

Philemon
B - 7488CA *The Spoken Word New Testament*

==

August 29, 1989
Archer Productions Studio, Nashville, Tennessee
Johnny Cash, narration. Prod. Dyann Rivkin.

Hebrews
B - 7488CA *The Spoken Word New Testament*

James
B - 7488CA *The Spoken Word New Testament*

==

August 30, 1989 - 1st session (10a-1p)
Stargem Recording Studio, Nashville, Tennessee
Johnny Cash, vocal, guitar; W.S. Holland, drums; Roy Huskey, bass; Jordanaires, background vocals; Hargus Robbins, piano; Reggie Young, guitar. Prod. Bob Moore.

89-1309   **HIDDEN SHAME** (Elvis Costello)
B - M/P-842-155-2 *Boom Chicka Boom*

89-1310   **MONTEAGLE MOUNTAIN** (Richard McGilbony)
B - M/P-842-155-2 *Boom Chicka Boom*

NOTE: Another session was held on September 7, 1989 at Stargem Studio, Nashville, to possibly overdub Cash vocal on the *Boom Chicka Boom* project. Information provided by Hugh Waddell of the House of Cash.

==

<u>August 30, 1989</u> - <u>2nd session</u> (1p-4p)
<u>Stargem Recording Studio, Nashville, Tennessee</u>
Johnny Cash, vocal, guitar; W.S. Holland, drums; Roy Huskey, bass; Reggie Young, guitar. Prod. Bob Moore.

EVERYTHING IS ALRIGHT AT HOME

==

<u>September 1, 1989</u>
<u>Archer Productions Studio, Nashville, Tennessee</u>
Johnny Cash, narration. Prod. Dyann Rivkin.

First Peter
B - 7488CA *The Spoken Word New Testament*

Second Peter
B - 7488CA *The Spoken Word New Testament*

First John
B - 7488CA *The Spoken Word New Testament*

Second John
B - 7488CA *The Spoken Word New Testament*

Third John
B - 7488CA *The Spoken Word New Testament*

Jude
B - 7488CA *The Spoken Word New Testament*

Revelations (Chapter 1-7)
B - 7488CA *The Spoken Word New Testament*

==

<u>September 5, 1989</u>
<u>Archer Studios Production, Nashville, Tennessee</u>
Johnny Cash, narration. Prod. Dyann Rivkin.

Revelations (Chapter 8-22)
B - 7488CA *The Spoken Word New Testament*

==

<u>September 6, 1989</u>
<u>Bradley's Barn, Mt. Juliet, Tennessee</u>
Sandy Kelly, vocal; JOHNNY CASH, vocal; remaining musicians unknown. Prod. Owen Bradley, Jr.

RING OF FIRE (June Carter-Merle Kilgore)
C - K-TEL/KCD-303 *Twenty Single Hits*

WOODCARVER (Pam & Rusty Wolfe)
A - K-TEL/KTS-036 b/w **Carlingford** (w/o Cash)
B - K-TEL/OCE-2465 *I Need To Be In Love*

NOTE: Information for this session was provided by Hugh Waddell of the House of Cash. There was also another session (overdub?) in October.
===

1989
Unknown Session(s) Dates
Johnny Cash, vocal, guitar; Earl Ball, piano; Ray Edenton, acoustic guitar; W.S. Holland, drums; Roy Huskey, Jr. or Bob Moore, bass; Jordanaires, background vocals; Billy Sanford, guitar; Reggie Young, electric guitar. Prod. Bob Moore.

89-1302   **A BACKSTAGE PASS** (John R. Cash)
   B - M/P-842-155-2 *Boom Chicka Boom*

89-1305   **DON'T GO NEAR THE WATER** (John R. Cash)
   B - M/P-842-155-2 *Boom Chicka Boom*

89-1307   **HARLEY** (Chick Rains-Michael Martin Murphey)
   B - M/P-842-155-2 *Boom Chicka Boom*

89-1311   **THAT'S ONE YOU OWE ME** (Jim Elliott-Mark D. Sanders)
   B - M/P-842-155-2 *Boom Chicka Boom*

89-1312   **I SHALL BE FREE** (John R. Cash)
   A - M/P-876-428-4 b/w **Farmer's Almanac**

89-1313   **VETERAN'S DAY** (Tom Russell)
   B - M/P-842-725-2 *Boom Chicka Boom*

NOTE: **A BACKSTAGE PASS** was probably done earlier in the year. It gives the impression, on record at least, that it was recorded before a "live" audience. This could also be the same song recorded on the October 24, 1986 sessions but titled then as **WHACKOS AND WEIRDOS. DON'T GO NEAR THE WATER** is a re-make of the same song recorded on February 19, 1974 and released as a single and on the CBS album *Ragged Old Flag* (KC-32917). All or part of these titles could have been recorded at Stargem Recording Studio, Nashville and/or Bradley's Barn, Mt. Juliet, Tennessee. **VETERAN'S DAY** was added to the European release of *Boom Chicka Boom* and was assigned a different album/compact disc number that the United States release.
===

September 6, 1990 - 2 sessions (10a-1p;2p-5p)
JMI Recording Studio, Nashville, Tennessee
Johnny Cash, vocal, guitar; Earl Ball, keyboard; W.S. Holland, drums; Steve Logan, bass; Kerry Marx, electric guitar. Prod. Jack Clement.

GREATEST COWBOY OF THEM ALL (John R. Cash)
(see overdub/release session: September 18, 1990 - 2nd session)

HEY PORTER (John R. Cash)
(see overdub/release session: September 18, 1990 - 1st session)

==

September 7, 1990 - 2 sessions (10a-1p;2p-5p)
JMI Recording Studio, Nashville, Tennessee
Johnny Cash, vocal, guitar; Earl Ball, keyboard; W.S. Holland, drums; Steve Logan, bass;
Kerry Marx, electric guitar. Prod. Jack Clement.

REDNECK LOVE

I'M AN EASY RIDER (John R. Cash)
C - M/P-848-051-2 *The Mystery Of Life*

COUNTRY BOY (John R. Cash)

==

September 18, 1990 - 1st session (11a-1p)
JMI Recording Studio, Nashville, Tennessee
Mark Howard, electric guitar; Roy Huskey, bass; Marty Stuart, guitar. Overdub session
only. Prod. Jack Clement.

WANTED MAN (Bob Dylan-John R. Cash)
C - M/P-848-051-2 *The Mystery Of Life*

HEY PORTER (John R. Cash)
C - M/P-848-051-2 *The Mystery Of Life*

ANGEL AND THE BADMAN (John R. Cash)
C - M/P-848-051-2 *The Mystery Of Life*

COUNTRY BOY (John R. Cash)

==

September 18, 1990 - 2nd session (2p-5p)
JMI Recording Studio, Nashville, Tennessee
Mark Howard, electric guitar; Roy Huskey, bass; Marty Stuart, guitar. Overdub session
only. Prod. Jack Clement.

GREATEST COWBOY OF THEM ALL (John R. Cash)
C - M/P-848-051-2 *The Mystery Of Life*

==

September 25, 1990 (10a-1p)
JMI Recording Studio, Nashville, Tennessee
Jody Maphis, guitar; Kerry Marx, guitar. Prod. Jack Clement.

90-2404   **BEANS FOR BREAKFAST** (John R. Cash)
A - M/P-878-292-7 b/w **Goin' By The Book**
C - M/P-848-051-2 *The Mystery Of Life*

==

1990
Studio Unknown
Martin Delray, vocal, guitar; JOHNNY CASH, vocal; remaining musicians unknown.
Prod. Blake Mevis-Nelson Larkin.

GET RHYTHM (John R. Cash)
A - ATLANTIC/PRCD-3429-2

==

1990
Reflections Studio, Nashville, Tennessee
Tommy Cash, vocal, guitar; JOHNNY CASH, vocal; Tom T. Hall, vocal; George Jones, vocal; Michael Black, Lisa Carrie, Ellen Dockery, vocal harmony; remaining musicians unknown. Prod. Jack Gale-Jim Pierce.

THOUGHTS ON THE FLAG (Tom T. Hall)
C - PLAYBACK/PB-4501 *Twenty-fifth Anniversary Album* (Tommy Cash)

==

1990
Reflections Studio, Nashville, Tennessee
Tommy Cash, vocal, guitar; JOHNNY CASH, vocal; Michael Black, Lisa Carrie, Ellen Dockery, vocal harmony; remaining musicians unknown. Prod. Jack Gale-Jim Pierce.

GUESS THINGS HAPPEN THAT WAY (Jack Clement)
C - PLAYBACK/PB-4501 *Twenty-fifth Anniversary Album* (Tommy Cash)

==

March 14, 1991 (10a-1p)
LSI Recording Studio, Nashville, Tennessee
Johnny Cash, vocal, guitar; W.S. Holland, drums; Steve Logan, bass; Kerry Marx, electric guitar; Bobby Wood, piano. Prod. Mike Daniel.

GOD'S HANDS (Jim Dowell-Kent Blazy-Rob Crosby)

DON'T TAKE YOUR GUNS TO TOWN (John R. Cash)

==

June 24, 1991 - 2 sessions (10a-1p;2p-5p)
Germantown Studio, Nashville, Tennessee
William Baxter, steel guitar, dobro; Anita, Helen Carter, June Carter Cash, solo vocals -1; Stuart Duncan, mandolin, fiddle; Jack Hale, keyboards; Paul Hollowell, piano, keyboards; Kerry Marx, guitar; Ronald Tutt, drums; Glenn Worf, bass; Unknown saxophone -2. Prod. Ralph Jungheim.

AWAY IN A MANGER (Luther-Kilpatrick-Muller)
(see overdub/release session: August 1991)

BLUE CHRISTMAS -2 (B. Hayes-J. Johnson)
(see overdub/release session: August 1991)

FIRST NOEL -1 (Traditional/Arr: Jack Hale Jr)
(see overdub/release session: August 1991)

IT CAME UPON A MIDNIGHT CLEAR -1 (Sears-Willis)
(see overdub/release session: August 1991)

HARK, THE HERALD ANGELS SING (Wesley-Mendelssohn)
(see overdub/release session: August 1991)

Here Was A Man (narration) (Johnny Bond-Tex Ritter)
(see overdub/release session: August 1991)

I'LL BE HOME FOR CHRISTMAS (Gannon-Kent)
(see overdub/release session: August 1991)

JOY TO THE WORLD (Watts-Handel)
(see overdub/release session: August 1991)

NOTE: Musician Union files lists "employer's" name as Delta Music Inc. for this session date as well as those done on June 25, 1991. Additional information provided by Jack Hale Jr, December 1991. Cash overdubbed his vocals in August 1991.

==

June 25, 1991 - 2 sessions (10a-1p;2p-5p)
Germantown Studio, Nashville, Tennessee
William Baxter, steel guitar, dobro; Anita, Helen Carter, June Carter Cash, solo vocals -1; Jack Hale, keyboards; Paul Hollowell, piano, keyboards; James Horn; Kerry Marx, guitar; Ronald Tutt, drums; Glenn Worf, bass; Unknown flute -2. Prod. Ralph Jungheim.

O CHRISTMAS TREE -1 (Traditional/Arr: J. Hale Jr)
(see overdub/release session: August 1991)

O COME ALL YE FAITHFUL (Traditional/Arr: J. Hale Jr)
(see overdub/release session: August 1991)

O LITTLE TOWN OF BETHLEHEM -2 (P. Brooks-L. Redner)
(see overdub/release session: August 1991)

SILENT NIGHT (Mohr-F. Gruber)
(see overdub/release session: August 1991)

WE WISH YOU A MERRY CHRISTMAS (FIGGY PUDDIN') -1
(Carter-Hale)
(see overdub/release session: August 1991)

WHAT CHILD IS THIS (W.C. Dix)
(see overdub/release session: August 1991)

WHITE CHRISTMAS (Irving Berlin)
(see overdub/release session: August 1991)

NOTE: James Horn is listed on the Musician Union contract as "3 hours" but it is unknown if this was for the first or second session. Additional information provided by Jack Hale Jr, December 1991. Cash overdubbed his vocals August 1991.
===

August 1991
Reflections Studio, Nashville, Tennessee.
Johnny Cash, vocal overdub; possible additional vocal harmony added at this session - vocalists unknown -1. Prod. Ralph Jungheim.

BLUE CHRISTMAS (B. Hayes-J. Johnson)
C - LASER LIGHT/LL-15417 *Country Christmas*

SILENT NIGHT -1 (Mohr-F. Gruber)
C - LASER LIGHT/LL-15417 *Country Christmas*

WHITE CHRISTMAS (Irving Berlin)
C - LASER LIGHT/LL-15417 *Country Christmas*

Here Was A Man (narration) (Tex Ritter-Johnny Bond)
C - LASER LIGHT/LL-15417 *Country Christmas*

JOY TO THE WORLD -1 (Handel-Watts)
C - LASER LIGHT/LL-15417 *Country Christmas*

O LITTLE TOWN OF BETHLEHEM -1 (L. Redner-P. Brooks)
C - LASER LIGHT/LL-15417 *Country Christmas*

WHAT CHILD IS THIS (W.C. Dix)
C - LASER LIGHT/LL-15417 *Country Christmas*

AWAY IN A MANGER (Luther-Kilpatrick-Muller)
C - LASER LIGHT/LL-15417 *Country Christmas*

O COME ALL YE FAITHFUL -1 (Traditional)
C - LASER LIGHT/LL-15417 *Country Christmas*

HARK, THE HERALD ANGELS SING -1 (Wesley-Menderssohn)
C - LASER LIGHT/LL-15417 *Country Christmas*

I'LL BE HOME FOR CHRISTMAS (Gannon-Kent)
C - LASER LIGHT/LL-15417 *Country Christmas*

August 1991
Possibly Reflections Studio, Nashville, Tennessee
Anita, Helen Carter, June Carter Cash, vocals. Prod. Ralph Jungheim.

WE WISH YOU A MERRY CHRISTMAS (FIGGY PUDDIN')
(Carter-Hale)
C - LASER LIGHT/LL-15417 *Country Christmas*

FIRST NOEL (Traditional)
C - LASER LIGHT/LL-15417 *Country Christmas*

O CHRISTMAS TREE (Traditional)
C - LASER LIGHT/LL-15417 *Country Christmas*

IT CAME UPON A MIDNIGHT CLEAR (Sears-Willis)
C - LASER LIGHT/LL-15417 *Country Christmas*

1991
Quad Studios, Nashville, Tennessee
Johnny Cash, vocal; One Bad Pig: Phillip Owens, vocal, drums; Paul Q-Pek, vocal, guitar; Daniel Tucek, vocal, bass; Casey Womack, vocal. Prod. Billy Smiley.

MAN IN BLACK (John R. Cash)
B - MYRRH/WORD/7016937380 *I Scream Sunday* (One Bad Pig)

NOTE: "One Bad Pig" is a Christian rock group.

1991
Studio Location Unknown
Johnny Cash, vocal; Razzy Bailey, vocal; remaining musicians and producer unknown.

LONG BLACK VEIL (Marijohn Wilken-Danny Dill)
B - CURB/D2-77494 *Best Of Johnny Cash*

NOTE: It is not certain if this was a "true" duet or if there was a vocal overdub session involved. It also appears this, or at least a portion of the final master, was recorded live.

January 13, 1992 (10a-1p)
Music Mill Studio, Nashville, Tennessee
Johnny Cash, vocal; David Briggs; Kerry Marx, guitar; Brent Rowan, guitar; William Wilson; Glenn Worf, bass. Prod. Harold Shedd.

WHEN WE MEET AT THE RIVER

==

January 15, 1992 (10a-1p; 2p-6p)
Music Mill Studio, Nashville, Tennessee
Johnny Cash, vocal; June Carter Cash, vocal. Prod. Harold Shedd.

WHEN I LOOK (Dottie West-Mark Gray)

NOTE: This was originally intended as a Mercury/Polygram release but it was used later by the House of Cash in a video project entitled *"Return To The Promised Land"* (World Wide Pictures). See notes for sessions dated February 1992, Mid-July/Mid-August 1992 and Late August 1992. Information for this project was provided by Hugh Waddell in conversation on November 23, 1993.

==

February 1992
Recorded and video taped on location in Israel.
Johnny Cash, vocal -1, acoustic guitar -2; June Carter Cash, vocal -3, acoustic guitar -4; John Carter Cash, vocal -5, guitar -6. Prod. Johnny Cash-June Carter Cash-Hugh Waddell.

OVER THE NEXT HILL I'LL BE HOME (John R. Cash) -1,2
(see overdub session dated Mid-August 1992)

OLD RUGGED CROSS (George Bernard) -1,3,6
(see overdub session dated Mid-August 1992)

I WON'T HAVE TO CROSS JORDAN ALONE -1,2
(Thomas Ramsey-Charles Durham)

WAITING ON THE FAR SIDE BANKS OF JORDAN -1,2,3,4
(Terry Smith)
(see overdub session dated Mid-August 1992)

LET ME HELP YOU CARRY THE WEIGHT (Kostas) -1,3,6
(see overdub session dated Mid-August 1992)

LORD, TAKE THESE HANDS (John Carter Cash) -5,6

FISHERS OF MEN (Harry Clarke) -1,3,5,6
(see overdub session dated Mid-August-1992)

WHAT ON EARTH WOULD YOU DO FOR HEAVEN'S SAKE -1,2
(John R. Cash)

GOSPEL SHIP (A.P. Carter) -3,4

I SAW A MAN (Arthur Smith) -1,2,3,5,6

NOTE: This project was originally intended for The Nashville Network but picked up instead by World Wide Pictures in 1993 and distributed in a video cassette format in retail outlets in October 1993. The majority of the above material was overdubbed with additional instrumentation in August 1992 at the Bob Cummings Production facility in Nashville, Tennessee. As the video was being edited on digital equipment (D2) format, Hugh Waddell of the House of Cash, had four digital audio tracks on which were recorded the musicial tracks to accompany the vocals. With the exception of **I SAW A MAN**, all the listed songs were used in the video project *"Return To The Promised Land."*

==

March 1992
Big Javelina Studio, Nashville, Tennessee
Marty Stuart, vocal, guitar; JOHNNY CASH, vocal.   Prod. Richard Bennett-Tony Brown-Marty Stuart.

DOIN' MY TIME (Jimmie Skinner)
C - MCAD-10596 *This One's Gonna Hurt You* (Marty Stuart)

==

Mid-July/Mid-August 1992
Bob Cummings Productions, Nashville, Tennessee
Pete Cummings, electric guitar -1; Joel Edwards, bass -2, keyboard -3; Lee Owens, acoustic guitar -4; David Schnauffer, dulcimer -5, jews harp -6; Hugh Waddell, drums -7; Ben Wade, dulcimer -8. Prod. Johnny Cash-June Carter Cash-Hugh Waddell.

OVER THE NEXT HILL I'LL BE HOME (John R. Cash) -1,2,7

OLD RUGGED CROSS (George Bernard) -3
(see overdub session dated Late August 1992)

WAITING ON THE FAR SIDE BANKS OF JORDAN -1,2,3,4,7
(Terry Smith)

LET ME HELP YOU CARRY THE WEIGHT (Kostas) -5,8
(see overdub session dated Late August 1992)

FISHERS OF MEN (Harry Clarke) -4,5

RETURN TO THE PROMISED LAND -1,2,4,7
(John R. Cash-David Skinner-Hugh Waddell)

NOTE: With the exception of Hugh Waddell of the House of Cash, all the musicians appearing above were actually involved in the editing of *"Return To The Promised Land"* at Bob Cummings Productions and are not "studio musicians." Because the completion date of this project was not until 1993, and due to the unusual nature of its production, contracts were not filed with the Musicians Union in Nashville until the summer of 1993.

==

Late August 1992
Bob Cummings Productions, Nashville, Tennessee
Johnny Cash, vocal; June Carter Cash, vocal. Prod. Johnny Cash-June Carter Cash-Hugh Waddell.

OLD RUGGED CROSS (George Bernard)

LET ME HELP YOU CARRY THE WEIGHT (Kostas)

RETURN TO THE PROMISED LAND
(John R. Cash-David Skinner-Hugh Waddell)

NOTE: The first two titles are re-makes of the material originally done in February 1992 on location in Israel.

November 30, 1992
The Castle Studio, Franklin, Tennessee
Mark O'Conner, violin; JOHNNY CASH, vocal; Charlie Daniels, vocal, violin; Marty Stuart, vocal; Travis Tritt, vocal; Sam Bacco, percussion; John Cowan, vocal harmony; Jerry Douglas, lap steel; Mike Lawler, B-3 organ; Brent Mason, electric guitar; Dana McVicker, vocal harmony; Gary Smith, piano; Harry Stinson, drums, vocal harmony; Glenn Worf, electric bass. Prod. Greg Brown-Jim Ed Norman-Mark O'Connor.

THE DEVIL COMES BACK TO GEORGIA (T. Crain-C. Daniels-
T. Degregorio-F. Edwards-C. Hayward-M. Kott-J. Marshall-M. O'Connor-
B. Spicher-E.K. Story-M. Stuart)
C - WARNER BROTHERS/9-45257-2 *Heroes* (Mark O'Connor)

NOTE: A music video was made in 1993 using this song and featuring Mark O'Connor, Johnny Cash, Charlie Daniels, Marty Stuart and Travis Tritt.

November 30, 1992
Woodland Recording Studio, Nashville, Tennessee
John Schneider, vocal; Johnny Cash, vocal; remaining musicians unknown.

HELL THIS AIN'T HEAVEN

NOTE: According to Hugh Waddell of the House of Cash on this date Cash and John Schneider recorded the above duet at Woodland Studio in Nashville. This was part of a "demonstration/speculative" project for Schneider. In all, fourteen songs were done with Cash appearing only on this title.

December 14, 1992 (10a-1p)
LSI Recording Studio, Nashville, Tennessee
Johnny Cash, vocals; Earl Ball, keyboard; W.S. Holland, drums; David Jones, guitar; Kerry Marx, guitar; Terry McMillan, possibly harmonica; David Rorick, bass. Prod. Johnny Cash.

IT AIN'T ME

BIG RIVER (John R. Cash)

I WALK THE LINE (John R. Cash)

January 15, 1993 (6p-9p)
LSI Recording Studio, Nashville, Tennessee
Johnny Cash, vocal; Kerry Marx, guitar; Terry McMillan, possibly harmonica; David Rorick, bass; Hugh Waddell, drums. Prod. Johnny Cash.

DRIVE ON (John R. Cash)

HEY ALRIGHT (John R. Cash)

LIKE A SOLDIER (John R. Cash)

I LOVE YOU TONIGHT (John R. Cash)

SHE SANG SWEET BABY JAMES (John R. Cash)

NOTE: Information from the Musicians Union and Hugh Waddell at the House Of Cash shows this session to be for "demonstration" recordings only.

January 15, 1993
LSI Recording Studio, Nashville, Tennessee
Johnny Cash, vocal; Kerry Marx, guitar; Terry McMillan, harmonica; David Rorick, bass; Hugh Waddell, drums. Prod. Johnny Cash.

HAVE YOU EVER BEEN TO LR (John R. Cash)

SOLDIER BOY (John R. Cash)

HELLO OUT THERE (John R. Cash)

POOR VALLEY GIRL (John R. Cash)

SPOTLIGHT (John R. Cash)

NOTE: See note for above session.

February 11, 1993
The Factory/Windmill Lane Studio, Westland Studio, Dublin, Ireland
Bono, guitar; JOHNNY CASH, vocal; Adam Clayton, bass guitar; The Edge, guitar, piano, synthesizers, background vocal; Brian Eno, synthesizer.   Prod. Brian Eno-The Edge.

THE WANDERER (Bono-U2)
C - ISLAND/CIDU29-518047-2 *Zooropa*

NOTE: The CD information states the recording of the material for *Zooropa* was done in March-May 1993. However, Cash was in Dublin in February 1993 and put down his vocal track at that time with additional music and vocals added later.

March 18, 1993
LSI Recording Studio, Nashville, Tennessee
Johnny Cash, vocal; Roy Ciaburri, bass; Don DeStefani. harmonica; Russ Gordon, guitar; Andrea Herbst, vocal; Chris Morrissey, drums. Prod. Eric Herbst.

BALLAD OF THE TWO-COOKIE KID (Eric Herbst)

NOTE: This was done as part of a continuing series of book-cassette packages for children from Better Place Publishing. The above listed musicians were not actually present in the studio when Cash did his vocal track.

May 17-20, 1993
Rick Rubin's Living Room, Los Angeles, California
Johnny Cash, vocal, acoustic guitar; June Carter Cash, vocal harmony -1; Billy Gibbons, vocal, guitar -2; unknown guitar -3. These are basically demonstration sessions only.

BURY ME NOT ON THE LONE PRAIRIE (take 1)
(arr: John R. Cash)

BURY ME NOT ON THE LONE PRAIRIE (take 2)
(arr: John R. Cash)

JUST THE OTHER SIDE OF NOWHERE (take 1)

JUST THE OTHER SIDE OF NOWHERE (take 2)

DRIVE ON (John R. Cash)

DELIA'S GONE (take 1) (K. Siberdorf-D. Toops)

DELIA'S GONE (take 2) (K. Siberdorf-D. Toops)

LONG BLACK VEIL (M. Wilken-D. Dill)

THE FOURTH MAN (Arthur Smith)

WHY ME LORD (take 1) (Kris Kristofferson)

WHY ME LORD (take 2) (Kris Kristofferson)

WAITING FOR A TRAIN (Jimmie Rodgers)

FLESH AND BLOOD (John R. Cash)

LIKE A SOLDIER (take 1) (John R. Cash)

CHILDREN GO HOW I SEND THEE (John R. Cash)

LOVING HER WAS EASIER (take 1) (Kris Kristofferson)

LOVING HER WAS EASIER (take 2) (Kris Kristofferson)

"T" FOR TEXAS (take 1) (Jimmie Rodgers)

"T" FOR TEXAS (take 2) (Jimmie Rodgers)

TO BEAT THE DEVIL (take 1) (Kris Kristofferson)

I WITNESSED A CRIME -2 (take 1) (Billy Gibbons)

BLACK BOOTS AND A SACK OF SILVER DOLLARS -2
(Billy Gibbons)

DOWN THERE BY THE TRAIN (Tom Waites)

EAST VIRGINIA BLUES (June Carter-Maybelle Carter)

NUMBER 13 (take 1) (Glenn Danzig)

THE BEAST IN ME (Nick Lowe)

WHAT ON EARTH (WILL YOU DO FOR HEAVEN'S SAKE)
(John R. Cash)

THE DRIFTER (Dolly Parton)

I WITNESSED A CRIME -3 (take 2) (Billy Gibbons)

BANKS OF THE OHIO -1 (A.P. Carter)

NUMBER 13 (take 2) (Glenn Danzig)

DRIVE ON (take 2) (John R. Cash)

LIKE A SOLDIER (take 2) (John R. Cash)

THE NEXT TIME I'M IN TOWN (Mark Knopfler)

BREAKIN' BREAD (Paul Overstreet)

TO BEAT THE DEVIL (take 2) (Kris Kristofferson)

FRIENDS IN CALIFORNIA (Waylon Jennings)

THE CARETAKER (John R. Cash)

THE WONDER

BAD NEWS (J.D. Loudermilk)

ALL GOD'S CHILDREN AIN'T FREE (John R. Cash)

ONE MORE RIDE (Bob Nolan)

NUMBER 13 (take 3) (Glenn Danzig)

NOTE: Billy Gibbons is a member of the musical group "ZZ Top" and Mark Knopfler, composer of **THE NEXT TIME I'M IN TOWN**, is a member of the rock group "Dire Straits". I mention this here to show the diversity and experimentation with which Cash has been involved since signing with American Records and Rick Rubin. See also the September sessions done at Ocean Way Studios below.
===

June 30, July 1-2, 1993
Rick Rubin's Living Room, Los Angeles, California
Johnny Cash, vocal, acoustic guitar; June Carter Cash, vocal -1; Glenn Danzig, guitar -2.

NUMBER 13 (Glenn Danzig) -2 (2 takes)

DRIVE ON (John R. Cash)

LIKE A SOLDIER (John R. Cash)

NEXT TIME I'M IN TOWN (Mark Knopfler)

BREAKIN' BREAD (Paul Overstreet) (2 takes)

TO BEAT THE DEVIL (Kris Kristofferson)

FRIENDS IN CALIFORNIA (Waylon Jennings) (2 takes)

THE CARETAKER (John R. Cash)

THE WONDER

BAD NEWS (J.D. Loudermilk)

ALL GOD'S CHILDREN AIN'T FREE (John R. Cash)

ONE MORE RIDE (Bob Nolan) (3 takes)

DOWN THERE BY THE TRAIN (Tom Waites) (3 takes)

EAST VIRGINIA BLUES (June Carter-Maybelle Carter) -1 (2 takes)

EAST VIRGINIA BLUES (June Carter-Maybelle Carter)

NUMBER 13 (Glenn Danzig) (2 takes)

THE BEAST IN ME (Nick Lowe) (2 takes)

===

<u>July 21-23, 1993</u>
<u>Rick Rubin's Living Room, Los Angeles, California</u>
Johnny Cash, vocal, acoustic guitar.

THE MAN WHO COULDN'T CRY (Loudin Wainwright III)

ALLEGHENY (Chris Gantry)

NEW CUT ROAD (Guy Clark)

NO EARTHLY GOOD (John R. Cash) (2 takes)

REDEMPTION (John R. Cash) (4 takes)

GETTYSBURG ADDRESS/STRANGEST DREAM

HOBO BILL'S LAST RIDE

MYSTERY OF NO. 5

THE BEAST IN ME (Nick Lowe) (2 takes)

IF I GIVE MY SOUL (Billy Joe Shaver)

I'M JUST AN OLD CHUNK OF COAL (Billy Joe Shaver)

GEORGIA ON A FAST TRAIN (Billy Joe Shaver)

I'M RAGGED BUT I'M RIGHT (George Jones)

JESUS WAS A CARPENTER (Christopher Wren)

IF I GIVE MY SOUL (Billy Joe Shaver) (incomplete)

IF I GIVE MY SOUL (Billy Joe Shaver) (3 takes)

BOLL WEEVIL SONG

WINGS IN THE MORNING (John R. Cash)

IN MY TIME OF DYING

I'VE BEEN EVERYWHERE

BIRD ON A WIRE (G. Cohan)

GO ON BLUES (John R. Cash) (2 takes)

OLD LONESOME

HEART OF GOLD (3 takes)

THE DRIFTER (Dolly Parton) (2 takes)

THE BEAST IN ME (Nick Lowe)

THE MAN WHO COULDN'T CRY (Loudin Wainwright III) (5 takes)

==
July 1993
Jack Clement Recording Studio, Nashville, Tennessee
Neil Young, vocal, guitar; JOHNNY CASH, vocal; remaining musicians unknown. Prod.
David Ferguson.

LITTLE DRUMMER BOY (K.K. Davis-H. Onarat-H. Simeone)

NOTE: This session was done as part of a Neil Young Christmas album project.
==
September 2-3, 1993
Ocean Way Recording Studio, Hollywood, California
Johnny Cash, vocal, acoustic guitar; Mike Campbell, guitar; Flea, bass -1; Chad Smith,
drums -2. Prod. Rick Rubin.

DARK AS A DUNGEON (Merle Travis)

GO ON BLUES (John R. Cash)

FARTHER ALONG (J.R. Baxter Jr)

LIKE A SOLDIER (John R. Cash)

WINGS IN THE MORNING (John R. Cash)

NO EARTHLY GOOD (John R. Cash)

BREAKIN' BREAD (Paul Overstreet)

DRIVE ON (John R. Cash)

WHY ME LORD (Kris Kristofferson)

REDEMPTION (John R. Cash)

GO ON BLUES (John R. Cash) -1, 2

THE DRIFTER (Dolly Parton)

CHILDREN GO HOW I SEND THEE (John R. Cash)

IF I GIVE MY SOUL (Billy Joe Shaver)

HEART OF GOLD

BIRD ON A WIRE (G. Cohan)

NOTE: Mike Campbell is a member of Tom Petty's band, "The Heartbreakers"; Flea and Chad Smith are members of the "Red Hot Chili Peppers." Sources at Ocean Way Studio said a session had been scheduled for September 1 but that was cancelled.
===

September 6 or 7, 1993 (12:30p-3:30p; 4p-7p; 7:30p-10:30p)
Ocean Way Recording Studio, Hollywood, California
Johnny Cash, vocal, acoustic guitar; David Bartel, guitar; Jonathan Bartel, bass; Bill Bateman, drums; Les Butler, harmonica; Gregory Hormel, guitar. Prod. Rick Rubin.

DEVIL'S RIGHT HAND (Steve Earl)

"T" FOR TEXAS (Jimmie Rodgers)

BAD NEWS (J. D. Loudermilk)

NOTE: The above listed musicians are members of the rock group "Red Devils."
===

September 7, 1993
Ocean Way Recording Studio, Hollywood, California
Johnny Cash, vocal, acoustic guitar; Unknown acoustic guitar. Prod. Rick Rubin.

BANKS OF THE OHIO (A.P. Carter)

JUST THE OTHER SIDE OF NOWHERE

THE BEAST IN ME (Nick Lowe)

THE FOURTH MAN (Arthur Smith)

NUMBER 13 (Glenn Danzig)

DARK AND BLOODY GROUND

DOWN THERE BY THE TRAIN (Tom Waites)

TO BEAT THE DEVIL (Kris Kristofferson)

NOTE: According to sources at Ocean Way Studio there was also a mastering session done on September 14, 1993. However, Cash was not present and they were not sure of the exact song titles involved. American Records plans an early 1994 release using some material from these September sessions.
===

September 16, 1993
Branson, Missouri
Johnny Cash, vocal, acoustic guitar; Earl Ball, piano; W.S. Holland, drums; David Jones, guitar; David Rorick. bass; Bob Wootton, electric guitar. Prod. Johnny Cash.

THE OLD ACCOUNT (John R. Cash)

PEACE IN THE VALLEY (T.A. Dorsey)

FARTHER ALONG (J.R. Baxter Jr)

NOTE: This session was held to provide the music tracks for Cash's October 26, 1993 appearance on the Billy Graham Crusade in Columbus, Ohio.
===

October 9. 1993
Jack Clement Recording Studio, Nashville, Tennessee
Johnny Cash, vocal, acoustic guitar.

LIKE A SOLDIER (John R. Cash)

THE NEXT TIME I'M IN TOWN (Mark Knopfler)

TENNESSEE STUD

THE DOOR (Rodney Crowell)

REDEMPTION (John R. Cash)

===

October 12, 1993
Cedar Hill Refuge Studio, Hendersonville, Tennessee
Johnny Cash, vocal, acoustic guitar.

LONG ROAD

TENNESSEE STUD

NEVER GROW OLD

WHERE COULD I GO

WHEN WE ALL GET TO HEAVEN

I SHALL NOT BE MOVED

DO LORD

HOW BEAUTIFUL HEAVEN MUST BE

IF WE NEVER MEET AGAIN
(Arthur Brumley)

LET THE LOWER LIGHTS BE BURNING (arr: John R. Cash)

I'M BOUND FOR GLORY

IN THE SWEET BYE AND BYE

WHERE THE SOUL

I'LL FLY AWAY (Arthur Brumley)

IN THE GARDEN

JUST A LITTLE TALK

SOFTLY AND TENDERLY

WHEN HE REACHED DOWN HIS HAND FOR ME (G.E. Wright)

WHEN THE ROLL IS CALLED UP YONDER

THE BEAST IN ME (Nick Lowe)

NOTE: Cedar Hill Refuge "studio" is in reality a cabin located in a wooded compound not far from Cash's home in Hendersonville, Tennessee. It is equipped with a digital 8-track recording system and, as can be seen in the following, extensively used by him throughout the latter months of 1993.

==

October 22, 1993
Cedar Hill Refuge Studio, Hendersonville, Tennessee
Johnny Cash, vocal, acoustic guitar.

TENNESSEE STUD

THE BEAST IN ME (Nick Lowe)

==

November 1, 1993
Cedar Hill Refuge Studio, Hendersonville, Tennessee
Johnny Cash, vocal, acoustic guitar.

OVER THE NEXT HILL (John R. Cash) (2 takes)

MY CHILDREN WALK IN TRUTH (John R. Cash)

BALLAD OF BARBARA (John R. Cash)

THE BEAST IN ME (Nick Lowe)

TALK TO ME

JUST AS I AM

WHEN THE ROLL IS CALLED UP YONDER

I AM A PILGRIM

IF I GIVE MY SOUL (Billy Joe Shaver)

DOWN THERE BY THE TRAIN (Tom Waites)

NUMBER 13 (Glenn Danzig)

===

December 5, 1993
Rick Rubin's Living Room, Los Angeles, California
Johnny Cash, vocal, acoustic guitar.

DEAD OR ALIVE (3 takes)

LET HER BLOW (John R. Cash)

BALLAD OF BARBARA (John R. Cash)

CASEY'S LAST RIDE (Kris Kristofferson) (2 takes)

THE BEAST IN ME (Nick Lowe) (5 takes)

DELIA'S GONE (K. Siberdorf-D. Toops) (6 takes)

GOIN' TO MEMPHIS (John R. Cash)

IF I GIVE MY SOUL (Billy Joe Shaver) (2 takes)

I'M JUST AN OLD CHUNK OF COAL (Billy Joe Shaver) (6 takes)

UNDERSTAND YOUR MAN (John R. Cash)

THE MAN WHO COULDN'T CRY (Loudin Wainwright III) (2 takes)

LIVE FOREVER (Billy Joe Shaver)

==

December 6, 1993
Rick Rubin's Living Room, Los Angeles, California
Johnny Cash, vocal, acoustic guitar.

LIVE FOREVER (Billy Joe Shaver) (2 takes)

REDEMPTION (John R. Cash) (2 takes)

BIRD ON A WIRE (G. Cohan) (2 takes)

LIKE A SOLDIER (John R. Cash)

DOWN THERE BY THE TRAIN (Tom Waites) (8 takes)

DRIVE ON (John R. Cash) (3 takes)

NO EARTHLY GOOD (John R. Cash)

TENNESSEE STUD

GO ON BLUES (John R. Cash)

IF I GIVE MY SOUL (Billy Joe Shaver)

NUMBER 13 (Glenn Danzig)

NOTE: The last four songs were done by Cash during an interview by MTV with Rick Rubin.
==

December 7, 1993
Rick Rubin's Living Room, Los Angeles, California
Johnny Cash, vocal, acoustic guitar.

NUMBER 13 (Glenn Danzig) (3 takes)

WHY ME LORD (Kris Kristofferson) (4 takes)

DARK AS A DUNGEON (Merle Travis)

FARTHER ALONG (J.R. Baxter Jr) (2 takes)

DOWN THERE BY THE TRAIN (Tom Waites)

EAST VIRGINIA BLUES (June Carter-Maybelle Carter) (2 takes)

BANKS OF THE OHIO (A.P. Carter) (2 takes)

BIG BATTLE (John R. Cash)

TWO TIMIN' WOMAN (John R. Cash) (3 takes)

OPEN PIT MINE

===

RELEASES

A. -- SINGLES

ATLANTIC

PRCD-3429-2: (Martin Delray)
"Get Rhythm"

CBS

38-04428 (1-84): "That's The Truth"
(b/w) "Joshua's Gone Barbados"

38-04513 (6-84): "Chicken In Black"
(b/w) "Battle Of Nashville"

38-04740 (3-85): "Three Bells" (b/w)
"They Killed Him"

38-04860 (5-85) (Ray Charles):
"Crazy Old Soldier" (w/Cash) (b/w)
"It Ain't Gonna Worry My Mind"

38-04881 (5-85): "Highwayman"
(w/Willie, Waylon, Kris) (b/w)
"Human Condition" (w/Willie)

38-05594 (9-85): "Desperados Waiting
For A Train" (w/Willie, Waylon,
Kris) (b/w) "Twentieth Century Is
Almost Over" (Willie only)

38-05672 (1-86): "I'm Leaving Now"
(b/w) "Easy Street"

38-05896 (5-86) (w/Waylon):
"Even Cowgirls Get The Blues" (b/w)
"American By Birth"

38-06287 (9-86) (w/Waylon):
"Ballad Of Forty Dollars" (b/w)
"Field Of Diamonds"

38-07129 (1986 (David Allan Coe):
"Tanya Montana" (b/w) "Ten
Commandments Of Love" (w/Cash)

38-69067 (7-89): "Ragged Old Flag"
(b/w) "I'm Leaving Now"
This single was issued by CBS as a result
of the Supreme Court ruling on the
burning of the American flag.

38-73233 (1-90) (w/Willie, Waylon,
Kris): "Silver Stallion" (b/w)
"American Remains"

38-73381 (6-90): "Born And Raised In
Black And White" (w/Willie,
Waylon, Kris) (b/w) "Texas"
(Willie only)

EZRA

EZRA-227 (1986): "Man In White" (mono) (b/w) "Man In White" (stereo)

K-TEL

K-Tel/KTS-036 (Sandy Kelly): "Woodcarver" (w/Cash) (b/w) "Carlingford"

MCA

MCA-52989 (12-86) (John Schneider): "Better Class Of Loser" (w/Cash, Waylon) (b/w) "Take The Long Way Home"

MERCURY/POLYGRAM

888-142-7 (w/Jerry Lee Lewis, Carl Perkins, Roy Orbinson): "Class Of '55" (b/w) "We Remember The King"

884-760-7 (6-86): "Rock And Roll (Fais Do Do)" (w/Jerry Lee Lewis, Carl Perkins, Roy Orbison) (b/w) "Birth Of Rock And Roll" (no Cash)

884-934-7 (9-86): "Sixteen Candles" (no Cash) (b/w) "Rock And Roll (Fais Do Do)" (w/Jerry Lee Lewis, Carl Perkins, Roy Orbison)

888-459-7 (4-87): "The Night Hank Williams Came To Town" (w/Waylon) (b/w) "I'd Rather Have You"

888-719-7 (7-87): "Sixteen Tons" (b/w) "Ballad Of Barbara"

888-838-7 (10-87): "Let Him Roll" (b/w) "My Ship Will Sail"

888-010-7 (12-87): "Letters From Home" (b/w) "W. Lee O'Daniel (And The Lightcrust Doughboys)"

870-237-7 (5-88): "Get Rhythm" (b/w) "Cry, Cry, Cry"

870-688-1 (11-88): "That Old Wheel" (w/Hank Williams Jr) (b/w) "Tennessee Flat-Top Box"

872-420-89 (2-89): "Get Rhythm" (b/w) "Ballad Of A Teenage Queen"

874-562-7 (7-89): "Last Of The Drifters" (w/Tom T. Hall) (b/w) "Water From The Wells Of Home" (w/John Carter Cash)

875-626-7 (1990): "Cat's In The Cradle" (b/w) "I Love You, Love You"

876-428-7 (4-90): "Farmer's Almanac" (b/w) "I Shall Be Free"

878-292-7 (11-90): "Goin' By The Book" (b/w) "Beans For Breakfast"

878-968-7 (2-91): "Mystery Of Life" (b/w) "I'm An Easy Rider"

WARNER BROTHERS

7-28979 (8-85) (Karen Brooks): "I Will Dance With You" (w/Cash) (b/w) "Too Bad For Love"

==============================

B. -- ALBUMS

==============================

AMERICAN/SMASH

A/S-830-002-1 (5-86)
CLASS OF '55 (w/Lewis, Perkins, Orbison)

Birth Of Rock And Roll (Carl Perkins); Sixteen Candles (Jerry Lee Lewis); Class Of '55 (all); Waymore's Blues (all); We Remember The King (all); Coming Home (Roy Orbison); Rock And Roll (Fais Do-Do) (all); Keep My Motor Running (Jerry Lee Lewis); I Will Rock And Roll With You (Cash); Big Train From Memphis (all).

NOTE: In the above listing "all" indicates Cash, Jerry Lee Lewis, Carl Perkins and Roy Orbison.   BIG TRAIN FROM MEMPHIS includes a number of guest vocalists.

ASTAN Germany)

AS.20086 (1984)
GREAT SONGS OF JOHNNY CASH
I Heard That Lonesome Whistle; Rock Island Line; Sugartime; Folsom Prison Blues; Born To Lose; Remember Me; Wreck Of The Old '97; Ballad Of A Teenage Queen; I Walk The Line; Home Of The Blues.

AXIS (Australia)

AX-1189 (1983)
ORIGINAL ROCKABILLY
I Forgot To Remember To Forget; Get Rhythm; Hey Porter; I Walk The Line; Ballad Of A Teenage Queen; I Love You Because; Cry, Cry, Cry; There You Go; Doin' My Time; Country Boy; Big River; Goodnight Irene.

BEAR FAMILY (Germany)

BFX-15127 (7-84)
BITTER TEARS
This album contains basically the same contents as appeared on the U.S. release CL-2248/CS-9048 with the addition of OLD APACHE SQUAW and BIG FOOT. The front cover is the same but

the inside and back covers are completely different.

BFX-15211 (1986)
SUN COUNTRY YEARS, 1950-1959
This is an eleven record set with Cash included on volume ten with: TRAIN OF LOVE; HOME OF THE BLUES; STORY OF A BROKEN HEART and BALLAD OF A TEENAGE QUEEN. Volume eleven includes: FOLSOM PRISON BLUES; IF THE GOOD LORD'S WILLING; I WAS THERE WHEN IT HAPPENED and I HEARD THAT LONESOME WHISTLE BLOW. These are supposedly all previously unreleased alternate takes.

BELLAPHON Germany)
(see also: Pickup, SR International)

BI-230.13.010 (1988)
THAT GOOD OLD TIMES
Folsom Prison Blues; Guess Things Happen That Way; Oh Lonesome Me; Wreck Of The Old '97; Born To Lose; Blue Train; I Forgot To Remember To Forget; I Love You Because; Luther's Boogie; Thanks A Lot; Hey Good Looking; Country Boy; I Walk The Line; Train Of Love; Big River; Sugartime.

BLOSSOM

TLA-50155 (1982)
ROCK ISLAND LINE
You Win Again; Born To Lose; Doin' My Time; Fools Hall Of Fame; Goodnight Irene; Give My Love To Rose; Home Of The Blues; Katy Too; Rock Island Line; So Doggone Lonesome.

BLUE (Switzerland)

BV/25-LP (1983)
JOHNNY CASH

Rock Island Line; I Heard That
Lonesome Whistle; Country Boy; I Walk
The Line; Cry, Cry, Cry; So Doggone
Lonesome; I Was There When It
Happened; If The Good Lord's Willing;
Wreck Of The Old '97; Folsom Prison
Blues; Doin' My Time.

BOOTLEG ALBUMS

JC-01
LIVING LEGEND JOHNNY CASH #1
American Trilogy (from the Goodpasture
Christian album CHS-79); One More Ride
(w/Marty Stuart from Sugarhill album
SuH-3726); Anillo De Fuego; I Still Miss
Someone (w/Earl Scruggs from the CBS
album PC-34090); Pepsi Cola
Commerical; The Love That Never Failed
(from the Sparc album SP-1001); What's
Good For You (Should Be Alright For
Me) (from CMH album CMH-6241);
Veteran's Day; Frozen Logger; Folsom
Prison Blues (original Sun version using
choir SLP-1245); No Earthly Good (from
Oak Ridge Boys KC-33935); Amazing
Grace (from EZRA album EZRA-223);
Hey Porter (from Sugarhill album SuH-
3726); Brakeman's Blues; Ragged Old
Flag (from Folk Era CD FE-2055CD);
My Ship Will Sail (w/Earl Scruggs from
CBS PC-34090).

JC-02
LIVING LEGEND JOHNNY CASH #2
I Will Dance With You (from CBS-11-
60516); Battle Of Nashville (from CBS-
38-04513); Outside Lookin' In (inst.-from
CBS-4-44264); Three Bells (from CBS-
38-94740); Ballad Of Barbara (from
CBS-4-45890); Cattle Call (inst. from-
CBS-4-43299); Human Condition (from
CBS-38-04881); I Shall Be Free; General
Lee; It Was Jesus; Bill's Theme (inst-from
CBS-4-43299); Help Me Make It
Through The Night (w/June Carter Cash);
They Killed Him; Spanish Harlem (inst-

from CBS-4-43299); Little Bit Of
Yesterday; Man In White.

JC-03
LIVING LEGEND JOHNNY CASH #3
World Needs A Melody (w/Carter
Family); Get Rhythm (w/Martin Delray);
Suffer Little Children (w/Glen Campbell);
Guess Things Happen That Way
(w/Tommy Cash); I Will Dance With You
(w/Karen Brooks); Your Love Is My
Refuge (w/Jack Routh); I Still Miss
Someone (w/Bill Monroe); Ring Of Fire
(w/Sandy Kelly); Crazy Old Soldier
(w/Ray Charles); Jealous Loving Heart
(w/Ernest Tubb); Love Me Tender
(w/Julie Andrews); Long Black Veil
(w/Razzy Bailey); Woodcarver (w/Sandy
Kelly); Thoughts On The Flag (w/Tommy
Cash); Mother Maybelle (w/Marty
Stuart); Amazing Grace (w/JoAnne Cash
Yates).

JC-04
LIVING LEGEND JOHNNY CASH #4
A Gunfight; Ben Dewberry's Final Run;
Sweet Kentucky/Sweet Kentucky
(instrumental); Goodnight Loving Trail;
I'm Never Gonna Cease My Wandering;
A Pub With No Beer; You're Right, I'm
Left, She's Gone; Jamaica Farewell; I'm
Moving Up; A Croft In Clachan; Love's
Been Good To Me; I Can Tell You
Everything You Ever Wanted To Know
About Drinking; Love Is A Gamble; Ride
Easy My Baby (w/June C. Cash);
Columbus Stockade Blues; America The
Beautiful.

JC-05
LIVING LEGEND JOHNNY CASH #5
Man Gave Names To All The Animals;
Jesus Is Lord (w/Joanne Cash Yates); Are
All The Children In; Lord Is It I/The Last
Supper; I Saw The Light; Wings In The
Morning; It Is No Secret; How Great
Thou Art; I Believe; These Men With
Broken Hearts; Old Time Religion
(w/Joanne Cash Yates & Tommy Cash);

Why Me Lord; I See Men As Trees Walking; Gospel Medley (w/Joanne Cash Yates); Christmas Can't Be Far Away; When The Saints Go Marching In (w/Carter Family).

JC-06
LIVING LEGEND JOHNNY CASH #6
On The Road Again (w/Willie, Waylon, Kris); Pretty Woman (w/Roy Orbison); Old Flames Don't Hold A Candle To You (w/June Carter); Rain (w/Larry Gatlin); Whole Lotta Shakin' Goin' On/Blue Suede Shoes (w/Carl Perkins & Jerry Lee Lewis); No Memories Hanging Around (w/Rosanne Cash); A Part Of Me (w/June Carter); One More Night (w/Jackie De Shannon); Waylon's Back In Town (Waylon Jennings); Have I Told You Lately That I Love You (June Carter); Mabelline (w/Eddie Rabbitt); Where The Soul Of Men Never Dies (w/Emmylou Harris); Take Me Home Country Roads (w/John Denver); Turn Your Radio On/What Would You Give In Exchange For Your Soul/In The Sweet By And By (w/Ricky Skaggs); Kawliga (w/Hank Williams Jr); You Are My Sun Shine (w/June Carter).

JC-07
LIVING LEGEND JOHNNY CASH #7
Medley #1: Paul Revere/Battle Of New Orleans/Gettsburg Address/Glory, Glory Hallelujah; Deportee (w/Johnny Rodriguez); Love Song To America; This Land Is Your Land; Ragged Old Flag; Trail Of Tears; Trail Of Tears As Told By Johnny Cash; Medley #2: We're Coming Father Abraham/Glory, Glory Hallelujah/Dixie.

CASTLE COMMUNICATIONS
(THE COLLECTOR SERIES)
(West Germany)

CCSLP-146 (2LP) (1986)
THE JOHNNY CASH COLLECTION

Wide Open Road; Cry, Cry, Cry; Folsom Prison Blues; So Doggone Lonesome; Mean Eyed Cat; New Mexico; I Walk The Line; I Love You Because; Straight A's In Love; Home Of The Blues; Rock Island Line; Country Boy; Doin' My Time.|| Big River; Ballad Of A Teenage Queen; Oh Lonesome Me; You're The Nearest Thing To Heaven; Always Alone; You Win Again; Hey, Good Lookin'; Blue Train; Katy Too; Fools Hall Of Fame; Ways Of A Woman In Love; Down The Street To 301.

CBS

2CSP-001 (Australia) (2LP) (1981)
COUNTRY CLASSICS
Ring Of Fire; What Is Truth; A Boy Named Sue; Sunday Morning Coming Down; I Still Miss Someone; Wreck Of The Old '97; Folsom Prison Blues; One Piece At A Time; I Walk The Line; Understand Your Man; Daddy Sang Bass; The Night They Drove Old Dixie Down; Tennessee Flat-Top Box; Big River; Walls Of A Prison; Don't Take Your Guns To Town.|| San Quentin; Long Black Veil; Orange Blossom Special; Remember The Alamo; Junkie And The Juicehead; In Them Old Cottonfields Back Home; I Got Stripes; Man In Black; If I Were A Carpenter (w/June Carter Cash); Ballad Of Ira Hayes; Hey Porter; Five Feet High And Rising; Forty Shades Of Green; Wabash Cannonball; Amazing Grace; In The Sweet By And By.

ASF-1051 (South Africa)
JOHNNY CASH SPECTACULAR
Daddy Sang Bass; A Boy Named Sue; Folsom Prison Blues; If I Were A Carpenter (w/June Carter Cash); A Thing Called Love; Jackson (w/June Carter Cash); I Walk The Line; Orange Blossom Special; Ring Of Fire; Don't Take Your Guns To Town; Blistered; Southwind; Sunday Morning Coming Down; I

Promise You; Papa Was A Good Man; Daddy.

M-9047 (Argentine)
EL MUNDO DE JOHNNY CASH
Blistered; If I Were A Carpenter (w/June Carter Cash); To Beat The Devil; I've Got A Thing About Trains; Wrinkled, Crinkled, Wadded Dollar Bill; Southwind; See Ruby Fall; The Devil To Pay; 'Cause I Love You; Sing A Traveling Song; Route 1 Box 144.

P-17627 (1982)
JOHNNY CASH SINGS HIS BEST HITS
Ghost Riders In The Sky; Man In Black; See Ruby Fall; Daddy Sang Bass; Ring Of Fire; One Piece At A Time; Kate; Any Old Wind That Blows; Flesh And Blood; Don't Take Your Guns To Town; Oney; Sunday Morning Coming Down; One On The Right Is On The Left; Folsom Prison Blues; Rosanna's Going Wild; A Thing Called Love; What Is Truth; A Boy Named Sue; The Matador; Understand Your Man.

CBS/EMBASSY-21091 (Europe) (1982)
AMERICAN SUPERSTARS
Ring Of Fire; Orange Blossom Special; The Night They Drove Old Dixie Down; Jackson (w/June Carter); Don't Take Your Guns To Town; I Walk The Line (live); A Boy Named Sue; San Quentin; If I Were A Carpenter (w/June Carter Cash); Folsom Prison Blues (live); Kate; (Ghost) Riders In The Sky

CBS-32304 (Europe) (1982)
BIGGEST HITS
Don't Take Your Guns To Town; Ring Of Fire; Understand Your Man; One On The Right Is On The Left; Rosanna's Going Wild; Folsom Prison Blues; Daddy Sang Bass; A Boy Named Sue; Sunday Morning Coming Down; Flesh And Blood; A Thing Called Love; Kate; One Piece At A Time; There Ain't No Good

Chain Gang (w/Waylon Jennings); Riders In The Sky; The Baron.

KC-33814 (9-75)
LOOK AT THEM BEANS
Texas '47; What Have You Got Planned Tonight Diana; Look At Them Beans; No Charge; I Hardly Ever Sing Beer Drinking Songs; Down The Road I Go; I Never Met A Man Like You Before; All Around Cowboy; Gone; Down At Drippin' Springs.
NOTE: This album was accidently omitted from volume one.

FC-39415 (8-84)
FRIENDSHIP (Ray Charles)
Cash/Charles duet on CRAZY OLD SOLDIER.

FC-39951 (10-85)
RAINBOW
I'm Leaving Now; Here Comes That Rainbow Again; They're All The Same; Easy Street; Have You Ever Seen The Rain; You Beat All I Ever Saw; Unwed Fathers; Love Me Like You Used To; Casey's Last Ride; Borderline (A Musicial Whodunit).

FC-40056 (5-85)
HIGHWAYMAN (w/Willie, Waylon, Kris)
Highwayman (w/Waylon, Willie, Kris); Last Cowboy Song (w/Waylon, Willie, Kris); Jim I Wore A Tie Today (w/Willie); Big River (w/Waylon, Willie, Kris); Committed To Parkview (w/Willie); Desperados Waiting For A Train (w/Waylon, Willie, Kris); Deportee (w/Willie, Johnny Rodriquez); Welfare Line (w/Waylon, Willie, Kris); Against The Wind (w/Waylon, Willie); Twentieth Century Is Almost Over (w/Willie).

FC-40571 (1986)
A MATTER OF LIFE (David Allan Coe)
Cash is included on THE TEN COMMANDMENTS OF LOVE.

CBS-54704 (Netherlands) (1985)
GOLDEN HIGHLIGHTS
Ring Of Fire; Orange Blossom Special;
The Night They Drove Old Dixie Down;
Jackson (w/June Carter); Don't Take
Your Guns To Town; I Walk The Line; A
Boy Named Sue; San Quentin; If I Were
A Carpenter (w/June Carter Cash);
Folsom Prison Blues; Kate; Ghost Riders
In The Sky.

CBS-54938 (Netherlands) (1986)
I LOVE COUNTRY-JOHNNY CASH
(THE STORYTELLER)
The Baron; A Boy Named Sue; Ballad Of
Ira Hayes; Highway Patrolman; The
Diplomat; No Charge; John's; To Beat
The Devil; Last Gunfighter Ballad; Don't
Take Your Guns To Town; The Cowboy
Who Started The Fight; The Gambler;
Reverend Mr. Black; All Around
Cowboy; Ghost Riders In The Sky; Who's
Gene Autry.

CBS-85032 (Europe) (1981)
A FREE MAN
Folsom Prison Blues; Ring Of Fire; In
The Old Cottonfield Fields Back Home; I
Walk The Line; If I Were A Carpenter
(w/June Carter Cash); Orange Blossom
Special; Jackson (w/June Carter); Sunday
Morning Coming Down; Five Feet High
And Rising; One Piece At A Time; Ghost
Riders In The Sky; City Of New Orleans;
Daddy Sang Bass; San Quentin; The
Night They Drove Old Dixie Down;
Reason To Believe; The Lady Came From
Baltimore; Man In Black; Bonanza.

CL-917351 (Netherlands) (1982)
THE MAN FROM ARKANSAS
Frankie's Man, Johnny; In The Jailhouse
Now; My Shoes Keep Walking Back To
You; Great Speckled Bird; I Forgot More
Than You'll Ever Know; Long Legged
Guitar Pickin' Man (w/June Carter); Kate;
A Thing Called Love; I'm So Lonesome I
Could Cry; What Do I Care; I Want To

Go Home; Don't Think Twice, It's All
Right; Don't Take Your Guns To Town;
Blistered; Reason To Believe; Streets Of
Laredo.

CHARLY (United Kingdom)

SUNLP-1015 (Portugal) (1988)
JOHNNY CASH'S TOP HITS
Cry, Cry, Cry; Luther Played The Boogie;
Folsom Prison Blues*; So Doggone
Lonesome*; Mean Eyed Cat**; Wide
Open Road+; Two Timin' Woman+;
There You Go; I Walk The Line; Country
Boy; Train Of Love+; Get Rhythm; Hey
Porter; Wide Open Road++.
NOTE: The liner notes indicate the
following: (*) first reissue from the Sam
Phillips mastertape 45 release; (**)
previously unissued; (+) previously
unissued in a mono standard record
pressing--I take this to mean "previously
unissued" because on the following album
(SUNLP-1047) the same notation is given
for a title that was obviously never
released; (++) featuring A.W. Kernodle
on steel guitar. But at this point I am not
sure what the difference is between
"previously unissued" and "previously
unissued in a mono standard record
pressing."

SUNLP-1047 (Portugal) (1988)
ROCK ISLAND LINE
Belshazar; If The Good Lord's Willing;
Wreck Of The Old '97; You Tell Me; Oh
Lonesome Me*; Big River; Doin' My
Time; Rock Island Line; Home Of The
Blues; Straight A's In Love; Come In
Stranger*; Blue Train; Next In Line; Hey
Good Lookin'*; Life Goes On; Katy Too.
NOTE: The liner notes indicate titles
denoted (*) to be "previously unissued in
a mono standard record pressing." The
version of HEY GOOD LOOKIN'
included here has definitely not been
released before but it is not certain if OH
LONESOME ME and COME IN

STRANGER are alternate versions. On this release OH LONESOME ME does not include any vocal harmony as is on the original version.

DEJA VU (Italy)

DVLP-2103 (1987)
THE JOHNNY CASH COLLECTION
Wreck Of The Old '97; Ballad Of A Teenage Queen; I Heard That Lonesome Whistle; Rock Island Line; Goodbye Little Darlin'; Train Of Love; Down The Street To 301; Give My Love To Rose; Come In Stranger; Get Rhythm; Folsom Prison Blues; I Walk The Line; Hey Porter; Guess Things (Can) Happen That Way; Ways Of A Woman In Love; There You Go; Big River; Sugartime; Blue Train; Doin' My Time

----

DUCHESSE (Europe)

DU-152078 (1990)
SAN QUENTIN AND OTHER HITS
A Boy Named Sue; Jackson; San Quentin; (Ghost) Riders In The Sky; Ring Of Fire; You're The Nearest Thing To Heaven; The Rebel-Johnny Yuma; One On The Right Is On The Left; It Ain't Me Babe; Ballad Of Ira Hayes; Orange Blossom Special; Goodbye Little Darlin', Goodbye; Understand Your Man; Don't Take Your Guns To Town; Straight A's In Love; I Love You Because.

EMI (Australia)

SCA-078 (1984)
20 GOLDEN GREATS
Hey Porter; Ballad Of A Teenage Queen; Guess Things Happen That Way; I Love You Because; Ways Of A Woman In Love; Hey, Good Lookin'; Down The Street To 301; Two Timin' Woman; You're The Nearest Thing To Heaven;

Goodnight Irene; I Walk The Line; Come In Stranger; Folsom Prison Blues; Rock Island Line; Wreck Of The Old '97; Straight A's In Love; Blue Train; Cold, Cold Heart; Oh, Lonesome Me; Big River.

EUROPA (Germany)

EU-111.404.2
JOHNNY CASH
Ring Of Fire; Don't Think Twice, It's Alright; The Rebel-Johnny Yuma; Remember The Alamo; Detroit City; Jackson (w/June Carter Cash); I Walk The Line; Casey Jones; I Still Miss Someone; Five Feet High And Rising; Don't Take Your Guns To Town; Bonanza.

EU-111.423.9 (1980)
JOHNNY CASH
Daddy Sang Bass; A Boy Named Sue; It Ain't Me, Babe; In The Jailhouse Now; Give My Love To Rose; Shanytown; Man In Black; A Thing Called Love; Folsom Prison Blues (live); Streets Of Laredo; If I Were A Carpenter (w/June Carter Cash); Orange Blossom Special.

EVEREST-EUROPA TIMELESS TREASURES (Italy)

E/E.LP 16-23 (1983)
JOHNNY CASH-16 ORIGNAL GOLDEN HITS!
Folsom Prison Blues (live); A Boy Named Sue; I Walk The Line; Understand Your Man; Don't Take Your Guns To Town; Guess Things Happen That Way; If I Were A Carpenter (w/June Carter); Ring Of Fire; One Piece At A Time; Daddy Sang Bass; I Got Stripes (live); Man In Black; One On The Right Is On The Left; Sunday Morning Coming Down; Blistered; What Do I Care.

HALLMARK (United Kingdom)

SHM-3146 (1984)
VERY BEST OF JOHNNY CASH
What Is Truth; All Over Again; I'm So
Lonesome I Could Cry; Understand Your
Man; Daddy Sang Bass; Busted; Let
There Be Country; Ghost Riders In The
Sky; A Thing Called Love; It Ain't Me,
Babe; Don't Take Your Guns To Town;
Wreck Of The Old '97; Ring Of Fire; If I
Were A Carpenter (w/June Carter Cash);
Green, Green Grass Of Home; Folsom
Prison Blues.

HOUSE OF CASH

HOC/CS-1001 (9-87)
WILDWOOD FLOWER (Carter Family)
Wildwood Flower; Dixie Darlin'; Banks
Of The Ohio; Worried Man Blues
(w/Johnny Cash); Storms Are On The
Ocean (w/Johnny Cash); Savior Of My
Natural Life; Ain't Gonna Work
Tomorrow; Fifty Miles Of Elbow Room;
Seven Bridges Road; Church In The
Wildwood (w/Johnny Cash).
NOTE: This was only released by the
House of Cash on cassette.   In 1988
Mercury/Polygram released it, also on
cassette.   However, in Europe it was
released by Mercury/Polygram on a long-
play album.

INSTANT (United Kingdom)

INS-5007 (1989)
BORN TO LOSE
I Walk The Line; Ballad Of A Teenage
Queen; Big River; Wreck Of The Old '97;
Guess Things Happen That Way; Born
To Lose; Give My Love To Rose; Folsom
Prison Blues; Rock Island Line; Luther
Played The Boogie; Straight A's In Love;
Get Rhythm; Next In Line; You're The
Nearest Thing To Heaven.

JANA

JANA-8709 (4-88)
AMAZING GRACE
(JoAnne Cash Yates)
Cash is included on AMAZING GRACE.

JANA-8901 (4-89)
JOANNE CASH YATE LIVE
Cash is included with a duet on four
songs: JESUS IS LORD; GOSPEL
MEDLEY; HOW BEAUTIFUL
HEAVEN MUST BE and LORD I'M
COMING HOME.   A video was also
made of this live performance.

JOKER (Italy)

SM-3988 (1982)
I WALK THE LINE
I Walk The Line; Blues Train; Down The
Street To 301; Goodbye, Little Darling;
Ways Of A Woman In Love; Rock Island
Line; Train Of Love; Hey Porter; Give
My Love To Rose; Guess Things Happen
That Way; Luther's Boogie; I Could
Never Be Ashamed Of You; Big River;
Get Rhythm.
NOTE: BLUE TRAIN was listed as
above on this album.

K-TEL

K-TEL/OCE-2465
I NEED TO BE IN LOVE (Sandy Kelly)
Cash is included with a duet on
WOODCARVER.

LOTUS (Italy)

LOP-14053 (1984)
20 GREATEST HITS
I Walk The Line; Blue Train; Down The
Street To 301; Goodbye, Little Darling;
Ways Of A Woman In Love; Rock Island

Line; Train Of Love; Folsom Prison Blues; Cry, Cry, Cry; I Heard That Lonesome Whistle; Hey Porter; Give My Love To Rose; Guess Things Happen That Way; Luther's Boogie; I Could Never Be Ashamed Of You; Big River; Get Rhythm; You're The Nearest Thing To Heaven; There You Go; Thanks A Lot.

LOUISIANA HAYRIDE

LH-973
LOUISIANA HAYRIDE SATURDAY NITE
Cash is included with HEY PORTER (12-55); LUTHER PLAYED THE BOOGIE (1957); BIG RIVER (1960) and HEY PORTER (1965).

MERCURY/POLYGRAM

M/P-834-491-4 (5-88) (Europe)
WILDWOOD FLOWER (Carter Family)
Same as the "House Of Cash" cassette HOC/CS-1001 and United States Mercury/Polygram cassette M/P-834.491.4.
NOTE: It was released in Europe on this long-play album.

OCEAN (United Kingdom)

OCNWL2032 (1989)
CLASSIC JOHNNY CASH
Cry, Cry, Cry; Folsom Prison Blues; So Doggone Lonesome; I Walk The Line; There You Go; Train Of Love; Next In Line; Don't Make Me Go; Home Of The Blues; Give My Love To Rose; Ballad Of A Teenage Queen; Guess Things Happen That Way; Come In Stranger; Ways Of A Woman In Love; You're The Nearest Thing To Heaven; Luther Played The Boogie; Thanks A Lot; Katy Too.
NOTE: The record number is written

differently on the record and cover. The sleeve has OCNWL2032 while the record has OCN 2032 WL.

OUT OF TOWN DISTRIBUTORS

OTD-8015 (1982)
EARLY YEARS
Blue Train; Don't Make Me Go; I Could Never Be Ashamed Of You; There You Go; Thanks A Lot; I Couldn't Keep From Crying; Ways Of A Woman In Love; If The Good Lord's Willing; Down The Street To 301; I Was There When It Happened.

OTD-8019 (1982)
EVERLASTING JOHNNY CASH
I Walk The Line; Big River; Always Alone; Mean Eyed Cat; Wreck Of The Old '97; Guess Things Happen That Way; Belshazah; Wide Open Road; You're My Baby; Luther's Boogie.

OTD-8025 (1982)
TRUCK STOP FAVORITES
I Heard That Lonesome Whistle; So Doggone Lonesome; Oh Lonesome Me; Give My Love To Rose; Home Of The Blues; Port Of Lonely Hearts; Goodnight Irene; I Couldn't Keep From Crying; Born To Lose; Don't Make Me Go.

OTD-8032 (1982)
HARD TIMES AND BLUES
Folsom Prison Blues; Come In Stranger; Goodnight Irene; Cold, Cold Heart; Country Boy; Train Of Love; Oh, Lonesome Me; Sugartime; Port Of Lonely Hearts; Remember Me.

OTD-8033 (1982)
THE BEGINNING
Get Rhythm; Doin' My Time; Katy Too; I Love You Because; New Mexico; Home Of The Blues; I Forgot To Remember To Forget; You Win Again; So Doggone Lonesome; My Treasure.

PLAYBACK

PLAYBACK/PB-4501
THE 25TH ANNIVERSARY ALBUM
(Tommy Cash)
Cash duets with Tommy Cash, George Jones and Tom T. Hall on THOUGHTS ON THE FLAG and with Tommy Cash on GUESS THINGS HAPPEN THAT WAY.

POLSKIE NAGRANIA (Poland)

MUZA SX 2454 (1987)
GREATEST HITS
Hey Porter; Cry, Cry, Cry; Folsom Prison Blues; Guess Things Happen That Way; Luther's Boogie; Rock Island Line; Goodnight Irene; Wreck Of The Old '97; Come In Stranger; Ballad Of A Teenage Queen; I Walk The Line; Get Rhythm; I Love You Because; Cold, Cold Heart; Big River; Give My Love To Rose; Straight A's In Love.

MUZA SX 2559 (1987)
JOHNNY CASH GREATEST HITS 2
Sugartime; Ways Of A Woman In Love; Blue Train; You're The Nearest Thing To Heaven; Home Of The Blues; Katy Too; Born To Lose; Don't Make Me Go; There You Go; Down The Street To 301; Life Goes On; Port Of Lonely Hearts; Belshazah; Country Boy; Wide Open Road; You Tell Me; Two Timin' Woman.

PREMIER (United Kingdom)

PMP-1004 (1986)
LADY
Kate; Oney; Any Old Wind That Blows; Lady Came From Baltimore; Ragged Old Flag; My Old Kentucky Home; Texas 1947; One Piece At A Time; Sold Out Of Flagpoles; Last Gunfighter Ballad;

Dialogue #2; Lady; Dialogue #3; After The Ball; I Would Like To See You Again; Gone Girl; I Will Rock And Roll With You; Ghost Riders In The Sky.
NOTE: "Dialogue #2" and "Dialogue #3" listed here are from *The Rambler* album as are LADY and AFTER THE BALL.

CBR-1015 (1984)
18 LEGENDARY PERFORMANCES
It's Just About Time; Straight A's In Love; I Just Thought You'd Like To Know; You're The Nearest Thing To Heaven; Rock Island Line; Cold, Cold Heart; Folsom Prison Blues; Hey, Good Lookin'; I Love You Because; Big River; Ballad Of A Teenage Queen; Goodbye, Little Darling; I Could Never Be Ashamed Of You; Next In Line; Port Of Lonely Hearts; Sugartime; There You Go; Two Timin' Woman.

QUALITY (Canada)

QTY.V-1619
JOHNNY CASH HITS
Train Of Love; Next In Line; Home Of The Blues; Big River; Come In Stranger; I Walk The Line; Ballad Of A Teenage Queen; Don't Make Me Go; Give My Love To Rose; Folsom Prison Blues; Guess Things Happen That Way; There You Go.

QTY.SV-2089 (1981)
GREATEST HITS
Folsom Prison Blues; I Walk The Line; Rock Island Line; You Win Again; Remember Me; Oh, Lonesome Me; Ballad Of A Teenage Queen; I Forgot To Remember To Forget; Wreck Of The Old '97; Guess Things Happen That Way.

RCA

AHL1-7184 (1-86)

SWEET MOTHER TEXAS (Waylon
Jennings)
Cash/Jennings duet on BE CAREFUL
WHO YOU LOVE.

RCA INTERNATIONAL (Germany)

RI.NL-45432 (1983)
TAKEOFF-I WALK THE LINE
I Walk The Line; Ways Of A Woman In
Love; Down The Street To 301; Guess
Things Happen That Way; Katy Too; I
Was There When It Happened; Hey
Porter; Give My Love To Rose; Blue
Train; Don't Make Me Go; Oh, Lonesome
Me; I Couldn't Keep From Crying; If The
Good Lord's Willing; Thanks A Lot;
Wide Open Road; Goodbye, Little
Darling.

REDITA (Netherlands)

REDITA-126
COTTON CHOPPER COUNTRY
Cash is included with LEAVE THAT
JUNK ALONE.

RHINO

RNLP-70229 (1987)
VINTAGE YEARS: 1955-1963
Hey Porter; I Walk The Line; Get
Rhythm; Folsom Prison Blues; Rock
Island Line; Home Of The Blues; Ballad
Of A Teenage Queen; Big River; Guess
Things Happen That Way; Always Alone;
Don't Take Your Guns To Town; I Still
Miss Someone; Seasons Of My Heart;
Ring Of Fire.

SCORE (France)

SCO-8966 (1981)
JOHNNY CASH

I Walk The Line; Rock Island Line;
Sugartime; Folsom Prison Blues; Born To
Lose; Remember Me; Wreck Of The Old
'97; Ballad Of A Teenage Queen; I Heard
That Lonesome Whistle; Home Of The
Blues.

SHOWCASE (United Kingdom)

SHLP-126 (1984)
FOLSOM PRISON BLUES
Ways Of A Woman In Love; If The Good
Lord's Willing; I Was There When It
Happened; Down The Street To 301;
Blue Train; Don't Make Me Go; I Could
Never Be Ashamed Of You; There You
Go; Thanks A Lot; I Couldn't Keep From
Crying; It's Just About Time; Straight A's
In Love; I Just Thought You'd Like To
Know; You're The Nearest Thing To
Heaven; Rock Island Line; Cold, Cold
Heart; Folsom Prison Blues; Hey, Good
Lookin'.

SONY/CBS (Japan)

SO.25AP-2256 (1982)
GREATEST HITS
Folsom Prison Blues; I Walk The Line;
Understand Your Man; Jackson; Orange
Blossom Special; A Boy Named Sue;
Ring Of Fire; Big River; I Still Miss
Someone; Daddy Sang Bass; Don't Take
Your Guns To Town; Sunday Morning
Coming Down; Man In Black; (Ghost)
Riders In The Sky.

SUCCESS (Netherlands)

SU.LP-205510 (1985)
BALLAD OF A TEENAGE QUEEN
I Love You Because; Cold, Cold Heart;
You're The Nearest Thing To Heaven;
Big River; There You Go; It's Just About
Time; Sugartime; Straight A's In Love;

Next In Line; Hey, Good Lookin'; Ballad Of A Teenage Queen; Port Of Lonely Hearts; Two Timin' Woman; Goodbye, Little Darling; Rock Island Line; I Could Never Be Ashamed Of You; I Just Thought You'd Like To Know; Folsom Prison Blues.

THOMAS NELSON ORGANIZATION

TNO-7488CA (9-90)
THE SPOKEN WORD NEW
 TESTAMENT
A 14-cassette tape package of Cash reading the New Testament.

TOPLINE (United Kingdom)

TOP-30112148 (1985)
HOME OF THE BLUES
Port Of Lonely Hearts; My Treasure; So Doggone Lonesome; Goodbye Little Darlin'; I Love You Because; Next In Line; Don't Make Me Go; Home Of The Blues; Belshazar; Leave That Junk Alone; Story Of A Broken Heart; You Win Again; I Could Never Be Ashamed Of You; It's Just About Time; I Just Thought You'd Like To Know; I Forgot To Remember To Forget.

W.A.A. (Canada)

W.A.A. 9026 (1983)
I WALK THE LINE
Hey Porter; Give My Love To Rose; Guess Things Happen That Way; Luther's Boogie; I Could Never Be Ashamed Of You; Blue Train; I Walk The Line; Ways Of A Woman In Love; Down The Street To 301; Goodbye, Little Darling.

WARNER BROTHERS

BSK.925-277.1 (1985)
I WILL DANCE WITH YOU
(Karen Brooks)
Cash/Brooks duet on I WILL DANCE WITH YOU.

WARWICK (United Kingdom)

WW-2083 (1988)
I WALK THE LINE
I Walk The Line; Cry, Cry, Cry; Hey Porter; Folsom Prison Blues; Get Rhythm; Luther Played The Boogie; Mean Eyed Cat; There You Go; Train Of Love; Give My Love To Rose; Big River; Ballad Of A Teenage Queen; Guess Things Happen That Way; Blue Train; Ways Of A Woman In Love; You're The Nearest Thing To Heaven.

WORD (see also: MYRRH)

WRD-3008 (United Kingdom) (1985)
WELCOME FRIEND
Man In Black; No Earthly Good; Papa Was A Good Man; A Song To Mama (w/Carter Family); That Silver Haired Daddy Of Mine (w/Tommy Cash); Daddy; Daddy Sang Bass; The Good Earth; Good Morning Friend; Best Friend; A Thing Called Love; Jesus Was A Carpenter; Were You There; Godshine; Welcome Back Jesus; Great Speckle Bird.

WRDR-3014 (United Kingdom) (1985)
JUST AS I AM
I Was There When It Happened; Softly And Tenderly; Old Rugged Cross; I Saw A Man; At The Cross; Just As I Am; He's Alive; Have Thine Own Way Lord; Let The Lower Lights Be Burning; Rock Of Ages; Lead Me Gently Home; When The Roll Is Called Up Yonder; When He Comes; Farther Along; He'll Understand And Say Well Done; In The Sweet Bye And Bye.

WR-8293 (1-86)
NO MORE NIGHT (Glen Campbell)
Cash/Campbell duet on SUFFER
LITTLE CHILDREN.

WS-8333 (5-86)
BELIEVE IN HIM
Believe In Him; Another Wide River To
Cross; God Ain't No Stained Glass
Window; Over There; Old Rugged Cross
(w/Jessi Colter); My Children Walk In
Truth; You're Driftin' Away; Belshazzar;
Half A Mile A Day; One Of These Days
I'm Gonna Sit Down And Have A Little
Talk With Paul.

WR-98334 (7-86)
THEY CAME TO AMERICA
Cash is included in a duet with a number
of performers singing LET AMERICA
BE AMERICA AGAIN.

===============================

C. -- COMPACT DISCS

===============================

A&M

393 718-2
THE LEGEND OF JESSE JAMES
Same as U.S. release A&M SP-3718.

ALLEGIANCE EXTRA

CDP-72926 (12-87)
ALLEGIANCE EXTRA - PLUS ONE
This CD is the same as Allegiance album
AV-5017 for Johnny Cash entitled *The
First Years* and the Carl Perkins release
The Heart And Soul Of Carl Perkins.

AMERICA/SMASH
(POLYGRAM) (West Germany)

A/S-830.002-2 M-1
CLASS OF '55
Same as long play album 830.002-1.

ARC RECORDS

TOP/CD-129
I WALK THE LINE
I Walk The Line; Ballad Of A Teenage
Queen; Big River; Wreck Of The Old 97;
Guess Things Happen That Way; Born
To Lose; Folsom Prison Blues; Give My
Love To Rose; Rock Island Line; Luther
Played The Boogie; Straight A's In Love;
Get Rhythm.

ATLANTIC

AT-7 82176-2 (1990)
GET RHYTHM (Martin Delray)
Cash sings duet on GET RHYTHM.

BEAR FAMILY RECORDS
(West Germany)

BCD-15247
JOHNNY CASH--1955-1957
UP THROUGH THE YEARS
Cry, Cry, Cry; Hey Porter; Folsom Prison
Blues; Luther Played The Boogie; So
Doggone Lonesome; I Walk The Line;
Get Rhythm; Train Of Love; There You
Go; Goodbye, Little Darlin'; I Love You
Because; Straight A's In Love; Next In
Line; Don't Make Me Go; Home Of The
Blues; Give My Love To Rose; Rock
Island Line; Wreck Of The Old '97;
Ballad Of A Teenage Queen; Big River;
Guess Things Happen That Way; Come
In Stranger; You're The Nearest Thing To
Heaven; Blue Train.

BCD-15517 (9-90) (5-CD)
THE MAN IN BLACK, 1954-1958
CD-1: Wide Open Road; You're My
Baby; My Treasure; My Treasure; Hey
Porter*; Folsom Prison Blues*; Wide
Open Road; (My) Two Timin' Woman;
Hey Porter; Cry, Cry, Cry; Wide Open
Road; Port Of Lonely Hearts; I Couldn't

Keep From Crying; New Mexico; Folsom Prison; So Doggone Lonesome; Mean Eyed Cat; Luther Played The Boogie; Rock And Roll Ruby; I Walk The Line; Brakeman's Blues*; Get Rhythm*; Get Rhythm; I Walk The Line; Train Of Love; Train Of Love; There You Go; One More Ride; I Love You Because; Goodbye Little Darling; I Love You Because; Straight A's In Love.

CD-2: Don't Make Me Go*; Next In Line; Don't Make Me Go; Don't Make Me Go; Home Of The Blues*; Give My Love To Rose*; Give My Love To Rose; Home Of The Blues; Rock Island Line; Wreck Of Old '97; Belshazzar; Country Boy; Leave That Junk Alone; Doin' My Time; Country Boy; If The Good Lord's Willing; I Heard That Lonesome Whistle Blow; I Was There When It Happened; Remember Me; I Was There When It Happened; Big River*; Ballad Of A Teenage Queen*; Goodnight Irene; Big River; Ballad Of A Teenage Queen; Come In Stranger; Guess Things Happen That Way*; Come In Stranger; Oh, Lonesome Me*; Guess Things Happen That Way; Oh, Lonesome Me.

CD-3: Sugartime*; Born To Lose; You're The Nearest Thing To Heaven; Born To Lose; Sugartime; Story Of A Broken Heart; Always Alone (incomplete); Always Alone; Story Of A Broken Heart (false starts); Story Of A Broken Heart; You Tell Me; Life Goes On; You Win Again*; I Could Never Be Ashamed Of You*; Hey Good Lookin'*; I Can't Help It*; Cold, Cold Heart*; Blue Train; Katy Too; Ways Of A Woman In Love; Fools Hall Of Fame*; Ways Of A Woman In Love; Thanks A Lot; It's Just About Time*; I Forgot To Remember To Forget*; I Just Thought You'd Like To Know; It's Just About Time; I Forgot To Remember To Forget; Down The Street To 301.

CD-4: Oh, What A Dream*; I'll Remember You*; Drink To Me; What Do

I Care; Suppertime; It Was Jesus; Oh, What A Dream*; I'll Remember You*; Mama's Baby; The Troubador; Run Softly Blue River; All Over Again; That's All Over; Frankie's Man Johnnie; Fool's Hall Of Fame; Walkin' The Blues; Lead Me Father; That's Enough; I Still Miss Someone; One More Ride; Pickin' Time; Don't Take Your Guns To Town; I'd Rather Die Young; Shepherd Of My Heart; Cold Shoulder.

NOTE: Those titles marked (*) in the above are considered to be released here for the first time.

CD-5: Lead Me Father (take 1-4); Lead Me Father (take 5-9); Lead Me Father (take 10-12); Lead Me Father; That's Enough (take 1-3); That's Enough; I Still Miss Someone (take 1-5); I Still Miss Someone (take 6-8); I Still Miss Someone (take 9-10); I Still Miss Someone; One More Ride (take 1-4); One More Ride (take 5-11); One More Ride; Pickin' Time (take 1-2); Pickin' Time; Don't Take Your Guns To Town (take 1-4); Don't Take Your Guns To Town (take 5-6); Don't Take Your Guns To Town; I'd Rather Die Young (take 1); I'd Rather Die Young; Shepherd Of My Heart (take 1-2); Shepherd Of My Heart; Cold Shoulder.

NOTE: Take 2 of LEAD ME FATHER is actually FEED ME FATHER.

BCD-15562 (7-91) (5-CD)
THE MAN IN BLACK, 1959-1962
CD-1: Snow In His Hair; I Saw A Man; Lead Me Gently Home; Are All The Children In; Swing Low, Sweet Chariot; I Call Him; The Old Account; He'll Be A Friend; These Things Shall Pass; It Could Be You; God Will; Great Speckled Bird; Were You There; He'll Understand And Say Well Done; God Has My Fortune Laid Away; When I've Learned; I Got Shoes; Let The Lower Lights Be Burning; If We Never Meet Again; When I Take My Vacation In Heaven; When He Reached Down His Hand For Me; Taller

Than Trees; I Won't Have To Cross Jordan Alone; My God Is Real; These Hands; Were You There; Peace In The Valley; A Day In The Grand Canyon. CD-2: I'll Remember You; I Got Stripes; You Dreamer You; Five Feet High And Rising; The Rebel-Johnny Yuma; Lorena; Second Honeymoon; Fable Of Willie Brown; Smiling Bill McCall; Johnny Yuma Theme; The Man On The Hill; Hank And Joe And Me; The Caretaker; Clementine; I Want To Go Home; Old Apache Squaw; Don't Step On Mother's Roses; My Grandfather's Clock; I Couldn't Keep From Crying; My Shoes Keep Walking Back To You; I Will Miss You When You Go; I Feel Better All Over; Bandana (instrumental); Wabash Blues (instrumental); Viel Zu Spat; Wo Ist Zu Hause, Mama; Heartbeat*; Hello Again*.
NOTE: (*) Roy Cash, Jr., (aka: Roy Rivers), is the nephew of Johnny Cash.
CD-3: Tall Man; Girl In Saskatoon; Locomotive Man; The Losing Kind; Five Minutes To Live; Forty Shades Of Green; The Big Battle; Blues For Two (instrumental); Jeri And Nina's Melody (instrumental); Why Do You Punish Me; Just One More; Seasons Of My Heart; Honky-Tonk Girl; I'm So Lonesome I Could Cry; Time Changes Everything; I'd Just Be Fool Enough; Transfusion Blues; Lovin' Locomotive Man; Five Minutes To Live; Mr. Lonesome; Forty Shades Of Green; Folsom Prison Blues; I Walk The Line; Hey Porter; I Forgot More Than You'll Ever Know About Her; There's A Mother Always Waiting; The Losing Kind.
CD-4: Tennessee Flat Top Box; Sing It Pretty Sue; A Little At A Time; So Do I; Bonanza; Shamrock Doesn't Grow In California; I'm Free From The Chain Gang Now; Delia's Gone; Lost On The Desert; I Forgot More Than You'll Ever Know About Her; Accidentally On Purpose; You Remembered Me; In The Jailhouse Now; Let Me Down Easy; In

Them Old Cottonfields Back Home; You Won't Have Far To Go; Delia's Gone; No One Will Ever Know; The Danger Zone; I'll Be All Smiles Tonight; Send A Picture Of Mother; Hardin Wouldn't Run; Sing It Pretty Sue; Blue Bandana (instrumental); So Doggone Lonesome (instrumental); Johnny Reb; Delia's Gone; I Walk The Line (take 6-slow); I Walk The Line (take 9-fast).
CD-5: Girl In Saskatoon (take 1); Girl In Saskatoon (take 2); Girl In Saskatoon (take 3); Girl In Saskatoon (take 4/5); Girl In Saskatoon (take 6); Girl In Saskatoon (take 7/8); Girl In Saskatoon (take 9); An Empty Chair* (take 1); An Empty Chair* (take 2/3/4); An Empty Chair* (take 5); Relief Is Just A Swallow Away* (take 1); Relief Is Just A Swallow Away* (take 2); Relief Is Just A Swallow Away* (take 3/4); Relief Is Just A Swallow Away* (take 5); Relief Is Just A Swallow Away* (take 6); Riot In Cell Block #9** (take 1); Riot In Cell Block #9** (take 2); Riot In Cell Block #9** (take 3); It's A Sin To Tell A Lie** (take 1); Rocket '69** (take 1); Rocket '69** (take 2); Blueberry Hill** (take 1).
NOTE: (*)-Roy Cash (aka: Roy Rivers); (**)-Ray Liberto, Jr., at this time, Cash's brother-in-law.   Information for this session was given on the CD box as being from May 9, 1960 while the actual session date given in the discography was May 10, 1960.

BCD-15563 (7-91) (4-CD)
COME ALONG AND RIDE THIS TRAIN
CD-1: Come Along And Ride This Train; Loading Coal; Slow Rider; Lumberjack; Dorraine Of Ponchartrain; Going To Memphis; When Papa Played The Dobro; Boss Jack; Old Doc Brown; Legend Of John Henry's Hammer; Tell Him I'm Gone; Another Man Done Gone (w/Anita Carter); Shifting, Whispering Sands* (w/Lorne Greene); Casey Jones; Nine Pound Hammer; Chain Gang; Busted;

Waiting For A Train; Roughneck; Pick A Bale Of Cotton; Cotton Pickin' Hands.
NOTE: (*) previously unissued.
CD-2: Hiawatha's Vision; Road To Kaintuck; Hammer And Nails (w/Statler Brothers); Shifting, Whispering Sands (Pt. 1); Ballad Of Boot Hill; I Ride An Old Paint; Hardin Wouldn't Run; Mr. Garfield; Streets Of Laredo; Johnny Reb; A Letter From Home; Bury Me Not On The Lone Prairie; Mean As Hell; Sam Hall; Twenty-five Minutes To Go; The Blizzard; Sweet Betsy From Pike; Green Grow The Lilacs; Rodeo Hand; Stampede; Shifting, Whispering Sands (Pt. 2); Remember The Alamo; Reflections.
CD-3: Introduction-Big Foot; As Long As The Grass Shall Grow; Apache Tears; Custer; Talking Leaves; Ballad Of Ira Hayes; Drums; White Girl; Old Apache Squaw; The Vanishing Race; Opening Dialogue; Paul Revere; Begin West Movement; Road To Kaintuck; To The Shining Mountains; Battle Of New Orleans; Southwestward; Remember The Alamo; Opening The West; Lorena; Gettysburg Address; The West; Big Foot; Like A Young Colt; Mr. Garfield; A Proud Land; The Big Battle; On Wheels And Wings; Come Take A Trip In My Airship; Reaching For The Stars; These Are My People.
CD-4: From Sea To Shining Sea; Whirl And The Suck; Call Daddy From The Mines; Frozen Four-Hundred-Pound-Fair-To-Middlin' Cotton Picker; Walls Of A Prison; The Masterpiece; You And Tennessee; She Came From The Mountains; Another Song To Sing; Flint Arrowhead; Cisco Clifton's Fillin' Station; Shrimpin' Sailin'; From Sea To Shining Sea; Hit The Road And Go; Dialogue #1; If It Wasn't For The Wabash River; Dialogue #2; Lady; Dialogue #3; After The Ball; Dialogue #4; No Earthly Good; Dialogue #5; A Wednesday Car; Dialogue #6; My Cowboy's Last Ride; Dialogue #7; Calilou; Dialogue #8; Come Along And Ride This Train.

NOTE: Neither take of COME ALONG AND RIDE THIS TRAIN have been used before this CD set. The opening track used the "Carter Family" as vocal harmony but they are absent from the closing track.

BELLAPHON (West Germany)

BI-287.07.031
JOHNNY CASH
Probably same as long-play album Pickup-220.07.031.

BI-287.13.006
THE SINGING STORY TELLER
Same as Bellaphon LP 220.13.006.

BI-287.13.007
JOHNNY CASH & JERRY LEE LEWIS SING HANK WILLIAMS
Probably same as Bellaphon LP 220.13.007.

BI-287.13.011
ROUGH CUT KING OF COUNTRY MUSIC
Probably same as Bellaphon LP 220.13.011.

BI-287.13.016
STORY SONGS OF THE TRAINS AND RIVERS
Probably same as Bellaphon LP 220.13.016.

BI-287.13.021
ORIGINAL GOLDEN HITS # 2
Same as Bellaphon LP 220.13.021.

BI-287.13.035
JOHNNY CASH & JERRY LEE LEWIS COUNTRY COMEBACK
Probably same as Bellaphon LP 220.13.035.

BI-288.07.002
ORIGINAL GOLDEN HITS #1

Folsom Prison Blues; Hey Porter; So Doggone Lonesome; There You Go; Next In Line; Cry, Cry, Cry; I Walk The Line; Don't Make Me Go; Train Of Love; Home Of The Blues; Get Rhythm; Guess Things Happen That Way; Just About Time; Luther's Boogie; Thanks A Lot; Big River.

BI-288.13.002
ORIGINAL CLASS OF '55
Same as Bellaphon LP 230.13.002.

BI-288.13.010
THAT GOOD OLD TIME
Probably the same as Bellaphon album 230.13.010.

BI-288.13.018
ORIGINAL GOLDEN HITS #3
Probably same as Bellaphon LP 220.13.002.

BI-289.13.009 (1991)
THE LEGEND
Folsom Prison Blues; Hey Porter; So Doggone Lonesome; There You Go; Next In Line; Cry, Cry, Cry; Ballad Of A Teenage Queen; Come In Stranger; Ways Of A Woman In Love; You're The Nearest Thing To Heaven; I Just Thought You'd Like To Know; Give My Love To Rose; I Walk The Line; Don't Make Me Go; Train Of Love; Home Of The Blues; Get Rhythm; Guess Things Happen That Way.

BI-289.13.010
THE MAN, THE WORLD, HIS MUSIC
Probably same as Bellaphon LP-320.13.010.

BI-290.13.001
20 SUPER HITS
Same as long play album BS-45009.

BIG COUNTRY

BG-2430712
(18) ORIGINAL HITS
Big River; Folsom Prison Blues; Ballad Of A Teenage Queen; Rock Island Line; You're The Nearest Thing To Heaven; Next In Line; There You Go; Cold, Cold Heart; Goodbye, Little Darling, Goodbye; Hey Good Lookin'; Two Timin' Woman; Straight A's In Love; Port Of Lonely Hearts; I Love You Because; I Just Thought You'd Like to Know; Sugartime; It's Just About Time; I Could Never Be Ashamed Of You.

CASTLE COMMUNICATIONS
(West Germany)

CCSCD-146
THE JOHNNY CASH COLLECTION
CD release of CCSLP-146.

CBS

CD-A-8122
THE FABULOUS JOHNNY CASH
Same as CBS U.S. album release CL-1253/CS-8122.

CD-A-8255
RIDE THIS TRAIN
Same as CBS U.S. album release CL-1464/CS-8255.

CK-9478 (10-87)
GREATEST HITS #1
Same as U.S. long play album release CL-2678/CS-9478.

CBS/A-13832 (1992)
HELLO, I'M JOHNNY CASH
Rosanna's Going Wild; Daddy Sang Bass; Don't Take Your Guns To Town; Ballad Of Ira Hayes; Long Black Veil; Five Feet High And Rising; One On The Right Is On The Left; Orange Blossom Special; What Do I Care; Man In Black; Don't

Think Twice, It's All Right; See Ruby Fall; Blistered; Happy To Be With You.

CBS/A-19845
MANY SIDES OF JOHNNY CASH
(Ghost) Riders In The Sky; Flesh And Blood; Last Gunfighter Ballad; One Piece At A Time; Ragged Old Flag; Ballad Of Ira Hayes; Look At Them Beans; Daddy Sang Bass; I Still Miss Someone; Ring Of Fire.

CBS/A-20726
CLASSIC CHRISTMAS
Same as U.S. release CBS JC-36866

CBS/A-21608 (1991)
GOSPEL GLORY
Daddy Sang Bass; Peace In The Valley; Softly And Tenderly; Amazing Grace; Rock Of Ages; In The Sweet By And By; He'll Understand And Say Well Done; He Turned The Water Into Wine; Great Speckled Bird; Were You There.

CDCBS-26466 (Europe)
HIGHWAYMAN
Same as U.S. album FC-40056, European album CBS-26466 and Australian album SBP-8066.

CD-32209 (Austria) (1989)
AT FOLSOM PRISON AND SAN QUENTIN
Same as U.S. CBS CD release CGK-33639.

CGK-33639 (2/90)
JOHNNY CASH AT FOLSOM PRISON AND SAN QUENTIN
Same as U.S. album CL-2839/CS-9639 and CS-9827. However, this CD includes only one of the SAN QUENTIN tracks.

CK-37570 (Rosanne Cash)
SOMEWHERE IN THE STARS
Same as U.S. album FC-37570.

CK-38317 (5-87)
BIGGEST HITS
Same as U.S. album FC-38317.

CK-39415
FRIENDSHIP (Ray Charles)
Same as U.S. album FC-39415.

CK-40056 (7-86)
HIGHWAYMAN
Same as U.S. album FC-40056.

CK-40347
HEROES (w/Waylon Jennings)
Folks Out On The Road; I'm Never Gonna Roam Again; American By Birth; Field Of Diamonds (Cash only); Heroes; Even Cowgirls Get The Blues; Love Is The Way; Ballad Of Forty Dollars; I Will Always Love You (Waylon only); One Too Many Mornings.

CGK-40637 (7-87)
COLUMBIA RECORDS 1958-1986
Oh, What A Dream*; I Still Miss Someone; Pickin' Time; Don't Take Your Guns To Town; Five Feet High And Rising; Folsom Prison Blues (live); San Quentin #2; A Boy Named Sue; Sunday Morning Coming Down; Man In Black; Seasons Of My Heart; Legend Of John Henry's Hammer; Ring Of Fire; Ballad Of Ira Hayes; Orange Blossom Special; One Piece At A Time; Ghost Riders In The Sky; Without Love; The Baron; Highway Patrolman.
NOTE: This is the first release of this alternate master of YOU DREAMER YOU.

AK-44059
16 BY FOUR
Cash is included with: I WALK THE LINE; A BOY NAMED SUE; RING OF FIRE and ORANGE BLOSSOM SPECIAL.

CK-45240 (2/90)
HIGHWAYMAN 2
(w/Waylon, Willie & Kris)
Silver Stallion; Born And Raised In Black
And White; Two Stories Wide; We're All
In Your Corner Tonight; American
Remains; Anthem '84; Angels Love Bad
Men; Songs That Make A Difference;
Living Legend; Texas (Willie only).

CK-45384 (2/90)
JOHNNY CASH PATRIOT
Song Of The Patriot; Paul Revere
(w/Dialogue); Gettysburg Address
(w/Dialogue); Man In Black; From Sea
To Shining Sea; Mr. Garfield; Sold Out
Of Flagpoles; Ballad Of Ira Hayes;
Singing In Vietnam Talking Blues;
Ragged Old Flag.
NOTE: On the actual disc this last title is
given as RAGGED OLD CROSS.

CK-46031
COLUMBIA COUNTRY CLASSICS #3
AMERICANA
Cash·is included with DON'T TAKE
YOUR GUNS TO TOWN;
TENNESSEE FLAT TOP BOX; A BOY
NAMED SUE and HIGHWAYMAN
(w/Willie, Kris, Waylon).

C3K-47991 (3-CD)
ESSENTIAL JOHNNY CASH
1955-1983
CD-1: Hey Porter; Cry, Cry, Cry; Folsom
Prison Blues; Luther Played The Boogie;
Get Rhythm; I Walk The Line; Home Of
The Blues; Give My Love To Rose; Rock
Island Line; Doin' My Time; Big River;
Ballad Of A Teenage Queen; Guess
Things Happen That Way; Ways Of A
Woman In Love; Thanks A Lot; Oh,
What A Dream; What Do I Care; All
Over Again; I Still Miss Someone; I'd Just
Be Fool Enough (To Fall); Walking The
Blues; Frankie's Man, Johnny; Tennessee
Flat Top Box; Sing It Pretty, Sue; Pickin'
Time; Five Feet High And Rising; Old
Account; Peace In The Valley; Were

You There (w/Carter Family). NOTE:
The first fifteen songs are Sun masters.
CD-2: Don't Take Your Guns To Town;
Ballad Of Boot Hill; Rebel-Johnny Yuma;
Big Battle; When The Roses Bloom
Again (w/Carter Family); Ballad Of Ira
Hayes; Legend Of John Henry's Hammer;
Dark As A Dungeon; Long Black Veil; I
Got Stripes; Twenty-five Minutes To Go;
The Wall; Busted; Bad News; Dirty Old
Egg-Sucking Dog; Orange Blossom
Special; Ring Of Fire; Understand Your
Man; Jackson (w/June Carter); Blistered;
See Ruby Fall; Cisco Clifton's Fillin'
Station; Daddy Sang Bass.
CD-3: Folsom Prison Blues (live);
Cocaine Blues (live); A Boy Named Sue
(live); Wanted Man; Singin' In Viet Nam
Talkin' Blues; Man In Black; What Is
Truth; Flesh And Blood; Sunday Morning
Coming Down; Oney; One Piece At A
Time; Hit The Road And Go; Rockabilly
Blues (Texas 1955); I Will Rock And Roll
With You; No Expectations; (Ghost)
Riders In The Sky; Bull Rider; Highway
Patrolman; After The Ball; Without Love;
Last Time; I'm Gonna Sit On The Porch
And Pick On My Old Guitar.

CK-48952 (1992)
GOSPEL COLLECTION
It Was Jesus; I Saw A Man; Are All The
Children In; The Old Account; Lead Me
Gently Home; Swing Low, Sweet
Chariot; Snow In His Hair; Lead Me
Father; I Call Him; These Things Shall
Pass; He'll Be A Friend; God Will; He'll
Understand And Say Well Done; God
Must Have My Fortune Laid Away;
When I've Learned; I Got Shoes; Let The
Lower Lights Be Burning; If We Never
Meet Again; When I Take My Vacation
In Heaven; When The Saviour Reached
Down For Me; Taller Than Trees; I Won't
Have To Cross Jordan Alone; My God Is
Real (Yes, God Is Real); These Hands.

CDCBS-63601 (Europe)
NASHVILLE SKYLINE (Bob Dylan)

Same as U.S. album KCS-9825 and European album CBS-63601.

CSK-73572
AMERICAN REMAINS
Promotional CD containing only AMERICAN REMAINS (w/Willie, Kris, Waylon).

450366.2 (Europe)
BEST OF COUNTRY MUSIC #1
Cash is included with: THE BALLAD OF FORTY DOLLARS (w/Waylon Jennings); RING OF FIRE; I'M LEAVING NOW and HIGHWAYMAN (w/Waylon, Willie, Kristofferson).

450466.2 (Europe)
GREATEST YEARS 1958-1986
Same as U.S. album C2-40637 and European album CBS-450466.1.

450479.2 (Europe) (David Allan Coe)
A MATTER OF LIFE...AND DEATH
Same as U.S. album FC-40571.

451030.2 (Europe)
BEST OF COUNTRY MUSIC #2
Cash is included with EVEN COWGIRLS GET THE BLUES (w/ Waylon Jennings).

CBS-461129.2 (Austria)
I LOVE COUNTRY
I Walk The Line; City Of New Orleans; Ballad Of Ira Hayes; Legend Of John Henry's Hammer; San Quentin; (Ghost) Riders In The Sky; Last Gunfighter Ballad; Casey's Last Ride; The Gambler; Ballad Of Forty Dollars (w/Waylon); The Twentieth Century Is Almost Over; Folks Out On The Road (w/Waylon); A Boy Named Sue; The Baron; Don't Take Your Guns To Town; The Lady Came From Baltimore; I'm Leaving Now; Highway Patrolman; Johnny 99.

CBS-461131.2 (Austria)

COUNTRY MEN-I LOVE COUNTRY
Cash is included with: THE HIGHWAYMAN; THE LAST COWBOY SONG; DESPERADOS WAITING FOR A TRAIN (w/Waylon, Willie, Kristofferson) and EVEN COWGIRLS GET THE BLUES (w/Waylon Jennings).

CBS-461133.2 (Austria)
COUNTRY DUETS-I LOVE COUNTRY
Cash is included with THE CITY OF NEW ORLEANS (w/June Carter Cash).

CBS-462557.2 (Austria)
BEST OF JOHNNY CASH
Ring Of Fire; Orange Blossom Special; The Night They Drove Old Dixie Down; Jackson (w/June Carter Cash); Don't Take Your Guns To Town; I Walk The Line; A Boy Named Sue; San Quentin; If I Were A Carpenter (w/June Carter Cash); Folsom Prison Blues; Kate; (Ghost) Riders In The Sky; Daddy Sang Bass; Bonanza; In Them Old Cottonfields Back Home; Five Feet High And Rising; Man In Black; A Thing Called Love; Ballad Of Ira Hayes; In The Jailhouse Now.

CBS-462737 2 (Australia)
JOHNNY CASH AT SAN QUENTIN
Same as U.S. CBS release CS-9827 and European release CBS-63629.

CBS-463159-2 (Holland)
HIGHWAYMAN
Same as U.S. release CBS 26466.

CBS-466316 2
COUNTRY DUETS #2
I LOVE COUNTRY
Cash is included with EVEN COWGIRLS GET THE BLUES (w/Waylon); JACKSON (w/June Carter) and IF I WERE A CARPENTER (w/June Carter).

CBS-466652 2 (Europe) (1990)
HIGHWAYMAN 2
Cash as U.S. release CK-45240.

CBS-468116 2
20 FOOT-TAPPIN' GREATS--JOHNNY
CASH ITCHY FEET
Same as U.S. album release CBS-10009.

CBS-468847 2 (Australia)
HIGHWAYMEN PERFORM ON
THEIR OWN
Cash is included with FOLSOM PRISON
BLUES; A BOY NAMED SUE; DON'T
TAKE YOUR GUNS TO TOWN; RING
OF FIRE and THE HIGHWAYMAN
(w/Willie, Kris, Waylon).

CBS-469433-2
THE STORYTELLER
The Baron; A Boy Named Sue; Ballad Of
Ira Hayes; Highway Patrolman; The
Diplomat; No Charge; John's; To Beat
The Devil; Last Gunfighter Ballad; Don't
Take Your Guns To Town; Cowboy Who
Started The Fight; The Gambler;
Reverend Mr. Black; All Around
Cowboy; (Ghost) Riders In The Sky;
Who's Gene Autry.

CBS-902125.2 (United Kingdom)
JOHNNY CASH'S GREATEST HITS
Same as U.S. album release CL-2678/CS-
9478 and European release CBS-63062.

CD SOUNDS

CDFX-6757
COUNTRY LEGEND--JOHNNY CASH
I Heard That Lonesome Whistle; Cry,
Cry, Cry; Folsom Prison Blues; Country
Boy; Wreck Of The Old '97; I Love You
Because; I Walk The Line; Doing My
Time; If The Good Lord's Willing; Ballad
Of A Teenage Queen.

CeDe INTERNATIONAL

CD-66038
JOHNNY CASH-THE BEST OF
Next In Line; There You Go; Rock Island
Line; Get Rhythm; Big River; Born To
Lose; Train Of Love; Hey Porter; I Walk
The Line; Country Boy; I Heard That
Lonesome Whistle; Guess Things Happen
That Way; Wreck Of The Old '97; Folsom
Prison Blues; Ballad Of A Teenage
Queen; Doin' My Time.

CHARLY (United Kingdom)

CD/SUN-5 (1987)
COUNTRY MUSIC ORIGINALS #2
Cash is included with: HEY PORTER;
CRY, CRY, CRY; FOLSOM PRISON
BLUES; SO DOGGONE LONESOME.

CD/SUN-8
COUNTRY MUSIC ORIGINALS #3
Cash is included with: GET RHYTHM; I
WALK THE LINE; THERE YOU GO;
TRAIN OF LOVE; DON'T MAKE ME
GO; NEXT IN LINE; HOME OF THE
BLUES; GIVE MY LOVE TO ROSE.

CD/SUN-11
COUNTRY MUSIC ORIGINALS #4
Cash is included with: BIG RIVER;
BALLAD OF A TEENAGE QUEEN;
GUESS THINGS HAPPEN THAT
WAY; COME IN STRANGER; THE
WAYS OF A WOMAN IN LOVE;
YOU'RE THE NEAREST THING TO
HEAVEN; I JUST THOUGHT YOU'D
LIKE TO KNOW; IT'S JUST ABOUT
TIME; THANKS A LOT; LUTHER
PLAYED THE BOOGIE; I FORGOT
TO REMEMBER TO FORGET; KATY
TOO.

CD/SUN-13
COUNTRY MUSIC ORIGINALS #5
Cash is included with: YOU TELL ME;
GOODBYE LITTLE DARLIN',

GOODBYE; I LOVE YOU BECAUSE; STRAIGHT A's IN LOVE; STORY OF A BROKEN HEART; DOWN THE STREET TO 301; MEAN EYED CAT; PORT OF LONELY HEARTS; OH LONESOME ME; LIFE GOES ON; SUGARTIME; MY TREASURE; BLUE TRAIN; BORN TO LOSE; WIDE OPEN ROAD and BELSHAZZAR.

CCD-18 (4-87)
JOHNNY CASH--COUNTRY BOY
I Walk The Line; Wide Open Road; Cry, Cry, Cry; Hey Porter; Folsom Prison Blues; Get Rhythm; Luther Played The Boogie; Mean Eyed Cat; There You Go; Train Of Love; Straight A's In Love; Give My Love To Rose; Goodnight Irene; Rock Island Line; Country Boy; If The Good Lord's Willing; Big River; Ballad Of A Teenage Queen; Come In Stranger; Guess Things Happen The Way; Life Goes On; Blue Train; Katy Too; Ways Of A Woman In Love; Thanks A Lot.

CD-146
1955 TO 1958 RECORDINGS
Same as Charly albums SUNLP-1015 and SUNLP-1047 with the addition of DON'T MAKE ME GO and THANKS A LOT.

CDCD-1054 (1992)
GET RHYTHM
Cry, Cry, Cry; Luther Played The Boogie; Folsom Prison Blues; So Doggone Lonesome; Mean Eyed Cat; Wide Open Road; Two Timin' Woman; There You Go; I Walk The Line; Country Boy; Train Of Love; Get Rhythm; Hey Porter; Give My Love To Rose; Oh Lonesome Me; Rock Island Line; Big River; Ballad Of A Teenage Queen; Blue Train; You Win Again.

CMH

CD-8000 (1992)

ONCE UPON A TIME--MARTY STUART
Cash is included with a duet on MOTHER MAYBELLE.

COUNTRY MUSIC FOUNDATION
(Canada)

CMF-SP1/SED-10684
COUNTRY MUSIC HALL OF FAME-20TH ANNIVERSARY COLLECTION #1
Cash is included with SUNDAY MORNING COMING DOWN.

COUNTRY STARS

CTS-55406 (Europe) (1989)
I WALK THE LINE
Cry, Cry, Cry; Folsom Prison Blues; So Doggone Lonesome; I Walk The Line; There You Go; Train Of Love; Next In Line; Don't Make Me Go; Home Of The Blues; Give My Love To Rose; Ballad Of A Teenage Queen; Guess Things Happen That Way; Come In Stranger; Ways Of A Woman In Love; You're The Nearest Thing To Heaven; It's Just About Time; Luther Played The Boogie; Thanks A Lot; Katy Too; Straight A's In Love; Mean Eyed Cat; Oh Lonesome Me; Get Rhythm; Rock Island Line; Big River.

CRC (France)

CRC-30352-X
KINGS OF COUNTRY
(Cash and Jim Reeves)
Cash material: I Walk The Line; Hey Porter; Folsom Prison Blues; Get Rhythm; Mean Eyed Cat; Train Of Love; Big River; Ballad Of A Teenage Queen; Guess Things Happen That Way; Blue Train; Ways Of A Woman In Love.

CURB

D2-77494 (1991)
BEST OF JOHNNY CASH
Ring Of Fire; A Boy Named Sue; Sunday Morning Coming Down; Folsom Prison Blues (live at Folsom); I Walk The Line (Sun); Ballad Of A Teenage Queen (Sun); Guess Things Happen That Way (Sun); Ways Of A Woman In Love (Sun); Get Rhythm (Sun); That Old Wheel (w/Hank Williams Jr); Long Black Veil (w/Razzy Bailey).

DELTA (LASER LIGHT)

DELTA/15-417
COUNTRY CHRISTMAS
Blue Christmas; Silent Night; White Christmas; Figgy Puddin' (Carter Family); Here Was A Man; Joy To The World; O Little Town Of Bethlehem; What Child Is This; First Noel (Carter Family); Away In A Manger; O Christmas Tree (Carter Family); O Come All Ye Faithful; It Came Upon A Midnight Clear (Carter Family); Hark! The Herald Angels Sing; I'll Be Home For Christmas.

DIXIE FROG

DFG-8412
JIMMY TITTLE
Same as album of same title and number.

DOUBLE GOLD

DBG 2-53007
50 GOLDEN COUNTRY HITS (2-CD)
Cash is included with: FOLSOM PRISON BLUES; GUESS THINGS HAPPEN THAT WAY; I WALK THE LINE and BALLAD OF A TEENAGE QUEEN.

DUCHESSE

CD-35078 (Europe) (1990)
SAN QUENTIN AND OTHER HITS
A Boy Named Sue; Jackson (w/June Carter); San Quentin; (Ghost) Riders In The Sky; Ring Of Fire; You're The Nearest Thing To Heaven; The Rebel-Johnny Yuma; One On The Right Is On The Left; It Ain't Me Babe; Ballad Of Ira Hayes; Orange Blossom Special; Goodbye Little Darlin', Goodbye; Understand Your Man; Don't Take Your Guns To Town; Straight A's In Love; I Love You Because.

DUNHILL

DSZ009 (1986)
LEGENDS
Cash is included with: I WALK THE LINE; FOLSOM PRISON BLUES; GET RHYTHM; BALLAD OF A TEENAGE QUEEN; GUESS THINGS HAPPEN THAT WAY and ROCK ISLAND LINE.

EMI (Australia)

CDMID-166220
20 GOLDEN GREATS
Hey Porter; Ballad Of A Teenage Queen; Guess Things Happen That Way; I Love You Because; Ways Of A Woman In Love; Hey Good Lookin'; Down The Street To 301; Two Timin' Woman; You're The Nearest Thing To Heaven; Goodnight Irene; I Walk The Line; Come In Stranger; Folsom Prison Blues; Rock Island Line; Wreck Of The Old '97; Straight A's In Love; Blue Train; Cold, Cold Heart; Oh Lonesome Me; Big River.

ENTERTAINERS, THE

CD-0208 (Europe) (1990)
HIS 30 GREATEST HITS

I Walk The Line; Hey Porter; Rock Island Line; Train Of Love; Folsom Prison Blues; Blue Train; Down The Street To 301; Goodbye Little Darling Goodbye; Ways Of A Woman In Love; Give My Love To Rose; Cry, Cry, Cry; I Could Never Be Ashamed Of You; Big River; Get Rhythm; Luther Played The Boogie; You're The Nearest Thing To Heaven; Cold, Cold Heart; I Love You Because; There You Go; Just About Time; Sugartime; Straight A's In Love; Next In Line; Hey Good Lookin'; Ballad Of A Teenage Queen; I Just Thought You'd Like To Know; Home Of The Blues; So Doggone Lonesome; Don't Take Your Guns To Town; Country Boy.

EVERGREEN

2690522 CD
SUPER HITS
Folsom Prison Blues; Goodbye, Little Darlin'; There You Go; Big River; Straight A's In Love; Rock Island Line; Ballad Of A Teenage Queen; Next In Line; You're The Nearest Thing To Heaven; I Love You Because.

FOLK ERA

FE2055CD
WE THE PEOPLE
Cash is included with narration and four songs: BATTLE OF NEW ORLEANS; REMEMBER THE ALAMO; RAGGED OLD FLAG and BALLAD OF IRA HAYES.

GALAXIS

CD 9002
18 GOLDEN HITS
Same as "Spectrum Spec" 85008.

GIANTS (Europe)

GIANTS OF COUNTRY
GTS-76605
Cash is included with FOLSOM PRISON BLUES; BALLAD OF A TEENAGE QUEEN; I WALK THE LINE; BIG RIVER and NEXT IN LINE.

GREENLINE SRL (Italy)

SUN/CD-502 (1990)
ORIGINAL SUN - SINGLES
COLLECTION 1955-1959
Hey Porter; Cry, Cry, Cry; Folsom Prison Blues; So Doggone Lonesome; Get Rhythm; I Walk The Line; There You Go; Train Of Love; Don't Make Me Go; Next In Line; Home Of The Blues; Give My Love To Rose; Big River; Ballad Of A Teenage Queen; Guess Things Happen That Way; Come In Stranger; Ways Of A Woman In Love; You're The Nearest Thing To Heaven; I Just Thought You'd Like To Know; It's Just About Time; Thanks A Lot; Luther Played The Boogie; I Forgot To Remember To Forget; Katy Too; You Tell Me; Goodbye Little Darling; Straight A's In Love; I Love You Because.

HAPPY DAYS (Holland)

2605242
THE COUNTRY COLLECTION
20 GOLDEN HITS
Cash is included with PORT OF LONELY HEARTS.

HOLLYWOOD NITES (France)

HNC-0007
I WALK THE LINE
I Walk The Line; Rock Island Line; You Win Again; Hey Good Lookin'; Cold, Cold Heart; Sugartime; Born To Lose;

Big River; I Hear That Lonesome Wind Blow (?); Goodnight Irene; Folsom Prison Blues; I Forgot To Remember To Forget; Wreck Of The Old '97; Oh Lonesome Me.

HOTLINE (Europe)

447.059-2 (1987)
JOHNNY CASH
Same as Topline CD-521.

INNOVATIVE MUSIC PRODUCTION

PCD-813
JOHNNY CASH
I Walk The Line; Born To Lose; Hey Good Lookin'; Guess Things Happen That Way; Oh Lonesome Me; You're The Nearest Thing To Heaven; Get Rhythm; You Win Again; Folsom Prison Blues; I Could Never Be Ashamed Of You; Ballad Of A Teenage Queen; Rock Island Line; Country Boy; Ways Of A Woman In Love; Hey Porter; Wreck Of The Old '97; I Couldn't Keep From Crying; I Love You Because.

INSTANT

INS-5007
BORN TO LOSE
Same as album of same title and number.

INTERPRESS (Europe)

CD-11002 (1988)
16 GREATEST HITS (16 TONS)
I Walk The Line; Folsom Prison Blues; A Boy Named Sue; Understand Your Man; Ballad Of A Teenage Queen; Hey Porter; Orange Blossom Special; Don't Take Your Guns To Town; Guess Things Happen That Way; It Ain't Me, Babe; Next In Line; Ring Of Fire; Rock Island

Line; (Ghost) Riders In The Sky; Born To Lose; Wreck Of The Old '97; I Love You Because.

INTERTAPE (Europe)

CD-500.063 (1987)
JOHNNY CASH
I Walk The Line; Ballad Of A Teenage Queen; Big River; Guess Things Happen That Way; Born To Lose; Get Rhythm; Wreck Of The Old '97; Give My Love To Rose; Luther Played The Boogie; Hey Porter; Mean Eyed Cat; Train Of Love; You're The Nearest Thing To Heaven; Rock Island Line; Cold, Cold Heart; Folsom Prison Blues.

ISLAND

CIDU29-518047-2 (7-93)
ZOOROPA (U2)
Cash is included on THE WANDERER.

K-TEL

KCD-303
I NEED TO BE IN LOVE (Sandy Kelly)
Cash/Kelly duet on WOODCARVER.

KCD-325 (1990) (Ireland)
20 SINGLE HITS
Cash is included with two duets with Sandy Kelly: WOODCARVER and RING OF FIRE.

LASERLIGHT (see: DELTA)

LAURIE

PCD-4501 (1990) (Tommy Cash)
TWENTY-FIFTH ANNIVERSARY ALBUM

Same as U.S. "Playback" label release
PB-4501.

LIVING LEGEND RECORDS (Italy)

LLRCD-081 (1990)
BOB DYLAN MEETS GEORGE
HARRISON AND JOHNNY CASH
One Too Many Mornings; Good Old
Mountain Dew; I Still Miss Someone;
Careless Love; Matchbox; Big River;
That's All Right Mama; I Walk The Line;
You Are My Sunshine.

LOTUS (Europe)

CD 0211
GENTLEMEN OF COUNTRY AND
WESTERN
Cash is included with four songs: HEY
PORTER; FOLSOM PRISON BLUES; I
WALK THE LINE and BIG RIVER.

MASTERS MUSIC (Germany)

MM-85032
COUNTRY COLLECTION --
GREATEST HITS
Cash is included with PORT OF
LONELY HEARTS.

MASTERPIECE (United Kingdom)

CD-CST-11 (1988)
COUNTRY STORE COLLECTION
Same as the albums released on
Masterpiece and Starblend but with four
additional songs: GHOST RIDERS IN
THE SKY; SONG OF THE PATRIOT;
THE GAMBLER and IT'LL BE HER.

MCA

MCAD-5789/JVC-534 (John Schneider)

TAKE THE LONG WAY HOME
Same as U.S. album MCA-5789.

MCAD-10596 (Marty Stuart)
THIS ONE'S GONNA HURT YOU
Cash/Stuart duet on DOIN' MY TIME.

MERCURY/POLYGRAM

CDP-170 (1990)
FARMER'S ALMANAC
This is a promotional release with
FARMER'S ALMANAC as the only Cash
song.

SACD-217
JANUARY 1991
Cash is included with GOIN' BY THE
BOOK; THE GREATEST COWBOY
OF THEM ALL and BEANS FOR
BREAKFAST. (This is a promotional
album).

CDP-320 (1990)
GOIN' BY THE BOOK
This is a promotional CD which contains
only GOIN' BY THE BOOK.

CDP-397
THE MYSTERY OF LIFE
Cash is included with MYSTERY OF
LIFE. (This is a promotional CD).

CDP-469
WANTED MAN
Cash is included with WANTED MAN
from the *Mystery Of Life* CD. (This is a
promotional CD.)

M/P-832-031-2 (4-87)
JOHNNY CASH IS COMING TO
TOWN
The Big Light; Ballad Of Barbara; I'd
Rather Have You; Let Him Roll; The
Night Hank Williams Came To Town
(w/Waylon); Sixteen Tons; Letters From
Home; W. Lee O'Daniel (And The

Lightcrust Dough Boys); Heavy Metal (Don't Mean Rock And Roll To Me); My Ship Will Sail.

M/P-834-526-2 (6-88)
CLASSIC CASH - HALL OF FAME SERIES
Get Rhythm; Tennessee Flat-Top Box; Long Black Veil; A Thing Called Love; I Still Miss Someone; Cry, Cry, Cry; Blue Train; Sunday Morning Coming Down; Five Feet High And Rising; Peace In The Valley; Don't Take Your Guns To Town; Home Of The Blues; Guess Things Happen That Way; I Got Stripes; I Walk The Line; Ring Of Fire; Ballad Of Ira Hayes; Ways Of A Woman In Love; Folsom Prison Blues; Suppertime.
NOTE: This album of re-makes was originally intended to be released only in Europe. It was released first in Europe in April 1988 during a Cash tour there. It then was also released in the United States as a promotional package through the Country Music Hall of Fame as part of their exhibition on the career of Johnny Cash. Then, later in the year, it was made available in record stores.

M/P-834-778-2 (10-88)
WATER FROM THE WELLS OF HOME
Ballad Of A Teenage Queen (w/Rosanne Cash, Everly Brothers); As Long As I Live (w/Emmylou Harris, Waylon, Jessi Colter); Where Did We Go Right (w/June Carter Cash); Last Of The Drifters (w/Tom T. Hall); Call Me The Breeze (w/John Carter Cash); That Old Wheel (w/Hank Williams Jr); Sweeter Than The Flowers (w/Waylon, Emmylou Harris, Jessi Colter); A Croft In Clachan (Ballad Of Rob MacDunn) (w/Glen Campbell); New Moon Over Jamaica (w/Paul McCartney, June Carter Cash, Linda McCartney, Tom T. Hall); Water From The Wells Of Home (w/John Carter Cash).

M/P-842-155-2 (1-90)
BOOM CHICKA BOOM
A Backstage Pass; Cat's In The Cradle; Farmer's Almanac; Don't Go Near The Water; Family Bible; Harley; I Love You, Love You; Hidden Shame; Monteagle Mountain; That's One You Owe Me.
NOTE: This LP/CD was released in Europe with an added track, VETERAN'S DAY, and renumbered as 842-725-2.

M/P-848-051-2 (2-91)
THE MYSTERY OF LIFE
The Greatest Cowboy Of Them All; I'm An Easy Rider; Hey Porter; Beans For Breakfast; Goin' By The Book; Wanted Man; I'll Go Somewhere And Sing My Songs Again (w/Tom T. Hall); The Hobo Song; Angel And The Badman.

MONDANE (Switzerland)

BL-87066
JOHNNY CASH
Rock Island Line; I Heard That Lonesome Whistle; Country Boy; I Walk The Line; Cry, Cry, Cry; So Doggone Lonesome; I Was There When It Happened; If The Good Lord's Willing; Wreck Of The Old '97; Folsom Prison Blues; Doin' My Time.

MUSIC CLUB (United Kingdom)

MCCD-082 (1992)
BEST OF THE SUN YEARS 1955-1961
Cry, Cry, Cry; So Doggone Lonesome; Folsom Prison Blues; I Walk The Line; There You Go; Train Of Love; Next In Line; Wreck Of The Old '97; Home Of The Blues; Give My Love To Rose; Ballad Of A Teenage Queen; Big River; Guess Things Happen That Way; Come In Stranger; You're The Nearest Thing To Heaven; Luther Played The Boogie; Katy

Too; Straight A's In Love; Oh Lonesome Me; Get Rhythm.

MUSIC STARS (Denmark)

CD-600688
16 GOLDEN HITS
(Cash, M. Robbins, Don Williams)
Cash is included with six songs:
FOLSOM PRISON BLUES; GUESS THINGS HAPPEN THAT WAY; JUST ABOUT TIME; KATY TOO; I FORGOT TO REMEMBER TO FORGET and COME IN STRANGER.

CD-690888
16 USA TOP HITS, VOLUME SIX
Cash is included with I WALK THE LINE.

CD-790189
OH, WHAT A DREAM
Cash is included with six songs: OH, WHAT A DREAM; DON'T TAKE YOUR GUNS TO TOWN; SEASONS OF MY HEART; I STILL MISS SOMEONE; FIVE FEET HIGH AND RISING and PICKIN' TIME.

MYRRH

MYRRH/WORD/70169837380
I SCREAM SUNDAY (One Bad Pig)
Cash is included with a duet of MAN IN BLACK.

OBJECT

OROO20
I WALK THE LINE/THE COLLECTOR
I Walk The Line; Rock Island Line; You Win Again; Hey Good Lookin'; Cold, Cold Heart; Sugartime; Born To Lose; Big River; I Hear That Lonesome Wind Blow; Goodnight Irene; Folsom Prison

Blues; I Forgot To Remember To Forget; Wreck Of The Old '97; Oh Lonesome Me.
NOTE: It is assumed I HEAR THAT LONESOME WIND BLOW is actually I HEARD THAT LONESOME WHISTLE BLOW.

OCEAN (United Kingdom)

OCNWD-2032 (1989)
THE CLASSIC
Same as album release on same label.

OVERSEAS (Japan)

30 CP-Q102 (1986)
GREATEST HITS - 20
Hey Porter; Cry, Cry, Cry; Folsom Prison Blues; Get Rhythm; Guess Things Happen That Way; Come In Stranger; Ways Of A Woman In Love; It's Just About Time; I Just Thought You'd Like To Know; Katy Too; I Walk The Line; Next In Line; Home Of The Blues; Ballad Of A Teenage Queen; Straight A's In Love; I Love You Because; Down The Street To 301; Oh Lonesome Me; Wide Open Road; Rock Island Line.

PICKWICK

PWK-010
JOHNNY CASH
Same as "Innovative Music Production" (I.M.P.) PCD-813.

PWK-014
GREAT COUNTRY LOVE SONGS COLLECTION
Fools Hall Of Fame; Blue Train; I Heard That Lonesome Whistle; I Just Thought You'd Like To Know; Port Of Lonely Hearts; Cold, Cold Heart; Give My Love To Rose; Train Of Love; So Doggone Lonesome; Story Of A Broken Heart; Two Timin' Woman; I Couldn't Keep

From Crying; Remember Me; Don't Make Me Go; Always Alone; Goodbye, Little Darlin'.

P.M.C.

002016-1
JOHNNY CASH AND DON WILLIAMS THE COUNTRY KINGS
Cash is included with five songs: FOLSOM PRISON BLUES; SUGARTIME; HEY PORTER; TWO TIMIN' WOMAN and STRAIGHT A'S IN LOVE.

POLYSTAR

834-801-2
ONE MILLION DOLLARS CASH
Same as long play album "Polystar" 834801-1.

POLYTEL ELITE (Canada)

845-419-2
SINGS I WALK THE LINE
Same as "Share" SH-5000.

POP CORN (Holland)

PC-004
COUNTRY SUPER SONGS
Cash is included with I WALK THE LINE.

PRIMA

PXCD-115
THE LEGEND
It's Just About Time; Straight A's In Love; I Just Thought You'd Like To Know; You're The Nearest Thing To Heaven; Rock Island Line; Cold, Cold Heart; Folsom Prison Blues; Hey Good Lookin'; I Love You Because; Big River; Ballad Of A Teenage Queen; Goodbye Little Darlin'; I Could Never Be Ashamed Of You; Next In Line; Port Of Lonely Hearts; Sugartime; There You Go; Two Timin' Woman.

PXCD-122
KIND OF COUNTRY
Cash is included with COLD, COLD HEART and HEY GOOD LOOKIN'.

QUALITY MUSIC (Italy)

Q-157221
CARL PERKINS AND FRIENDS A ROCKABILLY SESSION
Cash is included with an interview.

RCA

RCA-2023-2-R (1990)
ELVIS PRESLEY
THE MILLION DOLLAR QUARTET
See session dated "December 4, 1956" in Appendix A of this volume.

RHINO

R3-73002
LIL' BIT O' GOLD-JOHNNY CASH
This is a "mini" disc which includes: I WALK THE LINE; FOLSOM PRISON BLUES; GUESS THINGS HAPPEN THAT WAY and BALLAD OF A TEENAGE QUEEN.

R2-70950
SUN YEARS
Folsom Prison Blues; Hey Porter; I Walk The Line; Get Rhythm; Guess Things Happen That Way; Rock Island Line; Home Of The Blues; Luther Played The Boogie; Mean Eyed Cat; Big River; Next In Line; Come In Stranger; Train Of

Love; There You Go; Ballad Of A
Teenage Queen; So Doggone Lonesome;
Ways Of A Woman In Love; Give My
Love To Rose.

SIGNAL

SIG-50490
BEST OF COUNTRY SONGS
Cash is included with THERE YOU GO
and YOU'RE THE NEAREST THING
TO HEAVEN.

SONY (See CBS)

SONET

SPCD-4
SPOTLIGHT--JOHNNY CASH
Folsom Prison Blues; Cold, Cold Heart;
Big River; Oh Lonesome Me; Next In
Line; I Forgot To Remember To Forget;
Goodnight Irene; Get Rhythm; Ballad Of
A Teenage Queen; Cry, Cry, Cry; I Walk
The Line; Luther's Boogie; Katy Too; I
Heard That Lonesome Whistle; Hey
Good Lookin'; I Love You Because; Hey
Porter; Wreck Of The Old '97; You Win
Again; Rock Island Line.

SOUND SENSATION (Canada)

EGBR-2518
FABULOUS JOHNNY CASH
Folsom Prison Blues; Guess Things
Happen That Way; Get Rhythm; Oh
Lonesome Me; Straight A's In Love; Hey
Porter; I Walk The Line; Ballad Of A
Teenage Queen; Ways Of A Woman In
Love; Big River; Rock Island Line; Give
My Love To Rose; Story Of A Broken
Heart; Next In Line; There You Go; Train
Of Love.

SOUNDWINGS (Europe)

102.1008-2
BALLAD OF A TEENAGE QUEEN
18 GREATEST HITS
You're The Nearest Thing To Heaven;
Rock Island Line; Cold, Cold Heart;
Folsom Prison Blues; Hey Good Lookin';
I Love You Because; It's Just About
Time; Straight A's In Love; I Just
Thought You'd Like To Know; Goodbye
Little Darling; I Could Never Be
Ashamed Of You; Next In Line; Port Of
Lonely Hearts; Sugartime; There You Go;
Two Timin' Woman; Big River; Ballad Of
A Teenage Queen.

SPECTRUM (Europe)

SPEC-U-4065 (1988)
I WALK THE LINE
I Walk The Line; Cry, Cry, Cry; Hey
Porter; Folsom Prison Blues; Get
Rhythm; Luther Played The Boogie;
Mean Eyed Cat; There You Go; Train Of
Love; Give My Love To Rose; Big River;
Ballad Of A Teenage Queen; Guess
Things Happen That Way; Blue Train;
Ways Of A Woman In Love; You're The
Nearest Thing To Heaven.

SPEC-85008
18 GOLDEN HITS
You're The Nearest Thing To Heaven;
Rock Island Line; Cold, Cold Heart;
Folsom Prison Blues; Hey Good Lookin';
I Love You Because; It's Just About
Time; Straight A's In Love; I Just
Thought You'd Like To Know; Goodbye
Little Darling; I Could Never Be
Ashamed Of You; Next In Line; Port Of
Lonely Hearts; Sugartime; There You Go;
Two Timin' Woman; Big River; Ballad Of
A Teenage Queen.

SPEC-85012
COUNTRY SUPERSTARS
20 GOLDEN HITS

Cash is included with two songs:
FOLSOM PRISON BLUES and YOU'RE
THE NEAREST THING TO HEAVEN.

STARBLEND/SOLITAIRE
COLLECTION

CDCC-8
LEGENDS
Cash is included with THE GREATEST
LOVE AFFAIR.

CDCST-11 (United Kingdom)
COUNTRY STORE COLLECTION
Same as the album released with same
label, title and number.

STARLITE

CDS-51010
THE BEST OF JOHNNY CASH
I Walk The Line; Blue Train; Down The
Street To 301; Goodbye Little Darlin';
Ways Of A Woman In Love; Rock Island
Line; Train Of Love; Folsom Prison
Blues; Hey Porter; Give My Love To
Rose; Cry, Cry, Cry; I Could Never Be
Ashamed Of You; Big River; Get
Rhythm; Luther's Boogie; You're The
Nearest Thing To Heaven.

STEP ONE RECORDS

SOR-0049 (1989) (2-CD)
ERNEST TUBB COLLECTION WITH
GUESTS
Cash is included with two duets with
Tubb on JEALOUS LOVING HEART
and SOLDIER'S LAST LETTER.

SUCCESS

209-1 CD
COUNTRY MUSIC EXPRESS #3
Cash is included with COUNTRY BOY.

2038CD
COUNTRY MUSIC EXPRESS #1
Cash is included with I LOVE YOU
BECAUSE and COLD, COLD HEART.

2044CD
COUNTRY SHOW #1
Cash is included with: FOLSOM
PRISON BLUES; I LOVE YOU
BECAUSE; BALLAD OF A TEENAGE
QUEEN; ROCK ISLAND LINE and
HEY GOOD LOOKIN'.

2055CD (Switzerland)
BALLAD OF A TEENAGE QUEEN
I Could Never Be Ashamed Of You;
Cold, Cold Heart; I Love You Because;
You're The Nearest Thing To Heaven;
Big River; There You Go; It's Just About
Time; Sugartime; Straight A's In Love;
Next In Line; Hey Good Lookin'; Ballad
Of A Teenage Queen; Goodbye Little
Darling Goodbye; Rock Island Line; I
Just Thought You'd Like To Know;
Folsom Prison Blues.

2068CD
BEST OF COUNTRY & WESTERN
#1
Cash is included with THERE YOU GO
and FOLSOM PRISON BLUES.

SUGAR HILL

SH-CD-3726
BUSY BEE CAFE (Marty Stuart)
Same as U.S. album SH-3726.

SUN (Canada)

841-053-2
SINGING STORY TELLER
Same as U.S. album release SUN-115.

841-059-2

STORY SONGS OF THE TRAINS
AND RIVERS
Same as U.S. album release SUN-104.

841-565-2
ROUGH CUT KING OF COUNTRY
MUSIC
Same as U.S. album release SUN-122.

841-575-2
JOHNNY CASH AND JERRY LEE
LEWIS SING HANK WILLIAMS
Same as U.S. album release SUN-125.

TAKE OFF

CD-70103
ALL TIME COUNTRY HITS #1
Cash is included with FOLSOM PRISON
BLUES.

TAMMY (Taiwan)

CD-20115
STARPORTRAIT (Cash & W. Nelson)
Cash is included with nine songs:
FOLSOM PRISON BLUES; I CAN'T
HELP IT; YOU WIN AGAIN; MY
TREASURE; HEY PORTER;
STRAIGHT A's IN LOVE; TWO TIMIN'
WOMAN; OH LONESOME ME and
SUGARTIME.

TELEDISC (CBS Special Product)

HELLO, I'M JOHNNY CASH (1989)
CTD21/1: Folsom Prison Blues; I Walk
The Line; Guess Things Happen That
Way; Jackson (w/June Carter); Ballad Of
A Teenage Queen; Daddy Sang Bass;
One Piece At A Time; Don't Take Your
Guns To Town; Ring Of Fire; There Ain't
No Good Chain Gang; (w/Waylon
Jennings); Big River; Give My Love To
Rose; One On The Right Is On The Left;
Hey Porter; Bad News; Get Rhythm;

Ways Of A Woman In Love; A Boy
Named Sue.
CTD21/2: Man In Black; Understand
Your Man; Cry, Cry, Cry; Tennessee
Flat-Top Box; Girl From The North
Country (w/Bob Dylan); Forty Shades Of
Green; Orange Blossom Special; Frankie's
Man, Johnny; Sunday Morning Coming
Down; (Ghost) Riders In The Sky; I Got
Stripes; If I Were A Carpenter (w/June
Carter Cash); A Thing Called Love;
Ballad Of Ira Hayes; It Ain't Me, Babe;
Five Feet High And Rising; I Still Miss
Someone; Were You There When They
Crucified My Lord (w/Carter Family).

THAT'S COUNTRY (Europe)

TC-001 (1990)
COUNTRY BOY
Country Boy; Folsom Prison Blues;
Straight A's In Love; You're The Nearest
Thing To Heaven; Ballad Of A Teenage
Queen; Two Timin' Woman; I Just
Thought You'd Like to Know; There You
Go; Next In Line; Hey Good Lookin'; It's
Just About Time; Goodbye Little Darling;
I Could Never Be Ashamed Of You; Port
Of Lonely Hearts.

TC-002 (1990)
I WALK THE LINE
I Walk The Line; Rock Island Line; Train
Of Love; I Love You Because; Guess
Things Happen That Way; Born To Lose;
Get Rhythm; Big River; Cold, Cold
Heart; Ways Of A Woman In Love;
Wreck Of The Old '97; Thanks A Lot;
Hey Porter; Sugartime.

TOPLINE RECORDS

TOP.CD-521
HOME OF THE BLUES
Port Of Lonely Hearts; My Treasure; So
Doggone Lonesome; Goodbye Little
Darling; I Love You Because; Next In

Line; Don't Make Me Go; Home Of The Blues; Belshazar; Leave That Junk Alone; Story Of A Broken Heart; You Win Again; I Could Never Be Ashamed Of You; It's Just About Time; I Just Thought You'd Like To Know; I Forgot To Remember To Forget.

UNIVERSAL

UVLD-12500 (w/N.G. Dirt Band)
WILL THE CIRCLE BE UNBROKEN, VOL. 2
Same as U.S. album release UVL2-12500.

WARNER BROTHERS

WBROS-3422-2
ROSES IN THE SNOW
(Emmylou Harris)
Same as U.S. album BSK-3422.

WBROS-45257-2 (9-93)
HEROES (Mark O'Connor)
Cash is included on THE DEVIL COMES BACK TO GEORGIA.

WOODFORD MUSIC (Holland)

WMCD-5537 (1990)
FOLSOM PRISON BLUES
Folsom Prison Blues; Cry, Cry, Cry; So Doggone Lonesome; Mean Eyed Cat; Wreck Of The Old '97; Get Rhythm; Don't Make Me Go; Ballad Of A Teenage Queen; Come In Stranger; Train Of Love;

Wide Open Road; Luther Played The Boogie; Thanks A Lot; Oh Lonesome Me.

WMCD-5538 (1990)
I WALK THE LINE
I Walk The Line; There You Go; Home Of The Blues; Life Goes On; Goodbye Little Darlin'; Ways Of A Woman In Love; I Love You Because; Guess Things Happen That Way; Big River; Next In Line; Hey Porter; Give My Love To Rose; Katy Too; You're The Nearest Thing To Heaven

WMCD-5539 (1990)
COUNTRY BOY
Country Boy; Straight A's In Love; Two Timin' Woman; Belshazzer; You Tell Me; It's Just About Time; Rock Island Line; Hey Good Lookin'; Blue Train; Doin' My Time; Cold, Cold Heart; I Could Never Be Ashamed Of You; Sugartime; If The Good Lord's Willing.

YESTERDAYS GOLD

SPA/CD-YDG-74607
24 GOLDEN OLDIES-VOLUME FIVE
Cash is included with I WALK THE LINE.

SPA/CD-YDG-74610
HE'LL HAVE TO GO
24 GOLDEN COUNTRY HITS
Cash is included with I WALK THE LINE and BALLAD OF A TEENAGE QUEEN.

==

BILLBOARD CHART LISTINGS

SINGLES: Country Charts

	1955 NOV 26
CRY, CRY, CRY	14

(no records on charts: December 3, 1955 - February 4, 1956)

===

	1956 FEB		MAR						APR
	11	18	25	3	10	17	24	31	7
FOLSOM PRISON BLUES	14	10	9	8	10	12	10	9	6
SO DOGGONE LONESOME	14	10	9	8	10	12	10	9	6

	APR		MAY				JUN		
	14	21	28	5	12	19	26	2	9
FOLSOM PRISON BLUES	6	6	7	9	6	5	7	6	9
GET RHYTHM									8
I WALK THE LINE									8
SO DOGGONE LONESOME	6	6	7	9	6	5	7	6	9

	JUN		JUL				AUG		
	16	23	30	7	14	21	28	4	11
FOLSOM PRISON BLUES		11			15				
I WALK THE LINE	7	4	5	5	4	3	3	3	3
SO DOGGONE LONESOME	10	11	12	13	15				

	AUG	SEP					OCT		
	18	25	1	8	15	22	29	6	13
I WALK THE LINE	2	2	3	3	3	3	3	3	3

	OCT	NOV					DEC		
	20	27	3	10	17	24	1	8	15
I WALK THE LINE	3	3	3	4	3	4	4	4	4

	DEC	
	22	29
I WALK THE LINE	4	3
THERE YOU GO	10	9
TRAIN OF LOVE	10	9

==

	1957 JAN				FEB				MAR
	5	12	19	26	2	9	16	23	2
I WALK THE LINE	2	2	3	4	4	4	9	8	9
THERE YOU GO	7	4	2	2	3	3	3	2	2
TRAIN OF LOVE	7	4	2	2	3		7	2	2

	MAR				APR				MAY
	9	16	23	30	6	13	20	27	6
I WALK THE LINE	11	11	12	15					
THERE YOU GO	2	2	2	2	2	3	3	4	8
TRAIN OF LOVE	2	2	2	2	2	3	3	4	8

	MAY		JUN				JUL		
	13	20	27	3	10	17	24	1	8
DON'T MAKE ME GO						10	9	10	10
NEXT IN LINE			14	12	11	10	9	10	10
THERE YOU GO	11	10	9	10	13		14	15	
TRAIN OF LOVE		10	9	10	13				

	JUL		AUG					SEP	
	15	22	29	5	12	19	26	2	
DON'T MAKE ME GO	9	9	12		12	11			
NEXT IN LINE	9	9	12	13	12	11	14	14	

(no records on charts: September 9, 1957)

	SEP		OCT					NOV	
	16	23	30	7	14	21	28	4	11
GIVE MY LOVE TO ROSE					6	7	8	6	7
HOME OF THE BLUES	14	9	7	5	6	7	8	6	7

	NOV		DEC				
	18	25	2	9	16	23	30
GIVE MY LOVE TO ROSE	7	10	10	11	14	12	12
HOME OF THE BLUES	7	10	10	11	14	12	12

==

1958								
JAN				FEB				MAR
6	13	20	27	3	10	17	24	3
BALLAD OF A TEENAGE QUEEN			8	4	3	1	1	1
BIG RIVER								1
GIVE MY LOVE TO ROSE	14	13	13	14	15	14	16	
HOME OF THE BLUES	14	13	13	14	15	14	16	

MAR			APR				MAY
10	17	24	31	7	14	21	28	5
BALLAD OF A TEENAGE QUEEN	1	1	1	1	1	2	2	2	4
BIG RIVER	1	1	1	1		2		2	4

MAY			JUN				JUL
12	19	26	2	9	16	23	30	7
BALLAD OF A TEENAGE QUEEN	5	5	5	7	11	11	15	18	
COME IN STRANGER				8	5	4	3	1	1
GUESS THINGS HAPPEN THAT WAY			20	8	5	4	3	1	1

JUL			AUG				SEP
14	21	28	4	11	18	25	1	8
COME IN STRANGER	1	1	1						
GUESS THINGS HAPPEN THAT WAY	1	2	2	3	3	2	3	3	8
WAYS OF A WOMAN IN LOVE							20	7	3
YOU'RE THE NEAREST THING TO HEAVEN								7	3

SEP			OCT				NOV
15	22	29	6	13	20	27	3	10
ALL OVER AGAIN					17	30	8	4	7
COME IN STRANGER		12							
GUESS THINGS HAPPEN THAT WAY	12	9	14	13					
WHAT DO I CARE					17	19	12	15	15
YOU'RE THE NEAREST THING TO HEAVEN	3	2	2	2	2	5	15	5	5

	NOV		DEC				
	17	24	1	8	15	22	29
ALL OVER AGAIN	7	9	4	10	9	8	8
WAYS OF A WOMAN IN LOVE	16	24	23	25			
WHAT DO I CARE	9	7	8	8	7	12	12
YOU'RE THE NEAREST THING TO HEAVEN	5	6	15	14	23		

===

1959								
	JAN				FEB			MAR
	5	12	19	26	2	9	16	23	2
ALL OVER AGAIN	11	12	17	22	23	22	24		
DON'T TAKE YOUR GUNS TO TOWN			20	10	10	4	2	1	1
IT'S JUST ABOUT TIME			30						
WHAT DO I CARE	9	14	24						

	MAR				APR			MAY
	9	16	23	30	6	13	20	27	4
DON'T TAKE YOUR GUNS TO TOWN	1	1	1	1	2	3	3	4	6
FRANKIE'S MAN, JOHNNY									27
LUTHER PLAYED THE BOOGIE				21	13	10	8	8	10
THANKS A LOT				30		24	20	14	19

	MAY			JUN					JUL
	11	18	25	1	8	15	22	29	6
DON'T TAKE YOUR GUNS TO TOWN	11	16	20	28					
FRANKIE'S MAN, JOHNNY	12	20	11	9	15	11	11	13	24
LUTHER PLAYED THE BOOGIE	9	8	9	10	18	17	19		
THANKS A LOT	13	12	15	22					
YOU DREAMER YOU	23	18	14	13	20	25	23	20	21

	JUL			AUG					SEP
	13	20	27	3	10	17	24	31	7
FIVE FEET HIGH AND RISING							25	24	15
FRANKIE'S MAN, JOHNNY	30								
I GOT STRIPES	30	18	18	13	9				
KATY TOO		21	16	19	12	11	12	11	11
YOU DREAMER YOU	26	27							

	SEP		OCT				NOV		
	14	21	28	5	12	19	26	2	9
FIVE FEET HIGH AND RISING	14	16	22	25	25			24	
GOODBYE, LITTLE DARLING									25
I GOT STRIPES	6	4	4	4	4	4	4	5	6
KATY TOO	13	15	28						

	NOV		DEC				
	16	23	30	7	14	21	28
GOODBYE, LITTLE DARLING	22	25	26		30		
I GOT STRIPES	12	16	14	16		27	23

===

	1960
	JAN
	4
LITTLE DRUMMER BOY	24

(no records on charts: January 11, 1960 - February 8, 1960)

	FEB		MAR				APR		
	15	22	29	7	14	21	28	4	11
I LOVE YOU BECAUSE				20	25				
STRAIGHT A's IN LOVE	27	18	16	24	24	27		30	27

	APR	MAY					JUN	
	18	25	2	9	16	23	30	6	13
SEASONS OF MY HEART	24	25	18	12	11	16	14	10	
SMILING BILL McCALL				20	18	15	13	20	30
STRAIGHT A's IN LOVE	25			30					

	JUN	JUL				AUG	
	20	27	4	11	18	25	1
SEASONS OF MY HEART	10	10	13	14	20	24	29
SMILING BILL McCALL	27	26					

(no records on charts: August 8, 1960 - August 15, 1960)

	AUG	SEP				OCT
	22	29	5	12	19	26	3
SECOND HONEYMOON	21	19	21	15	24	22	24

(no records on charts: October 10, 1960 - December 19, 1960)

	DEC
	26
MEAN EYED CAT	30

==

(no records on charts: January 2, 1961 - January 30, 1961)

	1961 FEB				MAR				APR
	6	13	20	27	6	13	20	27	3
OH LONESOME ME	26	27	17	16	13	16	19	22	24

(no records on charts: April 10, 1961 - June 5, 1961)

	JUN	
	12	19
THE REBEL-JOHNNY YUMA	24	29

(no records on charts: June 26, 1961 - December 11, 1961)

	DEC	
	18	25
TENNESSEE FLAT-TOP BOX	21	14

==

	1962 JAN				FEB				MAR
	6	13	20	27	3	10	17	24	3
TENNESSEE FLAT-TOP BOX	19	23	12	16	11	14	18	11	18

	MAR			APR		
	10	17	24	31	7	14
TENNESSEE FLAT-TOP BOX	20	20	21			
THE BIG BATTLE				27	25	24

(no records on charts: April 21, 1962 - July 7, 1962)

	JUL		AUG				SEP		
	14	21	28	4	11	18	25	1	8
IN THE JAILHOUSE NOW	26	16	13	8	13	12	19	27	24

	SEP
	15
IN THE JAILHOUSE NOW	30

(no records on charts: September 22, 1962 - March 30, 1963)

==

	1963 APR		
	6	13	20
BUSTED	18	13	16

(no records on charts: April 27, 1963 - June 1, 1963)

	JUN				JUL			AUG	
	8	15	22	29	6	13	20	27	3
RING OF FIRE	28	12	10	5	4	3	2	1	1

	AUG				SEP			OCT	
	10	17	24	31	7	14	21	28	5
RING OF FIRE	1	1	1	1	1	2	2	2	7

	OCT		NOV					DEC	
	12	19	26	2	9	16	23	30	7
RING OF FIRE	8	8	9	11	11	20	21	20	
THE MATADOR					20	11	7	7	4

	DEC		
	14	21	28
THE MATADOR	2	2	4

===

	1964 JAN				FEB				
	2	11	18	25	1	8	15	22	29
THE MATADOR	2	3	4	4	7	16	18	29	
UNDERSTAND YOUR MAN								30	18

	MAR				APR			MAY	
	7	14	21	28	4	11	18	25	2
DARK AS A DUNGEON	49								
UNDERSTAND YOUR MAN	7	5	2	2	1	1	1	1	1

	MAY				JUN			JUL	
	9	16	23	30	6	13	20	27	4
UNDERSTAND YOUR MAN	1	2	3	3	5	6	7	9	17

	JUL		AUG					SEP	
	11	18	25	1	8	15	22	29	5
BAD NEWS			35	32	19	19	17	14	13
BALLAD OF IRA HAYES	42	19	18	15	20	17	15	12	6
UNDERSTAND YOUR MAN	22	33							

	SEP		OCT						NOV
	12	19	26	3	10	17	24	31	7
BAD NEWS	13	11	8	8	12	22	40	43	
BALLAD OF IRA HAYES	5	3	3	3	4	8	16	18	16
IT AIN'T ME, BABE									47

	NOV		DEC				
	14	21	28	5	12	19	26
BALLAD OF IRA HAYES	30	44					
IT AIN'T ME, BABE	36	31	27	20	12	11	8

==

	1965 JAN					FEB			
	2	9	16	23	30	6	13	20	27
IT AIN'T ME, BABE	7	6	7	6	4	5	9	9	15
ORANGE BLOSSOM SPECIAL								44	28

	MAR				APR				MAY
	6	13	20	27	3	10	17	24	1
IT AIN'T ME, BABE	20	23	27	31	47				
ORANGE BLOSSOM SPECIAL	15	6	3	3	3	5	7	7	12

	MAY				JUN
	8	15	22	29	5
ORANGE BLOSSOM SPECIAL	22	27	30	30	38

(no records on charts: June 12, 1965 - July 3, 1965)

	JUL				AUG				SEP
	10	17	24	31	7	14	21	28	4
MR. GARFIELD	46	39	35	24	21	19	19	17	17
SONS OF KATIE ELDER									50

	SEP		OCT					
	11	18	25	2	9	16	23	30
MR. GARFIELD	15	15	20	23				
SONS OF KATIE ELDER	40	35	16	13	12	10	10	24

(no records on charts: November 6, 1965 - November 13, 1965)

	NOV	DEC				
	20	27	4	11	18	25
HAPPY TO BE WITH YOU	49	37	34	22	17	15

==

	1966 JAN					FEB			
	1	8	15	22	29	5	12	19	26
HAPPY TO BE WITH YOU	9	14	19	16	21	25	33	45	
ONE ON THE RIGHT IS ON THE LEFT							45	41	21

	MAR				APR				
	5	12	19	26	2	9	16	23	30
ONE ON THE RIGHT IS ON THE LEFT	12	8	8	5	3	3	3	2	2

	MAY				JUN	
	7	14	21	28	4	11
ONE ON THE RIGHT IS ON THE LEFT	4	6	14	17	23	26

(no records on the charts: June 18, 1966 - June 25, 1966)

	JUL					AUG			
	2	9	16	23	30	6	13	20	27
EVERYBODY LOVES A NUT	46	37	24	22	19	17	24	26	26

(no records on charts: September 3, 1966)

	SEP			OCT	
	10	17	24	1	8
BOA CONSTRICTOR	41	39	42	39	43

(no records on charts: October 15, 1966 - December 17, 1966)

	DEC	
	24	31
YOU BEAT ALL I EVER SAW	66	60

===

	1967 JAN				FEB				MAR
	7	14	21	28	4	11	18	25	4
JACKSON									71
YOU BEAT ALL I EVER SAW	53	41	35	34	31	20	20	23	23

	MAR			APR					MAY
	11	18	25	1	8	15	22	29	6
JACKSON	55	40	26	21	15	8	4	4	2
YOU BEAT ALL I EVER SAW	31	42							

	MAY			JUN			JUL		
	13	20	27	3	10	17	24	1	8
JACKSON	4	5	7	8	16	22	26		
LONG LEGGED GUITAR PICKIN' MAN							69	48	39

	JUL			AUG			SEP		
	15	22	29	5	12	19	26	2	9
LONG LEGGED GUITAR PICKIN' MAN	31	22	17	14	11	6	6	7	7

	SEP		OCT		
	16	23	30	7	14
LONG LEGGED GUITAR PICKIN' MAN	8	16	25	32	44

(no records on charts: October 21, 1967)

	OCT	NOV			DEC	
	28	4	11	18	25	2
THE WIND CHANGES	74	64	63	62	60	66

(no records on charts: December 9, 1967 - December 16, 1967)

	DEC	
	23	30
ROSANNA'S GOING WILD	44	39

===

	1968 JAN				FEB				MAR
	6	13	20	27	3	10	17	24	2
ROSANNA'S GOING WILD	33	27	20	7	5	5	2	2	5

	MAR			
	9	16	23	30
ROSANNA'S GOING WILD	7	7	16	21

(no records on charts: April 6, 1968 - May 25, 1968)

	JUN				JUL				
	1	8	15	22	29	6	13	20	27
FOLSOM PRISON BLUES (live)	47	41	13	9	8	6	2	1	1

	AUG					SEP			
	3	10	17	24	31	7	14	21	28
FOLSOM PRISON BLUES (live)	1	1	4	10	11	15	16	17	27

(no records on charts: October 5, 1968 - November 30, 1968)

	DEC			
	7	14	21	28
DADDY SANG BASS	50	31	23	19

===

	1969 JAN				FEB				MAR
	4	11	18	25	1	8	15	22	1
DADDY SANG BASS	1	1	1	1	1	1	3	4	6

	MAR				APR		
	8	15	22	29	5	12	19
DADDY SANG BASS	8	9	13	17	22	30	39

(no records on charts: April 26, 1969 - July 19, 1969)

	JUL AUG						SEP		
	26	2	9	16	22	30	6	13	20
A BOY NAMED SUE	54	42	15	7	1	1	1	1	1

	SEP OCT				NOV			
	27	4	11	18	25	1	8	15	22
A BOY NAMED SUE	3	8	11	13	20				
BLISTERED									68
GET RHYTHM			56	53	44	34	34	25	23

	NOV DEC				
	29	6	13	20	27
BLISTERED	42	15	11	4	4
GET RHYTHM	23	36	42	46	46
SEE RUBY FALL	42	15	11	4	4

===

	1970 JAN					FEB			
	3	10	17	24	31	7	14	21	28
BLISTERED	7	7	8	8	11	29	44		
IF I WERE A CARPENTER				70	39	10	5	4	3
ROCK ISLAND LINE									68
SEE RUBY FALL	7	7	8	8	11	29	44		

	MAR				APR				MAY
	7	14	21	28	4	11	18	25	2
IF I WERE A CARPENTER	2	3	3	9	10	17	24	36	49
ROCK ISLAND LINE	57	38	35	46	54	54			
WHAT IS TRUTH							37	18	12

	MAY				JUN				JUL
	9	16	23	30	6	13	20	27	4
WHAT IS TRUTH	8	5	4	3	3	8	9	16	17

	JUL	
	11	18
WHAT IS TRUTH	39	49

(no records on charts: July 25, 1970 - August 29, 1970)

	SEP				OCT				
	5	12	19	26	3	10	17	24	31
SUNDAY MORNING COMING DOWN	30	16	4	2	2	1	1	2	4

	NOV				DEC			
	7	14	21	28	5	12	19	26
BIG RIVER					73	71	65	41
FLESH AND BLOOD							30	16
SUNDAY MORNING COMING DOWN	5	11	14	15	28	50		

==

	1971 JAN					FEB			
	2	9	16	23	30	6	13	20	27
BIG RIVER	41	55	57	59					
FLESH AND BLOOD	6	4	2	2	1	2	4	6	22

	MAR	
	6	13
FLESH AND BLOOD	28	36

(no records on charts: March 20, 1971)

	MAR	APR				MAY			
	27	3	10	17	24	1	8	15	22
A GOOD MAN (June Cash)		72	62	54	41	39	32	27	27
MAN IN BLACK	40	18	14	10	5	3	3	8	8

	MAY	JUN				JUL			
	29	5	12	19	26	3	10	17	24
A GOOD MAN (June Cash)	36	42	45						
MAN IN BLACK	9	14	20	32					
SINGING IN VIET NAM TALKING BLUES					58	50	32	21	18

	JUL	AUG				SEP			
	31	7	14	21	28	4	11	18	25
A SONG TO MAMA						72	53	48	47
NO NEED TO WORRY							51	30	27
SINGING IN VIET NAM TALKING BLUES	18	26	26	31	46				

	OCT					NOV			
	2	9	16	23	30	6	13	20	27
A SONG TO MAMA	38	37	37	49	51	51	51		
NO NEED TO WORRY	21	17	16	15	17	17	19	19	27
PAPA WAS A GOOD MAN			57	46	45	31	26	16	16

	DEC			
	4	11	18	25
NO NEED TO WORRY	41			
PAPA WAS A GOOD MAN	19	22	27	37

===

(no records on charts: January 8, 1972 - January 22, 1972)

	1972 JAN	FEB				MAR			
	29	5	12	19	26	4	11	18	25
A THING CALLED LOVE	71	33	21	15	10	7	5	3	2

	APR				MAY				
	1	8	15	22	29	6	13	20	27
A THING CALLED LOVE	4	7	15	19	26	46	49		
KATE						72	29	20	12
TRAVELING MINSTREL BAND					75	75	71	43	42

	JUN				JUL				
	3	10	17	24	1	8	15	22	29
IF I HAD A HAMMER							47	45	34
KATE	4	2	2	2	4	11	26	37	
TRAVELING MINSTREL BAND	50	56							

	AUG				SEP				
	5	12	19	26	2	9	16	23	30
IF I HAD A HAMMER	32	30	29	34					
ONEY					52	41	30	11	9	7
WORLD NEEDS A MELODY									52

	OCT				NOV				DEC
	7	14	21	28	4	11	18	25	2
ONEY	6	5	3	3	3	2	2	14	23
WORLD NEEDS A MELODY	49	49	41	38	35	35	40		

(no records on charts: December 9, 1972 - December 16, 1972)

	DEC	
	23	30
ANY OLD WIND THAT BLOWS	48	34

==

	1973 JAN				FEB				MAR
	6	13	20	27	3	10	17	24	3
ANY OLD WIND THAT BLOWS	27	24	21	16	13	10	8	6	4
THE LOVIN' GIFT			59	50	45	40	35	28	28

	MAR			
	10	17	24	31
ANY OLD WIND THAT BLOWS	3	7	13	23
THE LOVIN' GIFT	27	28	46	

(no records on charts: April 7, 1973 - April 14, 1973)

	APR	MAY				JUN			
	21	28	5	12	29	26	2	9	16
CHILDREN	74	57	46	41	35	34	30	30	35

(no records on charts: June 23, 1973 - July 28, 1973)

	AUG				SEP		
	4	11	21	28	1	8	15
PRAISE THE LORD AND PASS THE SOUP	85	71	63	62	61	63	57

(no records on charts: September 22, 1973)

	SEP	OCT			NOV				
	29	6	13	20	27	3	10	17	24
ALLEGHENY	95	88	85	87	84	75	70	69	70
PICK THE WILDWOOD FLOWER								85	73

	DEC				
	1	8	15	22	29
ALLEGHENY	84				
PICK THE WILDWOOD FLOWER	70	62	50	41	37

==

	1974		
	JAN		
	5	12	19
PICK THE WILDWOOD FLOWER	34	42	64

(no records on charts: January 26, 1974 - February 16, 1973)

	FEB	MAR					APR	
	23	2	9	16	23	30	6	13
ORLEANS PARISH PRISON	90	86	77	71	62	56	52	59

(no records on charts: April 20, 1974)

	APR	MAY				JUN			
	27	4	11	18	25	1	8	15	22
RAGGED OLD FLAG	81	72	62	51	41	38	35	31	36

	JUN	JUL		
	29	6	13	20
RAGGED OLD FLAG	42	48	54	78

(no records on charts: July 27, 1974 - December 7, 1974)

	DEC		
	14	21	28
LADY CAME FROM BALTIMORE	80	64	79

==

	1975								MAR
	JAN				FEB				
	4	11	18	25	1	8	15	22	1
LADY CAME FROM BALTIMORE	39	31	25	19	16	14	30	51	64

(no records on charts: March 8, 1975 - April 5, 1975)

	APR		MAY						JUN
	12	19	26	3	10	17	24	31	7
MY OLD KENTUCKY HOME	86	78	63	58	46	42	42	44	67

(no records on charts: June 14, 1975 - July 19, 1975)

	JUL	AUG					SEP		
	26	2	9	16	23	30	6	13	20
LOOK AT THEM BEANS	83	73	61	51	41	32	25	22	17

	SEP	OCT	
	27	4	11
LOOK AT THEM BEANS	17	37	65

(no records on charts: October 18, 1975 - November 8, 1975)

	NOV			DEC			
	15	22	29	6	13	20	27
TEXAS '47	90	73	60	49	43	38	36

==

	1976 JAN					FEB			
	3	10	17	24	31	7	14	21	28
STRAWBERRY CAKE						88	78	67	60
TEXAS '47	36	35	45	54	62				

	MAR		
	6	13	20
STRAWBERRY CAKE	56	54	59

(no records on charts: March 27, 1976 - April 3, 1976)

	APR		MAY						JUN
	10	17	24	1	8	15	22	29	5
ONE PIECE AT A TIME	80	55	33	16	9	3	2	1	1

	JUN		JUL			
	12	19	26	4	10	17
ONE PIECE AT A TIME	2	8	14	36	53	95

(no records on charts: July 17, 1976)

	JUL		AUG				SEP	
	24	31	7	14	21	28	4	11
SOLD OUT OF FLAGPOLES	69	56	43	34	30	29	44	58

(no records on charts: September 18, 1976 - October 16, 1976)

	OCT		NOV				DEC		
	23	30	6	13	20	27	4	11	18
IT'S ALL OVER	77	66	53.	42	42	41	46	64	
OLD TIME FEELING					78	63	53	42	34

	DEC				
	25				
OLD TIME FEELING	27				

==

	1977				
	JAN				
	1	8	15	22	29
OLD TIME FEELING	27	26	26	42	50

(no records on charts: February 5, 1977 - February 19, 1977)

	FEB	MAR				APR			
	26	5	12	19	26	2	9	16	23
LAST GUNFIGHTER BALLAD	81	67	56	46	40	38	38	44	59

(no records on charts: April 30, 1977 -July 30, 1977)

	AUG				SEP				OCT
	6	13	20	27	3	10	17	24	1
LADY	84	74	64	54	49	47	46	58	63

(no records on charts: October 8, 1977 - October 15, 1977)

	OCT	NOV				DEC			
	22	29	5	12	19	26	3	10	17
AFTER THE BALL	78	66	56	46	38	34	32	40	51

	DEC	
	24	31
AFTER THE BALL	61	61

==

	1978
	JAN
	7
AFTER THE BALL	99

(no records on charts: January 14. 1978 - February 4, 1978)

	FEB			MAR				APR	
	11	18	25	4	11	18	25	1	8
I WOULD LIKE TO SEE YOU AGAIN	74	50	36	30	26	20	14	13	12

	APR			MAY
	15	22	29	6
I WOULD LIKE TO SEE YOU AGAIN	32	45	56	60

(no records on charts: May 15, 1978)

	MAY		JUN				JUL		
	20	27	3	10	17	24	1	8	15
THERE AIN'T NO GOOD CHAIN GANG	78	39	26	16	9	3	3	2	2

	JUL		AUG	
	22	29	5	12
THERE AIN'T NO GOOD CHAIN GANG	3	26	43	76

(no records on charts: August 19, 1978 - September 2, 1978)

	SEP				OCT			
	9	16	23	30	7	14	21	28
GONE GIRL	81	69	58	53	45	45	44	71

(no records on charts: November 4, 1978 - December 2, 1979)

	DEC	
	9	16
IT'LL BE HER	93	89

(no records on charts: December 23, 1978 - January 6, 1979)

==

| | 1979 | | | | | | | | |
	JAN			FEB			MAR		
	13	20	27	3	10	17	24	3	10
I WILL ROCK AND ROLL WITH YOU	85	75	57	49	37	31	28	24	23

	MAR			APR
	17	24	31	7
I WILL ROCK AND ROLL WITH YOU	21	63	98	98

(no records on charts: April 14, 1979 - May 12, 1979)

	MAY		JUN					JUL	
	19	26	2	9	16	23	30	7	14
GHOST RIDERS IN THE SKY	75	49	34	31	18	14	9	5	4

	JUL		AUG				SEP
	21	28	4	11	18	25	1
GHOST RIDERS IN THE SKY	3	2	6	42	54	72	97

(no records on charts: September 8, 1979 - October 13, 1979)

	OCT		NOV			DEC			
	20	27	3	10	17	24	1	8	15
I'LL SAY IT'S TRUE	72	62	49	44	42	61	84		
I WISH I WAS CRAZY AGAIN					62	50	40	32	26

	DEC	
	22	29
I WISH I WAS CRAZY AGAIN	24	24

==

	1980 JAN				FEB
	5	12	19	26	2
I WISH I WAS CRAZY AGAIN	22	22	32	58	63

(no records on charts: February 9, 1980 - April 12, 1980)

	APR		MAY		
	19	26	3	10	17
BULL RIDER	88	77	67	66	67

(no records on charts: May 24, 1980 - May 31, 1980)

	JUN				JUL			
	7	14	21	28	5	12	19	26
SONG OF THE PATRIOT	78	68	59	57	54	54	87	96

(no records on charts: August 2, 1980 - August 16, 1980)

	AUG		SEP			OCT		
	23	30	6	13	20	27	4	11
COLD LONESOME MORNING	88	77	70	64	54	53	72	99

(no records on charts: October 18, 1980 - November 22, 1980)

	NOV	DEC		
	29	6	13	20
THE LAST TIME	89	85	95	99

(no records on charts: December 27, 1980 - January 17, 1981)

==

	1981				
	JAN		FEB		
	24	31	7	14	21
WITHOUT LOVE	89	81	79	78	100

(no records on charts: February 28, 1981 - March 14, 1981)

	MAR		APR			MAY			
	21	28	4	11	18	25	2	9	16
THE BARON	76	64	48	38	27	24	19	15	13

	MAY		JUN			
	23	30	6	13	20	27
THE BARON	11	10	27	54	85	95

(no records on charts: July 4, 1981 - July 18, 1981)

	JUL	AUG			
	25	1	8	15	22
MOBILE BAY	83	74	64	60	93

(no records on charts: August 29, 1981 - January 16, 1982)

==

	1982				
	JAN		FEB		
	23	30	6	13	20
CHATTANOOGA CITY LIMITS SIGN	84	74	71	88	100
REVEREND MR. BLACK	84	74	71	88	100

(no records on charts: February 27, 1982 - April 10, 1982)

	APR	MAY					JUN		
	17	24	1	8	15	22	29	5	12
THE GENERAL LEE	62	47	40	37	32	30	27	26	46

	JUN		JUL
	19	26	3
THE GENERAL LEE	58	80	99

(no records on charts: July 10, 1982 - July 31, 1982)

	AUG				SEP			
	7	14	21	28	4	11	18	25
GEORGIA ON A FAST TRAIN	88	80	68	58	55	61	74	96

(no records on charts: October 2, 1982 - February 19, 1983)

==

	1983	
	FEB	MAR
	26	5
WE MUST BELIEVE IN MAGIC	84	84

(no records on charts: March 12, 1983 - September 17, 1983)

	SEP	OCT		
	24	1	8	15
I'M RAGGED BUT I'M RIGHT	76	75	85	99

(no records on charts: October 22, 1983 - May 5, 1984)

==

	1984				
	MAY			JUN	
	12	19	26	2	9
THAT'S THE TRUTH	85	84	92	96	100

(no records on charts: June 16, 1984 - July 7, 1984)

	JUL			AUG				SEP	
	14	21	28	4	11	18	25	1	8
CHICKEN IN BLACK	72	66	58	52	46	45	58	71	80

	SEP	
	15	22
CHICKEN IN BLACK	88	99

(no records on charts: September 29, 1984 - May 11, 1985)

==

	1985								
	MAY		JUN				JUL		
	18	25	1	8	15	22	29	6	13
HIGHWAYMAN	60	42	36	31	24	20	15	11	8

	JUL		AUG					SEP	
	20	27	3	10	17	24	31	7	14
DESPERADOS WAITING FOR A TRAIN									66
HIGHWAYMAN	7	5	4	2	1	11	21	41	46

	SEP		OCT				NOV		
	21	28	5	12	19	26	2	9	16
DESPERADOS WAITING FOR A TRAIN	53	47	39	37	28	25	21	18	15
HIGHWAYMAN	67	74							

	NOV		DEC			
	23	30	7	14	21	28
DESPERADOS WAITING FOR A TRAIN	15	36	50	74	91	95

==

	1986	
	JAN	
	(4)	11
DESPERADOS WAITING FOR A TRAIN	5	100

(no records on charts: January 18, 1986 - May 10, 1986)

	MAY			JUN				JUL	
	17	24	31	7	14	21	28	5	12
EVEN COWGIRLS GET THE BLUES	70	61	57	52	45	42	38	35	47

	JUL	
	19	26
EVEN COWGIRLS GET THE BLUES	65	82

(no records on charts: August 2, 1986 - March 21, 1987)

==

	1987								
	MAR	APR				MAY			
	28	4	11	18	25	2	9	16	23
THE NIGHT HANK WILLIAMS CAME TO TOWN	73	65	60	55	50	46	43	50	71

	MAY	JUN
	30	6
THE NIGHT HANK WILLIAMS CAME TO TOWN	85	96

(no records on charts: June 13, 1987 - December 5, 1987)

	DEC		
	12	19	26
W. LEE O'DANIEL (AND THE LIGHTCRUST DOUGHBOYS)	85	80	72

==

	1988 JAN	
	(2)	9
W. LEE O'DANIEL (AND THE LIGHTCRUST DOUGHBOYS)	72	91

(no records on charts: January 16, 1988 to September 17, 1988)

	SEP	OCT				NOV			
	24	1	8	15	22	29	5	12	19
THAT OLD WHEEL	77	62	54	46	44	39	38	33	25

	NOV	DEC				
	26	3	10	17	24	(31)
THAT OLD WHEEL	23	21	21	33	52	52

==

	1989 JAN				FEB
	7	14	21	28	4
THAT OLD WHEEL	75	80	87	94	97

(no records on charts: February 11, 1989 - February 18, 1989)

	FEB	MAR				APR			
	25	4	11	18	25	1	8	15	22
BALLAD OF A TEENAGE QUEEN	76	61	54	49	45	54	74	77	93

(no records on charts: April 29, 1989 to March 3, 1990)

==

	1990 MAR					APR			
	3	10	17	24	31	7	14	21	28
SILVER STALLION	70	59	52	46	34	31	28	27	25

	MAY				JUN
	5	12	19	26	2
SILVER STALLION	28	40	50	60	71

(no singles on the charts: June 9, 1990 to September 22, 1990)

	SEP		OCT	
	22	29	6	13
GOIN' BY THE BOOK	72	70	70	69

===

Most Played C&W In Juke Boxes

	1956 MAR		APR				
	17	24	31	7	14	21	28
SO DOGGONE LONESOME	5	7	8	5	5	5	8

	MAY				JUN		
	5	12	19	26	2	9	16
SO DOGGONE LONESOME	5	5	5	4	6	4	6

(no records on charts: June 23, 1956)

	JUN	JUL			AUG				
	30	7	14	21	28	4	11	18	25
I WALK THE LINE	4	4	2	1	2	1	2	1	1

	SEP					OCT			
	1	8	15	22	29	6	13	20	27
I WALK THE LINE	1	1	2	2	2	2	3	3	2

	NOV				DEC				
	3	10	17	24	1	8	15	22	29
I WALK THE LINE	2	2	3	4	3	3	4	4	3

===

	1957 JAN				FEB			
	5	12	19	26	2	9	16	23
I WALK THE LINE	3	3	4	2	5	6	8	4
THERE YOU GO		8	6	5	6	2	3	2

	MAR				APR				
	2	9	16	23	30	6	13	20	27
I WALK THE LINE	7				10				
THERE YOU GO	1	1	2	2	1	1	1	2	3

	MAY			
	6	13	20	27
THERE YOU GO	4	8	8	9

NOTE: This chart ceased to exist following the May 27, 1957 issue of BILLBOARD.

===

Most Played C&W By Jockeys

	1956 FEB			MAR				
	11	18	25	3	10	17	24	31
FOLSOM PRISON BLUES	10	12	11	9	14	11	10	8
SO DOGGONE LONESOME	15	14		7	7	7	9	

	APR			MAY			
	7	14	21	28	5	12	19
FOLSOM PRISON BLUES	9	7	4	10	14	8	15
SO DOGGONE LONESOME	7	6	8	8	11		12

(no records on charts: May 26, 1956)

	JUN				JUL			
	2	9	16	23	30	7	14	21	28
I WALK THE LINE		12	6	5	3	2	2	2	3
SO DOGGONE LONESOME	13								

	AUG				SEP			
	4	11	18	25	1	8	15	22	29
I WALK THE LINE	2	2	2	2	2	2	2	2	2

	OCT				NOV			
	6	13	20	27	3	10	17	24
I WALK THE LINE	3	3	2	1	3	3	3	3

	DEC				
	1	8	15	22	29
I WALK THE LINE	2	4	3	2	4
THERE YOU GO					11

===

1957

	JAN				FEB			
	5	12	19	26	2	9	16	23
I WALK THE LINE	4	10	8	11	7	10	6	15
THERE YOU GO		4	4	5	4	3	2	3
TRAIN OF LOVE		12	10	8	8	8	2	8

	MAR					APR			
	2	9	16	23	30	6	13	20	27
THERE YOU GO	2	2	2	2	3	5	5	5	12
TRAIN OF LOVE	13	12	11	12	13				

	MAY				JUN			
	6	13	20	27	3	10	17	24
THERE YOU GO	11	14	14		15			
NEXT IN LINE				15	12	10	11	14

	JUL					AUG	
	1	8	15	22	29	5	12
NEXT IN LINE	11	9	9	10	14	10	15
THERE YOU GO		13					

(no records on charts: August 19, 1957 - September 9, 1957)

	SEP			OCT			
	16	23	30	7	14	21	28
HOME OF THE BLUES	15		4	13	3	6	10
GIVE MY LOVE TO ROSE				15		13	

	NOV				DEC				
	4	11	18	25	2	9	16	23	30
HOME OF THE BLUES	6	6	7	4	11	9	6	5	5

===

1958

	JAN				FEB			
	6	13	20	27	3	10	17	24
HOME OF THE BLUES	7	4	6	6	10			
BALLAD OF A TEENAGE QUEEN		5	3	1	1	1	1	
BIG RIVER						11	14	12

	MAR					APR			
	3	10	17	24	31	7	14	21	28
BALLAD OF A TEENAGE QUEEN	1	1	1	1	1	1	2	2	2
BIG RIVER	9	4	5	4	6	4	4	4	7

	MAY			JUN					
	5	12	19	26	2	9	16	23	30
BALLAD OF A TEENAGE QUEEN	3	3	3	7	15	15			
BIG RIVER	13	15							
COME IN STRANGER					10		8	8	14
GUESS THINGS HAPPEN THAT WAY				4	6	10	6	1	2

	JUL			AUG				
	7	14	21	28	4	11	18	25
COME IN STRANGER	14	11	6	7	11		13	7
GUESS THINGS HAPPEN THAT WAY	1	1	2	2	3	3	2	3
WAYS OF A WOMAN IN LOVE							10	

	SEP				OCT		
	1	8	15	22	29	6	13
ALL OVER AGAIN							6
WHAT DO I CARE							11
GUESS THINGS HAPPEN THAT WAY	3	8	12	9	14	13	
COME IN STRANGER		12		12			
WAYS OF A WOMAN IN LOVE		11	5	7	2	7	4
YOU'RE THE NEAREST THING TO HEAVEN	11	6	9	8	5	9	7

NOTE: With the October 13, 1958 issue of BILLBOARD, this chart ceased to exist. The chart then became known as "The Billboard Hot C&W Sides" and was expanded to 30 positions.

===

Pop Charts

	1956 SEP		OCT				NOV		
	15	22	29	6	13	20	27	3	10
I WALK THE LINE	64	81	62	43	43	29	37	36	19

	NOV	DEC					
	17	24	1	8	15	22	29
I WALK THE LINE	19	23	19	22	27	27	88

===

	1957 JAN			FEB				
	5	12	19	26	2	9	16	23
I WALK THE LINE	37	75	83		91	99		100

(no records on charts: March 2, 1957 - June 24, 1957)

	JUL		
	1	8	15
NEXT IN LINE	99		100

(no records on charts: July 22, 1957 - October 7, 1957)

	OCT		NOV	
	14	21	28	4
HOME OF THE BLUES	97	88	93	88

(no records on charts: November 11, 1957 - January 27, 1958)

==

1958								
FEB				MAR				
3	10	17	24	3	10	17	24	31
BALLAD OF A TEENAGE QUEEN 63	32	32	36	20	18	28	22	16

	APR			MAY				JUN
	7	14	21	28	5	12	19	26	2
BALLAD OF A TEENAGE QUEEN 16	29	35	38	45	59	67	73	67
GUESS THINGS HAPPEN THAT WAY								56

	JUN				JUL			AUG
	9	16	23	30	7	14	21	28	4
BALLAD OF A TEENAGE QUEEN 83								
COME IN STRANGER	73	74	72	66	75	85	96	77
GUESS THINGS HAPPEN THAT WAY 38	29	24	27	25	17	12	11	21

	AUG			SEP				OCT
	11	18	25	1	8	15	22	29	6
GUESS THINGS HAPPEN THAT WAY 22	39	55	54	57	91			
COME IN STRANGER	87							
WAYS OF A WOMAN IN LOVE		62	58	30	24	25	65	70
ALL OVER AGAIN								88

	OCT		NOV				DEC	
	13	20	27	3	10	17	24	1	8
WAYS OF A WOMAN IN LOVE	75	75	77	89				
ALL OVER AGAIN	88	64	45	42	38	49	58	77	76
WHAT DO I CARE		90	83	70	69	53	52	60	78

	DEC		
	15	22	29
ALL OVER AGAIN	82		
IT'S JUST ABOUT TIME	78	62	54
I JUST THOUGHT YOU'D LIKE	85		
TO KNOW			

==

	1959								
	JAN				FEB				MAR
	5	12	19	26	2	9	16	23	2
IT'S JUST ABOUT TIME	51	47	57	83					
DON'T TAKE YOUR GUNS TO			71	49	39	33	32	34	33
TOWN									

	MAR				APR
	9	16	23	30	6
DON'T TAKE YOUR GUNS TO	38	49	68	73	86
TOWN					

(no records on charts: April 13, 1959 - April 20, 1959)

	APR	MAY			JUN		
	27	4	11	18	25	1	8
FRANKIE'S MAN, JOHNNY	77	71	74	79	70	57	72

(no records on charts: June 15, 1959 - July 6, 1959)

	JUL			AUG					SEP
	13	20	27	3	10	17	24	31	7
KATY TOO	87	85	81	69	66	77	74	79	
I GOT STRIPES				95	89	76	55	47	45
FIVE FEET HIGH AND RISING							88		

	SEP		OCT		
	14	21	28	5	12
I GOT STRIPES	53	43	49	61	66
FIVE FEET HIGH AND RISING	85	76			

(no records on charts: October 19, 1959 - December 14, 1959)

	DEC	
	21	28
LITTLE DRUMMER BOY	91	63

==

```
                            1960
                            JAN
                             4
LITTLE DRUMMER BOY          85
```

(no records on charts: January 11, 1960 - March 7, 1960)

```
                            MAR
                            14   21
STRAIGHT A's IN LOVE        84   87
```

(no records on charts: March 28, 1960 - June 27, 1960)

```
                            JUL
                             4   11   18   25
SECOND HONEYMOON            96   86   85   79
HONKY TONK GIRL                            92
DOWN THE STREET TO 301           89   86   85
```

(no records on charts: August 1, 1960 - December 26, 1960)

```
                            DEC
                            31
OH, LONESOME ME             97
```

(SMILING BILL McCALL was on the Pop charts in 1960 and peaked at 110. No further information is known at this time.)

==

```
                            1961
                            JAN
                             2
OH LONESOME ME              93
```

(no records on charts: January 9, 1961 - May 22, 1961)

```
                            MAY  JUN
                            29    5
THE REBEL-JOHNNY YUMA       111  108
```

(no records on charts: June 12, 1961 - October 30, 1961)

```
                            NOV                 DEC
                             6   13   20   27    4   11   18
TENNESSEE FLAT-TOP BOX      109  91  100   90   88   84   93
```

(no records on charts: December 25, 1961 - September 8, 1962)

	1962 SEP 15
BONANZA	94

(no records on charts: September 22, 1962 - May 25, 1963)

	1963 JUN					JUL			
	1	8	15	22	29	6	13	20	27
RING OF FIRE	72	59	48	37	35	24	23	20	17

	AUG			
	3	10	17	24
RING OF FIRE	17	19	30	39

(no records on charts: August 31, 1963 - October 19, 1963)

	OCT	NOV					DEC
	26	2	9	16	23	30	7
THE MATADOR	86	61	47	46	46	44	49

(no records on charts: December 14, 1963 - February 1, 1964)

	1964 FEB			MAR				APR
	8	15	22	29	7	14	21	28	4
DARK AS A DUNGEON	119							
UNDERSTAND YOUR MAN		86	71	56	42	40	35	39	43

(no records on charts: April 11, 1964 - October 24, 1964)

	OCT	NOV				DEC		
	31	7	14	21	28	5	12	19
IT AIN'T ME, BABE	100	98	79	64	58	58	61	68

(no records on charts: December 26, 1964 - February 6, 1965)

1965

	FEB			MAR		
	13	20	27	6	13	20
ORANGE BLOSSOM SPECIAL	95	92	90	89	80	86

(no records on charts: March 27, 1965 - August 21, 1965)

	AUG	SEP			
	28	4	11	18	25
SONS OF KATIE ELDER	124	122	120	119	121

(no records on charts: October 2, 1965 - February 19, 1966)

==

1966

	FEB	MAR				APR
	26	5	12	19	26	2
ONE ON THE RIGHT IS ON THE LEFT	83	73	58	52	46	55

(no records on charts: April 9, 1966 - June 25, 1966)

	JUL	
	2	9
EVERYBODY LOVES A NUT	97	96

(no records on charts: July 16, 1966 - August 27, 1966)

	SEP	
	3	10
BOA CONSTRICTOR	108	107

(no records on charts: September 17, 1966 - January 20, 1968)

==

1968

	JAN	FEB
	27	3
ROSANNA'S GOING WILD	91	91

(no records on charts: February 10, 1968 - May 18, 1968)

	MAY	JUN					JUL		
	25	1	8	15	22	29	6	13	20
FOLSOM PRISON BLUES (live)	96	84	75	55	44	33	32	32	32

	JUL	AUG	
	27	3	10
FOLSOM PRISON BLUES (live)	37	37	46

(no records on charts: August 17, 1968 - December 21, 1968)

	DEC
	28
DADDY SANG BASS	64

==

	1969								
	JAN				FEB				MAR
	4	11	18	25	1	8	15	22	1
DADDY SANG BASS	60	59	53	53	56	52	45	42	48

(no records on charts: March 8, 1969 - July 19, 1969)

	JUL	AUG					SEP		
	26	2	9	16	23	30	6	13	20
A BOY NAMED SUE	42	20	7	5	2	2	2	3	4

	SEP	OCT	
	27	4	11
A BOY NAMED SUE	11	17	22

(no records on charts: October 18, 1969 - November 1, 1969)

	NOV				DEC			
	8	15	22	29	6	13	20	27
BLISTERED	100	87	75	69	50	50	52	60
SEE RUBY FALL	100	87	75	69	50	50		
GET RHYTHM		94	79	71	60	68	70	

==

	1970							
	JAN	FEB				MAR		
	24	31	7	14	21	28	7	14
IF I WERE A CARPENTER	80	67	55	45	38	36	46	50
ROCK ISLAND LINE						93		

(no records on charts: March 21, 1970 - April 4, 1970)

	APR			MAY				
	11	18	25	2	9	16	23	30
WHAT IS TRUTH	66	46	31	28	20	20	19	31

(no records on charts: June 6, 1970 - August 22, 1970)

	AUG	SEP				OCT	
	29	5	12	19	26	3	10
SUNDAY MORNING COMING DOWN	62	59	58	53	49	46	53

(no records on charts: October 17, 1970 - December 5, 1970)

	DEC		
	12	19	26
FLESH AND BLOOD	81	76	60

==

	1971 JAN			
	2	9	16	23
FLESH AND BLOOD	55	54	55	64

(no records on charts: January 30, 1971 - March 13, 1971)

	MAR		APR			
	20	27	3	10	17	24
MAN IN BLACK	80	77	58	58	58	70

(no records on charts: May 1, 1971 - June 12, 1971)

	JUN		JUL
	19	26	3
SINGING IN VIET NAM TALKING BLUES	126	124	125

(no records on charts: July 10, 1971 - October 16, 1971)

	OCT		NOV
	23	30	6
PAPA WAS A GOOD MAN	110	109	104

(no records on charts: November 13, 1971 - January 29, 1972)

==

	1972 FEB
	5
A THING CALLED LOVE	103

(no records on charts: February 12, 1972 - May 6, 1972)

	MAY			JUN			
	13	20	27	3	10	17	24
KATE	95	95	78	77	75	75	77

(no records on charts: July 1, 1972 - September 2, 1972)

	SEP			
	9	16	23	30
ONEY	109	104	104	103

(no records on charts: October 7, 1972 - April 10, 1976)

===

	1976								
	APR	MAY					JUN		
	17	24	1	8	15	22	29	5	12
ONE PIECE AT A TIME	71	58	47	42	38	33	29	55	97

	JUN
	19
ONE PIECE AT A TIME	100

(no records on charts since June 26, 1976)

===

ALBUMS: Country Charts

BILLBOARD started their "Country Albums" listing with the issue for week ending January 11, 1964.

	1964		
	JAN		
	11	18	25
RING OF FIRE	1	4	6

	FEB				MAR			
	1	8	15	22	29	7	14	21	28
RING OF FIRE	6	1	1	1	1	1	1	1	1

	APR				MAY				
	4	11	18	25	2	9	16	23	30
RING OF FIRE	1	1	1	1	1	3	4	4	2

	JUN				JUL			
	6	13	20	27	4	11	18	25
RING OF FIRE	2	3	3	5	5	4	5	7
I WALK THE LINE						14	10	6

	AUG				SEP			
	1	8	15	22	29	5	12	19	26
RING OF FIRE	9	11							
I WALK THE LINE	3	3	3	2	1	1	1	1	2

	OCT				NOV			
	3	10	17	24	31	7	14	21	28
I WALK THE LINE	2	2	5	5	5	7	7	5	6
BITTER TEARS							19	15	5

	DEC			
	5	12	19	26
I WALK THE LINE	9	8	11	18
BITTER TEARS	4	4	5	3

===

	1965 JAN				FEB			
	2	9	16	23	30	6	13	20	27
BITTER TEARS	5	6	6	3	3	4	2	4	6

	MAR				APR			
	6	13	20	27	3	10	17	24
BITTER TEARS	6	10	13	19				
ORANGE BLOSSOM SPECIAL			16	8	6	6	5	4

	MAY				JUN			
	1	8	15	22	29	5	12	19
ORANGE BLOSSOM SPECIAL	4	3	3	4	4	7	13	15

(no records on charts: June 26, 1965 - March 26, 1966)

===

	1966 APR				MAY			
	2	9	16	23	30	7	14	21	28
MEAN AS HELL	30	26	14	7	5	5	4	4	8

	JUN				JUL			
	4	11	18	25	2	9	16	23	30
MEAN AS HELL	14	15	16	17	17	16	18	18	26
EVERYBODY LOVES A NUT	22	11	11	7	7	5	5	6	5

	AUG			
	6	13	20	27
EVERYBODY LOVES A NUT	5	12	13	21

(no records on charts: September 3, 1966 - November 5, 1966)

	NOV			DEC				
	12	19	26	3	10	17	24	31
HAPPINESS IS YOU	40	40	38	37	31	25	24	23

==

	1967 JAN				FEB				MAR
	7	14	21	28	4	11	18	25	4
HAPPINESS IS YOU	20	15	10	10	12	12	16	16	18

	MAR			APR					MAY
	11	18	25	1	8	15	22	29	6
HAPPINESS IS YOU	26	25	29	35	35	37	37	32	34

(no records on charts: May 13, 1967 - July 15, 1967)

	JUL		AUG			
	22	29	5	12	19	26
GREATEST HITS #1	35	14	9	7	6	5

	SEP				OCT				
	2	9	16	23	30	7	14	21	28
GREATEST HITS #1	3	3	1	1	1	2	10	10	9
CARRYIN' ON	31	26	20	15	11	8	8	8	5

	NOV			DEC					
	4	11	18	25	2	9	16	23	30
GREATEST HITS #1	10	10	11	11	10	27	33	33	37
CARRYIN' ON	5	6	9	10	15	17	17	32	

==

	1968 JAN				FEB			
	6	13	20	27	3	10	17	24
GREATEST HITS #1	37	32	32	27	31	34	34	44
FROM SEA TO SHINING SEA						39	32	26

	MAR				APR				
	2	9	16	23	30	6	13	20	27
GREATEST HITS #1	44	43	41						
FROM SEA TO SHINING SEA	20	17	16	16	10	9	15	24	24

	MAY	
	4	11
FROM SEA TO SHINING SEA	23	26

(no records on charts: May 18, 1968 - June 8, 1968)

	JUN			JUL			
	15	22	29	6	13	20	27
AT FOLSOM PRISON	24	17	11	8	2	1	1
GREATEST HITS #1				35	35	33	43

	AUG					SEP			
	3	10	17	24	31	7	14	21	28
AT FOLSOM PRISON	1	2	2	2	6	6	5	3	2
GREATEST HITS #1	39	36	32	30	28	25	29	27	24

	OCT			NOV					
	5	12	19	26	2	9	16	23	30
AT FOLSOM PRISON	1	2	3	4	4	4	3	4	10
GREATEST HITS #1	24	26	30						

	DEC			
	7	14	21	28
AT FOLSOM PRISON	10	6	6	7

==

	1969								
	JAN				FEB				MAR
	4	11	18	25	1	8	15	22	1
AT FOLSOM PRISON	7	12	10	10	11	15	15	14	13
HOLY LAND						43	24	23	17

	MAR				APR				MAY
	8	15	22	29	5	12	19	26	3
AT FOLSOM PRISON	9	7	7	12	10	9	9	10	20
HOLY LAND	16	14	11	9	9	6	6	6	10

	MAY				JUN				JUL
	10	17	24	31	7	14	21	28	5
AT FOLSOM PRISON	20	18	18	17	17	13	13	17	17
HOLY LAND	8	7	7	6	8	18	18	19	17
AT SAN QUENTIN									38

	JUL			AUG					SEP
	12	19	26	2	9	16	23	30	6
AT FOLSOM PRISON	26	26	30	27	23	23	24	25	21
HOLY LAND	20	27	27						
AT SAN QUENTIN	25	7	2	1	1	1	1	1	1

	SEP		OCT				NOV		
	13	20	27	4	11	18	25	1	8
AT FOLSOM PRISON	21	15	14	16	15	22	29	29	29
AT SAN QUENTIN	1	1	1	1	1	1	1	1	1
ORIGINAL GOLDEN HITS #1			35	29	16	12	12	10	7
ORIGINAL GOLDEN HITS #2			40	21	19	24	15	12	11

	NOV		DEC				
	15	22	29	6	13	20	27
AT FOLSOM PRISON	27	27	30	31	39	33	35
AT SAN QUENTIN	1	1	1	1	1	2	2
ORIGINAL GOLDEN HITS #1	5	4	6	6	5	9	9
ORIGINAL GOLDEN HITS #2	11	7	4	4	4	3	8
SHOWTIME			44	44	40	31	26
GET RHYTHM	43	38	38	36	31	30	32
STORY SONGS OF TRAINS AND RIVERS					22	16	14

==

	1970 JAN					FEB			
	3	10	17	24	31	7	14	21	28
AT SAN QUENTIN	2	4	3	3	3	5	7	6	6
ORIGINAL GOLDEN HITS #2	8	14	15	15	13	11	11	12	16
ORIGINAL GOLDEN HITS #1	9	11	12	12	20	22			
SHOWTIME	26	28	25	25	22	20	17	14	14
GET RHYTHM	32	41							
AT FOLSOM	40	40	36	36	35	35	40	40	
HELLO, I'M JOHNNY CASH							26	16	10
STORY SONGS OF TRAINS AND RIVERS	14	8	8	6	5	4	2	2	2

	MAR				APR				MAY
	7	14	21	28	4	11	18	25	2
AT SAN QUENTIN	6	5	6	8	8	9	8	8	10
ORIGINAL GOLDEN HITS #2	19	17	18	23	21	20	21	23	23
SHOWTIME	23	25	33	33	38				
HELLO, I'M JOHNNY CASH	3	3	3	1	1	1	1	2	3
AT FOLSOM					41	38	42		
STORY SONGS OF TRAINS AND RIVERS	10	14	14	14	14	15	15	18	18

	MAY				JUN				JUL
	9	16	23	30	6	13	20	27	4
AT SAN QUENTIN	14	14	12	13	14	21	23	25	25
ORIGINAL GOLDEN HITS #2	25								
WORLD OF JOHNNY CASH					45	32	20	16	8
HELLO, I'M JOHNNY CASH	3	3	3	3	4	3	3	3	7
SINGING STORY TELLER	45	45							
STORY SONGS OF TRAINS AND RIVERS	19	21	42						

	JUL		AUG						SEP
	11	18	25	1	8	15	22	29	5
AT SAN QUENTIN	30	37							
HELLO, I'M JOHNNY CASH	17	19	18	15	19	23	22	24	23
WORLD OF JOHNNY CASH	4	3	2	2	5	6	8	7	7

	SEP		OCT						NOV
	12	19	26	3	10	17	24	31	7
HELLO, I'M JOHNNY CASH	21	19	21	25	23	36	41	43	
WORLD OF JOHNNY CASH	5	4	7	7	10	9	9	8	14

	NOV		DEC				
	14	21	28	5	12	19	26
WORLD OF JOHNNY CASH	12	12	11	12	11	14	20
JOHNNY CASH SHOW	20	10	8	6	5	1	1
I WALK THE LINE (soundtrack)						44	27

===

	1971 JAN					FEB			
	2	9	16	23	30	6	13	20	27
WORLD OF JOHNNY CASH	24	28	28	30	34	37	39	37	
JOHNNY CASH SHOW	3	2	2	3	4	4	7	8	14
I WALK THE LINE (soundtrack)	15	10	9	9	18	17	14	14	12

	MAR				APR				MAY
	6	13	20	27	3	10	17	24	1
I WALK THE LINE (soundtrack)	21	23	25	36	39	42			
JOHNNY CASH SHOW	14	5	15	14	21	19	23	29	35

	MAY				JUN				JUL
	8	15	22	29	5	12	19	26	3
JOHNNY CASH SHOW	36	38	37	35	34	38	38		
MAN IN BLACK							19	13	3

	JUL				AUG				SEP
	10	17	24	31	7	14	21	28	4
MAN IN BLACK	2	2	1	1	4	3	4	6	4

	SEP			OCT					NOV
	11	18	25	2	9	16	23	30	6
MAN IN BLACK	4	4	5	7	11	11	14	17	18
GREATEST HITS #2							42	26	10

	NOV			DEC			
	13	20	27	4	11	18	25
MAN IN BLACK	18	35	36	43	44	44	42
GREATEST HITS #2	6	6	6	5	6	15	13

==

	1972								
	JAN					FEB			
	1	8	15	22	29	5	12	19	26
GREATEST HITS #2	11	7	6	10	9	9	8	9	9
MAN IN BLACK	42								

	MAR				APR				
	4	11	18	25	1	8	15	22	29
GREATEST HITS #2	15	15	13	13	21	24	25	28	30
A THING CALLED LOVE									31

	MAY				JUN				JUL
	6	13	20	27	3	10	17	24	1
GREATEST HITS #2	33	34							
A THING CALLED LOVE	16	8	8	3	3	3	2	2	2

	JUL				AUG				SEP
	8	15	22	29	5	12	19	26	2
A THING CALLED LOVE	3	3	2	2	7	8	8	11	15
AMERICA									32

	SEP			OCT					NOV
	9	16	23	30	7	14	21	28	4
A THING CALLED LOVE	25	27	30	31	41				
AMERICA	21	12	8	6	4	3	3	3	6
TRAVELING MINSTREL BAND								45	44

	NOV			DEC			
	11	18	25	2	9	16	23	30
AMERICA	6	7	8	8	13	18	22	27
JOHNNY CASH SONGBOOK	43	43						

==

	1973 JAN 6
AMERICA	35

(no records on charts: January 13, 1973 - January 27, 1973)

	FEB				MAR				
	3	10	17	24	3	10	17	24	31
ANY OLD WIND THAT BLOWS	36	30	22	15	11	8	6	5	9

	APR				MAY				JUN
	7	14	21	28	5	12	19	26	2
ANY OLD WIND THAT BLOWS	10	12	16	18	31				
GOSPEL ROAD					39	30	26	23	20

	JUN				JUL				AUG
	9	16	23	30	7	14	21	28	4
GOSPEL ROAD	17	14	13	12	13	26	35	36	46

(no records on charts: August 11, 1973 - September 22, 1973)

	SEP	OCT				NOV			
	29	6	13	20	27	3	10	17	24
JOHNNY CASH & HIS WOMAN	40	34	37	35	34	32	38	43	43
SUNDAY MORNING COMING DOWN	43	39	41	42	39	36	35	37	

	DEC				
	1	8	15	22	29
JOHNNY CASH & HIS WOMAN	37	36	36	33	32
SUNDAY MORNING COMING DOWN	39				

===

	1974 JAN 5
JOHNNY CASH & HIS WOMAN	36

(no records on charts: January 12, 1974 - June 8, 1974)

	JUN			JUL			AUG		
	15	22	29	6	13	20	27	3	10
RAGGED OLD FLAG	39	26	23	19	18	16	24	22	21
FIVE FEET HIGH AND RISING									38

	AUG		
	17	24	31
RAGGED OLD FLAG	27	44	
FIVE FEET HIGH AND RISING	33	33	42

(no records on charts: September 7, 1974 - November 2, 1974)

	NOV			
	9	16	23	30
JUNKIE & THE JUICEHEAD	50	49	48	48

(no records on charts: December 7, 1974 - October 4, 1975)

===

	1975								
	OCT		NOV						DEC
	11	18	25	1	8	15	22	29	6
LOOK AT THEM BEANS	45	41	41	38	38	41	41	40	45

(no records on charts: December 13, 1975 - March 27, 1976)

===

	1976							
	APR				MAY			
	3	10	17	24	1	8	15	22
STRAWBERRY CAKE	46	39	37	36	33	41	42	48

(no records on charts: May 29, 1976 - June 5, 1976)

	JUN			JUL				
	12	19	26	4	10	17	24	31
ONE PIECE AT A TIME	23	13	9	6	4	2	2	5

	AUG				SEP		
	7	14	21	28	4	11	18
ONE PIECE AT A TIME	7	8	12	16	22	39	49

(no records on charts: September 25, 1976 - February 26, 1977)

===

	1977						
	MAR				APR		
	5	12	19	26	2	9	16
LAST GUNFIGHTER BALLAD	45	37	31	30	29	29	39

(no records on charts: April 23, 1977 - July 23, 1977)

	JUL	AUG				SEP		
	30	6	13	20	27	3	10	17
THE RAMBLER	42	38	36	35	35	31	31	39

(no records on charts: September 24, 1977 - May 6, 1978)

===

	1978								
	MAY		JUN				JUL		
	13	20	27	3	10	17	24	1	8
I WOULD LIKE TO SEE YOU AGAIN	50	45	39	25	23	28	34	31	40

	JUL		AUG		
	15	22	29	5	12
I WOULD LIKE TO SEE YOU AGAIN	28	28	41	44	49

(no records on charts: August 19, 1978 - January 6, 1979)

===

	1979	
	JAN	
	13	20
GREATEST HITS #3	49	49

(no records on charts: January 27, 1979 - September 1, 1979)

	SEP				OCT				NOV
	8	15	22	29	6	13	20	27	3
SILVER	30	30	28	37	30	30	49	47	47

	NOV
	10
SILVER	49

(no records on charts: November 17, 1979 - January 12, 1980)

===

	1980					
	JAN		FEB			
	19	26	2	9	16	23
A BELIEVER SINGS THE TRUTH	45	44	43	50	45	50

(no records on charts: March 1, 1980 - June 27, 1981)

===

	1981								
	JUL				AUG				
	4	11	18	25	1	8	15	22	29
THE BARON	29	27	24	43	39	36	37	51	73

	SEP		
	5	12	19
THE BARON	73	68	75

(no records on charts: September 26, 1981 - April 17, 1982)

===

	1982								
	APR	MAY					JUN		
	24	1	8	15	22	29	5	12	19
THE SURVIVORS	29	23	21	21	21	25	25	27	40

	JUN	JUL		
	26	3	10	17
THE SURVIVORS	40	50	55	72

(no records on charts: July 24, 1982 - May 25, 1985)

===

	1985								
	JUN					JUL			
	1	8	15	22	29	6	13	20	27
HIGHWAYMAN	51	35	25	23	22	18	16	14	10

	AUG					SEP			
	3	10	17	24	31	7	14	21	28
HIGHWAYMAN	8	7	6	5	5	3	2	2	1

	OCT				NOV				
	5	12	19	26	2	9	16	23	30
HIGHWAYMAN	2	2	3	4	6	6	6	8	9

	DEC			
	7	14	21	28
HIGHWAYMAN	12	14	19	19

===

	1986 JAN				FEB				MAR
	(4)	11	18	25	1	8	15	22	1
HIGHWAYMAN	21	21	21	22	19	19	17	17	17

	MAR				APR				MAY
	8	15	22	29	5	12	19	26	3
HIGHWAYMAN	17	14	10	10	9	16	21	33	22

	MAY				JUN				JUL
	10	17	24	31	7	14	21	28	5
HIGHWAYMAN	22	22	29	29	34	32	28	29	28
HEROES							51	22	19
CLASS OF '55							55	48	42

	JUL			AUG					SEP
	12	19	26	2	9	16	23	30	6
HIGHWAYMAN	41	38	51	72					
HEROES	17	14	13	18	20	23	27	63	42
CLASS OF '55	19	18	16	19	17	15	17	15	15

	SEP			OCT				NOV	
	13	20	27	4	11	18	25	1	8
HEROES	39	45	52	59	46	73	74		
CLASS OF '55	17	18	24	31	29	34	34	37	60

	NOV			DEC	
	15	22	29	6
CLASS OF '55	73	68	68	73

(no records on charts: December 13, 1986 - May 9, 1987)

===

	1987 MAY			JUN				JUL	
	16	23	30	6	13	20	27	4	
JOHNNY CASH IS COMING TO TOWN	57	53	48	47	43	39	37	41	

	JUL			AUG					SEP
	11	18	25	1	8	15	22	29	5
JOHNNY CASH IS COMING TO TOWN	39	36	38	41	40	41	41	47	54

	SEP			OCT					NOV
	12	19	26	3	10	17	24	31	7
JOHNNY CASH IS COMING TO TOWN	55	56	63	59	64	64	68	70	72

(no records on charts: November 14, 1987 to December 10, 1988)

==

	1988	
	DEC	
	17	24
WATER FROM THE WELLS OF HOME	57	54

==

	1989								
	JAN				FEB				MAR
	7	14	21	28	4	11	18	25	4
WATER FROM THE WELLS OF HOME	52	50	48	48	50	48	52	55	53

	MAR			APR				
	11	18	25	1	8	15	22	29
WATER FROM THE WELLS OF HOME	51	55	54	60	58	59	60	69

	MAY	
	6	13
WATER FROM THE WELLS OF HOME	66	72

(no records on charts: May 20, 1989 to March 17, 1990)

==

	1990						
	MAR			APR			
	17	24	31	7	14	21	28
HIGHWAYMAN II	62	22	15	8	7	5	5

	MAY				JUN				
	5	12	19	26	2	9	16	23	30
HIGHWAYMAN II	4	5	7	8	8	8	14	15	15

	JUL				AUG			
	7	14	21	28	4	11	18	25
HIGHWAYMAN II	14	16	17	19	22	24	24	24
HIGHWAYMAN								75

	SEP				OCT				
	1	8	15	22	29	6	13	20	27
HIGHWAYMAN II	26	26	28	31	36	35	28	30	29
HIGHWAYMAN	59	59							

	NOV				DEC			
	3	10	17	24	1	8	15	22
HIGHWAYMAN II	33	36	49	58	58	59	59	58

==

	1991				
	JAN				FEB
	5	12	19	26	2
HIGHWAYMAN II	62	71	61	58	74

==

Pop Charts

	1958		
	DEC		
	8	15	22
FABULOUS JOHNNY CASH	20	19	24

(no records on charts: December 29, 1958 - February 2, 1956)

==

	1959					
	FEB			MAR		
	9	16	23	2	9	16
FABULOUS JOHNNY CASH	24	23	23	23	22	21

(no records on charts: March 23, 1959 - March 9, 1963)

==

	1963							
	MAR			APR				MAY
	16	23	30	6	13	20	27	4
BLOOD, SWEAT AND TEARS	134	87	80	82	99	113	117	132

	MAY			JUN			
	11	18	25	1	8	15	22
BLOOD, SWEAT AND TEARS	133	138	112	108	128	133	136

(no records on charts: June 29, 1963 - July 20, 1963)

	JUL	AUG					SEP		
	27	3	10	17	24	31	7	14	21
RING OF FIRE	149	110	108	95	72	70	43	39	33

	SEP	OCT			NOV				
	28	5	12	19	26	2	9	16	23
RING OF FIRE	33	27	26	33	41	39	61	48	52

	NOV	DEC			
	30	7	14	21	28
RING OF FIRE	73	62	53	55	70

===

	1964								
	JAN				FEB				
	4	11	18	25	1	8	15	22	29
RING OF FIRE	95	112	128	127	112	144	130	103	91

	MAR				APR				MAY
	7	14	21	28	4	11	18	25	2
RING OF FIRE	78	53	65	47	33	36	44	66	74

	MAY				JUN				JUL
	9	16	23	30	6	13	20	27	4
RING OF FIRE	73	66	59	56	56	73	60	63	68

	JUL		AUG						SEP
	11	18	25	1	8	15	22	29	5
RING OF FIRE	62	59	54	78	76	74	62	77	72
I WALK THE LINE			134	117	93	78	76	74	57

	SEP		OCT						NOV
	12	19	26	3	10	17	24	31	7
RING OF FIRE	74	74	66	106	106	102	144	146	146
I WALK THE LINE	54	53	53	57	55	67	92	108	144
BITTER TEARS									148

	NOV		DEC				
	14	21	28	5	12	19	26
I WALK THE LINE	146						
BITTER TEARS	130	91	74	59	51	47	54

===

	1965					
	JAN				FEB	
	2	9	16	23	30	6
BITTER TEARS	54	100	129	139	140	143

(no records on charts: February 13, 1965 - March 13, 1965)

	MAR		APR			MAY		
	20	27	3	10	17	24	1	8	15
ORANGE BLOSSOM SPECIAL	143	138	136	120	91	80	68	62	58

	MAY		JUN	
	22	29	5	12
ORANGE BLOSSOM SPECIAL	49	49	74	134

(no records on charts: June 19, 1965 - July 2, 1966)

==

	1966 JUL				AUG				SEP
	9	16	23	30	6	13	20	27	3
EVERYBODY LOVES A NUT	138	137	134	123	102	90	90	88	142

(no records on charts: September 10, 1966 - July 15, 1967)

==

	1967 JUL	AUG					SEP		
	22	29	5	12	19	26	2	9	16
GREATEST HITS #1	200	188	176	157	152	93	83	83	95

	SEP	OCT				NOV	
	23	30	7	14	21	28	4
GREATEST HITS #1	98	97	108	119	158	158	171
CARRYIN' ON			195	195	194		

(no records on charts: November 11, 1967 - June 8, 1968)

==

	1968 JUN		JUL				AUG		
	15	22	29	6	13	20	27	3	10
AT FOLSOM PRISON	160	94	84	51	45	40	35	33	25

	AUG		SEP				OCT	
	17	24	31	7	14	21	28	5	12
AT FOLSOM PRISON	20	19	13	13	17	17	17	18	16

	OCT	NOV					DEC	
	19	26	2	9	16	23	30	7	14
AT FOLSOM PRISON	18	41	40	38	38	37	39	40	38

	DEC	
	21	28
AT FOLSOM PRISON	35	35

==

	1969								
	JAN				FEB				MAR
	4	11	18	25	1	8	15	22	1
AT FOLSOM PRISON	30	33	33	32	42	42	38	53	44
HOLY LAND							124	97	97

	MAR				APR				MAY
	8	15	22	29	5	12	19	26	3
AT FOLSOM PRISON	39	39	40	40	39	37	42	41	41
HOLY LAND	75	72	62	62	54	54	58	55	72

	MAY				JUN				JUL
	10	17	24	31	7	14	21	28	5
AT FOLSOM PRISON	46	39	35	47	46	48	49	46	46
HOLY LAND	103	105	136	138	151	150	164	181	
AT SAN QUENTIN									52

	JUL			AUG					SEP
	12	19	26	2	9	16	23	30	6
AT FOLSOM PRISON	55	90	75	75	74	53	50	50	48
AT SAN QUENTIN	28	22	14	9	6	4	1	1	1
GREATEST HITS #1						188	187	189	179

	SEP		OCT				NOV		
	13	20	27	4	11	18	25	1	8
AT FOLSOM PRISON	40	47	43	39	33	43	42	44	44
AT SAN QUENTIN	1	2	2	2	3	3	2	5	3
GREATEST HITS #1	179	--	126	121	117	117	112	91	91
ORIGINAL GOLDEN HITS #1			130	95	95	103	104	103	103
ORIGINAL GOLDEN HITS #2			131	101	98	116	117	114	129
JOHNNY CASH					186	186			

	NOV			DEC			
	15	22	29	6	13	20	27
CHRISTMAS SPIRIT					7		
AT FOLSOM PRISON		58	58	53	53	52	62	64
AT SAN QUENTIN		·3	7	8	9	8	15	22
GREATEST HITS #1		88	85	82	96	115	111	108
ORIGINAL GOLDEN HITS #1		120	120	136	154	150	159	
ORIGINAL GOLDEN HITS #2		153						
GET RHYTHM					175	175	171	170	164
SHOWTIME								194
STORY SONGS OF TRAINS AND RIVERS								197

NOTE: *The Christmas Spirit* album was actually on a Christmas chart for this week.

==

	1970 JAN					FEB			
	3	10	17	24	31	7	14	21	28
AT FOLSOM PRISON	75	73	62	64	60	68	68	65	72
AT SAN QUENTIN	19	19	14	18	28	28	25	41	37
GREATEST HITS #1	99	97	108	108	103	110	108	112	115
HELLO, I'M JOHNNY CASH							46	27	13
GET RHYTHM	164								
SHOWTIME	192	181	199						
STORY SONGS OF TRAINS AND RIVERS	197								

	MAR			APR					MAY
	7	14	21	28	4	11	18	25	2
AT FOLSOM PRISON	72	78	79	75	76	75	75	104	104
AT SAN QUENTIN	37	33	54	68	86	86	82	87	85
GREATEST HITS #1	112	111	134	138	151	147	147	148	155
HELLO, I'M JOHNNY CASH	7	6	10	10	16	14	12	12	25

	MAY			JUN					JUL
	9	16	23	30	6	13	20	27	4
AT FOLSOM PRISON	116	116	119	128	127	120	127	124	131
AT SAN QUENTIN	86	110	117	118	113	110	116	116	130
GREATEST HITS #1	155	163	160	162	161	159	161	164	169
HELLO, I'M JOHNNY CASH	21	24	36	37	40	44	39	48	47
WORLD OF JOHNNY CASH					145	57	54	60	59
SINGING STORY TELLER		199	197	186					

	JUL		AUG						SEP
	11	18	25	1	8	15	22	29	5
AT FOLSOM PRISON	133	130	146	146	143	167	170	170	164
AT SAN QUENTIN	141	150	151	157	151	163	176	187	177
GREATEST HITS #1	170	168	168	156	150	176	176	174	168
HELLO, I'M JOHNNY CASH	82	89	94	99	99	95	129	132	144
WORLD OF JOHNNY CASH	84	76	71	75	79	80	80	79	92

	SEP		OCT						NOV
	12	19	26	3	10	17	24	31	7
AT FOLSOM PRISON	185	179	176	180	180				
AT SAN QUENTIN	177	174	172	174	173	171	178	178	
WORLD OF JOHNNY CASH	112	122	127	144	131	130	160	149	166

	NOV			DEC			
	14	21	28	5	12	19	26
WORLD OF JOHNNY CASH	183	174	163	165	176	173	171
JOHNNY CASH SHOW	70	54	53	47	47	45	44
I WALK THE LINE (soundtrack)					190	188	176

==

	1971 JAN					FEB			
	2	9	16	23	30	6	13	20	27
WORLD OF JOHNNY CASH	165	161	161	166					
JOHNNY CASH SHOW	57	63	57	69	62	77	82	82	110
I WALK THE LINE (soundtrack)	176	183	183						

	MAR	
	6	13
JOHNNY CASH SHOW	141	148

(no records on charts: March 20, 1971 - June 19, 1971)

	JUN	JUL					AUG		
	26	3	10	17	24	31	7	14	21
MAN IN BLACK	159	68	57	56	60	62	78	86	106

	AUG	SEP	
	28	4	11
MAN IN BLACK	153	194	181

(no records on charts: September 18, 1971 - October 16, 1971)

	OCT		NOV				DEC	
	23	30	6	13	20	27	4	11
GREATEST HITS #2	162	152	95	94	101	130	175	175

(no records on charts: December 18, 1971 - April 22, 1972)

==

	1972 APR	MAY				JUN			
	29	6	13	20	27	3	10	17	24
A THING CALLED LOVE	137	121	119	119	117	114	112	118	145

(no records on charts: July 1, 1972 - September 9, 1972)

	SEP			OCT			
	16	23	30	7	14	21	28
AMERICA	196	188	180	180	176	176	176

(no records on charts: November 4, 1972 - February 17, 1973)

==

	1973			
	FEB	MAR		
	24	3	10	17
ANY OLD WIND THAT BLOWS	191	190	188	192

(no records on charts: March 24, 1973 - July 10, 1976)

==

	1976	
	JUL	
	17	24
ONE PIECE AT A TIME	188	185

(no records on charts: July 31, 1976 - May 25, 1985)

==

	1985								
	JUN					JUL			
	1	8	15	22	29	6	13	20	27
HIGHWAYMAN	143	135	124	117	103	95	95	94	95

	AUG					SEP			
	3	10	17	24	31	7	14	21	28
HIGHWAYMAN	96	94	92	100	98	97	100	107	110

	OCT			NOV					
	5	12	19	26	2	9	16	23	30
HIGHWAYMAN	128	144	143	143	138	145	141	139	166

	DEC			
	7	14	21	28
HIGHWAYMAN	163	191	188	192

==

	1986			
	JAN			
	(4)	11	18	25
HIGHWAYMAN	192	189	186	181

(no records on charts: February 1, 1986 - June 14, 1986)

	JUN		JUL			AUG			
	21	28	5	12	19	26	2	9	16
CLASS OF '55	130	104	90	87	87	107	123	114	114

	AUG		SEP
	23	30	6
CLASS OF '55	145	173	189

(no records on charts since September 13, 1986)

===

APPENDIX A

PRE-1984 SESSIONS

Late 1954
Sun Record Company, Memphis, Tennessee
Johnny Cash, vocal, guitar. Prod. Sam Phillips.

SHOW ME THE GREEN

NOTE: This title was given in Colin Escott's notes included in the Bear Family 5-CD box set entitled *The Man In Black, 1954-1958* (BCD-15517). Unfortunately, the tape of this master could not be found. Given this approximate date, and assuming, as I did in volume one for this time period, that **WIDE OPEN ROAD, YOU'RE MY BABY** and perhaps **MY TREASURE** were done here as well, then this master of **SHOW ME THE GREEN** was probably just a demo tape. Marshall Grant, one of the original "Tennessee Two," disputes this date ("Late 1954") and emphatically states Cash never recorded anything at Sun without the Tennessee Two. (Telephone conversation with Marshall Grant - March 15, 1986.) Aural evidence, however, shows that Cash did record the above titles solo, probably only as demo tapes, as well as **LEAVE THAT JUNK ALONE,** at least one version of **COUNTRY BOY** and on at least one title a false start comment by Cash would indicate the demos were cut in the studio. In the same telephone conversation Grant admitted he had not heard, and was not aware of, the five-record set by Charly Records, *Johnny Cash--The Sun Years* (SB-103). Therefore, it is possible he does not know of the existence of some of the material included in it. Jack Clement also remembers Cash stopping by the Sun studio by himself and cutting demos but could not remember any exact titles. (Telephone conversation with Jack Clement - March 26, 1986.) And Cash, himself, says he definitely recorded solo at Sun prior to returning with Marshall Grant and Luther Perkins for regular session work. In addition to the above listed titles Cash says he recorded several others, including an early version of **BELSHAZAH**, but he is not sure whether or not Sam Phillips made and/or kept tapes of all the demo material. (Conversation with Johnny Cash - May 2, 1986 and March 22, 1989.)

==

April 2, 1956
Sun Record Company, Memphis, Tennessee

Johnny Cash, vocal, acoustic guitar; Marshall Grant, bass; Luther Perkins, electric guitar. Prod. Sam Phillips.

BRAKEMAN'S BLUES (incomplete) (Jimmie Rodgers)
C - BEAR FAMILY/BCD-15517 *The Man In Black, 1954-1958*

NOTE: This incomplete master was included in the above listed Bear Family box set. Because it was not included in volume one of the discography I have taken the liberty of listing it here. See volume one for complete details of this session date.
===

December 4, 1956
Sun Record Company, Memphis, Tennessee
Johnny Cash, vocal; W.S. Holland, drums; Jerry Lee Lewis, vocal, piano; Carl Perkins, vocal, guitar; Clayton Perkins, bass; J.B. Perkins, rhythm guitar; Elvis Presley, vocal, guitar. Possibly Smokey Joe Baugh, vocal; Charles Underwood, rhythm guitar. Any additional personnel and/or musicians present during this "session" are unknown at this time.

BLUEBERRY HILL (A. Lewis-V. Rose-L. Stock)

WILL THE CIRCLE BE UNBROKEN (A.P. Carter)

THERE ARE STRANGE THINGS HAPPENING EVERYDAY
(Sister Rosetta Tharpe)

BLUE MOON OF KENTUCKY (Bill Monroe)

NOTE: I had originally omitted this session from the first edition of the discography because of the apparent absence of Cash on any of the material. But in light of new evidence, and Cash himself, I now feel Cash did participate to some extent in the session and have decided to now include it here. There is a great deal of controversy surrounding this session as to both content and artists participating and, as one would suspect, considerable publicity and speculation as well. I will attempt to deal here with only Cash's part in the session or at least what is known to date.

In his book *"Man In Black"* (1975) Cash indicates this session was done during Perkins' second session in the "Summer of '55." He says he was first introduced to Jerry Lee Lewis and Jack Clement at this time. Cash says Elvis walked into the studio and they did **BLUEBERRY HILL, WILL THE CIRCLE BE UNBROKEN** and **THERE ARE STRANGE THINGS HAPPENING EVERYDAY**. In all eight or ten old hymn favorites were played. It was supposedly Clement's idea to turn on the recorder during this jam session (Cash/1975:79-82). And if Cash's chronology is correct this was done before **WILL THE CIRCLE BE UNBROKEN** which would lead to the speculation of still more tapes, somewhere, of this session. It could be that Cash was off a year and this all happened in 1956. Even by mid-summer 1955 Perkins had had more than two sessions for Sun Records.

In 1978 Shelby Singleton, now owner of the entire Sun master collection, planned to release an album entitled *The Million Dollar Quartet Volume 1* (SUN-1008) the cover of which suggested this to be "the" tapes. Whether this was indeed to be the long awaited session tape or merely a collection of separate Sun masters by Cash, Lewis, Perkins and Presley will probably never be known because RCA blocked its release.

In 1980 an album appeared entitled *Million Dollar Quartet-Authentic Studio Recordings, Memphis, December 4th, 1956* (OMD-001). The liner notes for the album state that Cash is not on any of the material but that he possibly arrived after these were done and leaves open the possibility he was on some additional tapes that have yet to surface. That he was there some time during the jam session is evidenced by at least three different pictures known to have been taken with the entire group--two of which are used on the album jacket. If the sequence of masters is correct on the OMD-001 album then Perkins' reference on side 2 to Sam Phillips leaving to get a photographer could mean that Cash was either there earlier and came back or did not arrive until well into the session. But as the liner notes state "it seems very unlikely that Cash merely showed up for picture taking and then left...."

In 1981 the OMD-001 album re-appeared with the same title only this time on a duplicate of the original Sun label and numbered SUN-1006. The liner notes for this album expand to include a portion of an article that appeared in the *"Memphis Press Scimitar"* by Robert Johnson under the date "5 Dec. 56." Johnson appears to have been in attendance for at least a portion of the session because he is the main source for Cash's part in the jam. He states that Cash did join in on **BLUEBERRY HILL**. But apparently Sam Phillips had not yet decided to start recording this impromptu session. In the May 1957 issue of *"16 Magazine"* the Johnson story is expanded and states that **ISLE OF GOLDEN DREAMS** was also done with Cash included. It is interesting to note that these two songs are absent from any of the albums mentioned here.

In April 1987 Cash stated he had recently received a letter from RCA accompanied by a tape, supposedly of this jam session, asking him to verify his presence, or lack of it, for future royalty purposes. He said that while he had not listened to the entire tape he is on it and singing falsetto (conversation with Johnny Cash, April 1987). The falsetto style was used by Cash during this period as witnessed by an alternate take of **FOLSOM PRISON BLUES** included in the Charly Record Company's *Johnny Cash--The Sun Years* (SB-103). He also mentioned the religious songs done and several Bill Monroe songs including **BLUE MOON OF KENTUCKY**. (The OMD-001 album, discussed above, includes **LITTLE CABIN ON THE HILL**, a Bill Monroe song.) This tended to contradict a February 1979 discussion when Cash told me he did not remember having been on any such session. A check of both RCA offices in Nashville and New York failed to locate anyone willing to admit to a possible future album using any such material.

In 1987 a double album surfaced entitled *The Complete Million Dollar Session--December 4th, 1956* (CDX-20), not from RCA but from Charly Records in London, England. This album includes forty titles but still no **BLUEBERRY HILL** or **ISLE OF GOLDEN DREAMS**. Elvis Presley does mention Cash during **AS WE TRAVEL ALONG THE JERICO ROAD** but in a manner that would indicate he (Cash) was not present at the time.

Cash stated in an interview with Bob Costas on the NBC television show *"Later With Bob Costas"* (October 1988) that he was at this session but the reason he was not heard on the recordings is that there was only one microphone and he was farthest from it. He also told how Jerry Lee Lewis literally took control of the piano from Presley--a fact proven by listening to the above material.

Finally, in 1990, RCA released a CD entitled *Elvis Presley with Jerry Lewis and Carl Perkins: The Million Dollar Quartet*. This was obviously slanted toward the promotion of Elvis but includes some very informative liner notes by Colin Escott. But again, aural evidence is lacking as to the presence of Cash. Another assumption could be that Sam Phillips called the press shortly before Carl Perkins and his group left to return to Jackson, Tennessee; that Cash was there in the beginning and began doing the gospel material referred to above, left and then returned in time for the photo session around the piano.

Unfortunately, the RCA CD release still does not answer with certainty Johnny Cash's participation in this famous "jam session."

I have elected to list the four songs above because of Cash's specific reference to them as given in this note.

===

August 13, 1958 (2p-8p)
Owen Bradley Studio, Nashville, Tennessee
Johnny Cash, vocal, guitar; Marshall Grant, bass; Murry Harman, Jr., drums; Luther Perkins, electric guitar. Prod. Don Law.

FEED ME FATHER (take 2) (John R. Cash)
C - BEAR FAMILY/BCD-15517 *The Man In Black, 1954-1958*

NOTE: Even though this session date was listed in volume one I have included this particular title here. This is actually **LEAD ME FATHER** but for some reason during the thirteen takes of this song, take 2 was sung as **FEED ME FATHER** with the lyrics changed slightly. See volume one for complete details of this session date.

===

August 14, 1959 (7p-9p)
Owen Bradley Studio, Nashville, Tennessee
Johnny Western, vocal, guitar; Marshall Grant, bass; Michael Kazak, drums; Anita Kerr Singers; Luther Perkins, electric guitar; Jimmy Wilson, piano. Prod. Don Law.

CO-62906   **TEN YEARS** (Jack Clement)
  A - CBS/4-41500 b/w **Only The Lonely**
  C - BEAR FAMILY/BCD-15552 *Johnny Western - Heroes And Cowboys*

NOTE: This session was mentioned in a footnote in volume one. Since then additional information has come to light making this deserving of an entry here. Johnny Cash is also given as "leader" for this session.

===

1959/1960
Possibly Owen Bradley Studio, Nashville, Tennessee
Johnny Cash, vocal, guitar; Marshall Grant, bass; Luther Perkins, electric guitar; Gordon Terry, fiddle; Johnny Western, guitar; remaining musicians unknown.

TUNE UP

TIJUANA JAIL

NOTE: Information for this "session" came from a conversation with Stew Carnall in July 1982 in Cheyenne, Wyoming. Carnall took over the management of Cash and the Tennessee Two in 1959 from Bob Neal and sold out to Saul Holiff in July 1961. The exact date is unknown but could have taken place before, after or during any one of the sessions for 1959 or 1960. The plan at the time, although never seriously pursued, was to release these two songs on a fictional "Spider Monkey" Records under the name "George Quatts." The song **TUNE UP** was nothing more than literally the musicians tuning up their instruments. This was obviously a continuation of the legendary antics of Cash, Grant and Perkins.

===

May 10, 1960 - (9p-12mid)
Radio Recorders, Hollywood, California
Johnny Cash, vocal, guitar; Marshall Grant, bass; Michael Kazak, drums; Luther Perkins, electric guitar; Jim Pierce, piano; Dick Stubbs, steel guitar; Gordon Terry, lead vocal -1. Prod. Don Law.

BATTLE OF NEW ORLEANS -1 (Don Helms)

RHCO-46617 **GIRL FROM SASKATOON** (John R. Cash-Johnny Horton)
    C - BEAR FAMILY/BCD-15562 *The Man In Black, 1959-1962*

NOTE: Also at this session Cash's then brother-in-law, Ray Liberto, Jr., did four songs while Cash's nephew, Roy Cash, Jr. (aka: Roy Rivers), did two songs. It is not known if Liberto and/or Cash, Jr. played instrumentally on the Cash masters. See the Bear Family 5CD box set listed above. The Bear Family booklet credits Don Helms as the composer of this version of **BATTLE OF NEW ORLEANS**, using "new words" but, unfortunately, this master is not included in the box set.

===

February 24, 1961 (8p-11p)
Radio Recorders, 7000 Santa Monica Boulevard, Hollywood, California
Johnny Western, vocal, guitar; Hubert Anderson, vibes; Bobby Bruce, violin; Buddy Clark, bass; Elliott Fisher, Frank Green, violins; Irving Kluyer, drums; Billy Latham, banjo -1; William Liebert, leader; Joseph Livoti, Anthony Olson, Myron Sandler, violins; Billy Strange, guitar; Olcott Vail, Garry White, violins; Unknown vocal background--possibly B.J. Baker Group. Prod. Don Law-Frank Jones.

RHCO-46879-18 **THE BIG BATTLE** -1 (John R. Cash)
    C - BEAR FAMILY/BCD-15552 *Johnny Western - Heroes And Cowboys*
    (see also overdub/release session: March 23, 1961)

RHCO-46879-22 **THE BIG BATTLE** (John R. Cash)
    (see also overdub session: March 23, 1961)

RHCO-46880 **FORTY SHADES OF GREEN** (John R. Cash)
    (see also overdub session: March 23, 1961)

RHCO-46880-8 **FORTY SHADES OF GREEN** (John R. Cash)
    C - BEAR FAMILY/BCD-15552 *Johnny Western - Heroes And Cowboys*
    (see also overdub session: March 23, 1961)

NOTE: Johnny Western provided the initial vocals at this session with Cash overdubbing his own vocal on March 23, 1961.

==

February 27/28, 1961 (9p-3a)
Radio Recorders, 7000 Santa Monica Boulevard, Hollywood, California
Johnny Western, vocal, guitar; B.J. Baker Group, vocals; Marshall Grant, bass; Ralph Hansell, vibes; W.S. Holland, drums; William Liebert, leader; Luther Perkins, electric guitar; Jimmy Wilson, piano. Prod. Don Law-Frank Jones.

RHCO-46881-11 **FORTY SHADES OF GREEN** (John R. Cash)
  (see overdub/release session: March 23, 1961)

RHCO-46882 **HE'LL UNDERSTAND AND SAY WELL DONE**
        (Arr: John R. Cash)
  (see overdub/release session: March 23, 1961)

RHCO-46998 **TALL MAN** (K. Darby)
  (see overdub/release session: March 23, 1961)

RHCO-46999 **GOD MUST HAVE MY FORTUNE LAID AWAY** (T. Harris)
  (see overdub/release session: March 23, 1961)

RHCO-47000 **WHEN I'VE LEARNED** (B. Killen-R. Baker-D. Wilson)
  (see overdub/release session: March 23, 1961)

NOTE: In volume one I had given this session with Johnny Cash as the artist. However, after further conversations with Johnny Western and the location of additional data I have elected to revise this session and include the overdub session of March 23, 1961. Western did confirm *two* sessions and the absence of Cash who then came in on March 23, 1961 and overdubbed his vocals. See above session for February 24, 1961 for Johnny Western's release of **FORTY SHADES OF GREEN** and **THE BIG BATTLE.**

==

March 23, 1961
Radio Recorders, 7000 Santa Monica Boulevard, Hollywood, California
Johnny Cash, vocal, guitar. Overdub session only. Prod. Don Law-Frank Jones.

RHCO-46879-18 **THE BIG BATTLE** (John R. Cash)
  A - CBS/4-42301 b/w **When I've Learned**
  B - CBS/CL-2053/CS-8853 *Ring Of Fire*
  C - BEAR FAMILY/BCD-15562 *The Man In Black, 1959-1962*

RHCO-46880 **FORTY SHADES OF GREEN** (John R. Cash)
  A - CBS/4-41995 b/w **The Rebel-Johnny Yuma**
  B - CBS/CL-2053/CS-8853 *Ring Of Fire*
  C - BEAR FAMILY/BCD-15562 *The Man In Black, 1959-1962*

RHCO-46881-11 **FORTY SHADES OF GREEN** (John R. Cash)
  C - BEAR FAMILY/BCD-15562 *The Man In Black, 1959-1962*

RHCO-46882 **HE'LL UNDERSTAND AND SAY WELL DONE**
(Arr: John R. Cash)
B - CBS/CL-1722/CS-8522 *Hymns From The Heart*
C - BEAR FAMILY/BCD-15562 *The Man In Black, 1959-1962*

RHCO-46998 **TALL MAN** (K. Darby)
A - CBS/4-42147 b/w **Tennessee Flat-Top Box**
B - CBS-67284 *International Superstar*
C - BEAR FAMILY/BCD-15562 *The Man In Black, 1959-1962*

RHCO-46999 **GOD MUST HAVE MY FORTUNE LAID AWAY** (T. Harris)
B - CBS/CL-1722/CS-8522 *Hymns From The Heart*
C - BEAR FAMILY/BCD-15562 *The Man In Black, 1959-1962*

RHCO-47000 **WHEN I'VE LEARNED** (B. Killen-R. Baker-D. Wilson)
A - CBS/4-42301 b/w **The Big Battle**
B - CBS/CL-1722/CS-8522 *Hymns From The Heart*
C - BEAR FAMILY/BCD-15562 *The Man In Black, 1959-1962*

===

July 19/20, 1961 (2p-6p;8p-1a)
Columbia Studio, Hollywood, California
Johnny Cash, vocal, guitar; Marshall Grant, bass; W.S. Holland, drums; Luther Perkins, electric guitar; Johnny Western, guitar. Prod. Don Law-Frank Jones.

RHCO-70271 **BLUE BANDANA** (instrumental)
C - BEAR FAMILY/BCD-15562 *The Man In Black, 1959-1962*

RHCO-70272 **SO DOGGONE LONESOME** (John R. Cash) (instrumental)
C - BEAR FAMILY/BCD-15562 *The Man In Black, 1959-1962*

RHCO-70275-6 **I WALK THE LINE** (John R. Cash) (slow)
C - BEAR FAMILY/BCD-15562 *The Man In Black, 1959-1962*

RHCO-70275-9 **I WALK THE LINE** (John R. Cash) (fast)
C - BEAR FAMILY/BCD-15562 *The Man In Black, 1959-1962*

NOTE: The above four entries fill in the gaps with master numbers not included in volume one. They were used in the above-listed Bear Family 5-CD boxed set for the first time. For additional material recorded on these dates, see the 1985 publication.
===

May 11, 1966
Sofia Gardens, Cardiff, Wales
Bob Dylan, vocal, piano; Johnny Cash, vocal.

I STILL MISS SOMEONE (John R. Cash-Roy Cash Jr)
B - TMQBRE-85002/3 *Up To Me* (Bob Dylan)

NOTE: Information for this impromptu "session" was taken from Michael Krogsgaard's excellent discography entitled *Positively Bob Dylan* (1991) from Popular Culture, Ink Press. The song was done backstage before a concert at the Sofia Gardens in Cardiff, Wales. I had originally thought not to include it but because it did appear on a "bootleg" extended-play set in Sweden and the significance of the individuals involved, I have listed it here. This song was also used in the motion picture *"Eat The Documentary"* February 8, 1971.

===

April 9, 1969
Probably Columbia Studio, Nashville, Tennessee
Anita, Helen, June, Maybelle Carter, vocals; remaining musicians unknown. Prod. Johnny Cash.

NCO-99037   **SUNNY SIDE OF SPAIN**

NCO-99038   **BREAK MY MIND**
    A - CBS/4-44982 b/w **If I Live Long Enough**

NCO-99039   **IF I LIVE LONG ENOUGH**
    A - CBS/4-44982 b/w **Break My Mind**

NOTE: Information for this session was provided by Kurt Rokitta, Essen, Germany.

===

July 24, 1969
Columbia Studio, Nashville, Tennessee
Johnny Cash, vocal, guitar; possibly Norman Blake, dobro; Anita, Helen, possibly Maybelle Carter, vocals -1; June Carter Cash, vocals -2; Marshall Grant, bass; W.S. Holland, drums; Carl Perkins, electric guitar; Bob Wootton, electric guitar. Prod. Bob Johnston.

NCO-99211   **COME ALONG AND RIDE THIS TRAIN** -1,-2 (take 1)
    (John R. Cash)
    C - BEAR FAMILY/BCD-15563 *Come Along And Ride This Train*

NCO-99211   **COME ALONG AND RIDE THIS TRAIN** (take 2) (John R. Cash)
    C - BEAR FAMILY/BCD-15563 *Come Along And Ride This Train*

NOTE: This previously unissued master was used on the above Bear Family 4-CD boxed set as the opening track on the first disc (take 1) and the closing track on the fourth disc (take 2). Take 1 included the "Carter Family" members listed above but they were not on take 2. The take designations are mine.

===

August 1/2, 1974 (soundtrack)
House of Cash Studio, Hendersonville, Tennessee
Johnny Cash, vocal, guitar; Norman Blake, rhythm guitar; Marshall Grant, upright bass; Bob Johnson, mandocello, mandolin. Prod. Nicholas Webster-Dyann Rivkin.

    RIDIN' THE RAILS #1 (John R. Cash)

TOM THUMB #1 (instrumental) (Bill Walker)

TOM THUMB #2 (instrumental) (Bill Walker)

TOM THUMB #3 (instrumental) (Bill Walker)

RIVER TRAIN (instrumental) (Bill Walker)

MEN OF THE RAILS-CANALMEN
(Arr: & Adapted: John R. Cash-Robert Johnson)

RAILROAD LAMENT-WAGONER'S SONG
(Arr: & Adapted: Bill Walker-Robert Johnson)

RAILROAD LAMENT-WAGONER'S SONG (instrumental)
(Arr: & Adapted: Bill Walker-Robert Johnson)

ROAD TO BE MADE (Robert Johnson)

DAYS OF YORE-LORENA (Arr: & Adapted: John R. Cash)

COLLAGE OF YESTERDAY-YANKEE DOODLE-DIXIE
(instrumental) (Arr: Bill Walker)

NIGHT THEY DROVE OLD DIXIE DOWN (J. Robbie Robertson)

DAYS OF YORE-LORENA (instrumental)
(Arr: & Adapted: John R. Cash)

NIGHT THEY DROVE OLD DIXIE DOWN (instrumental)
(J. Robbie Robertson)

RAILROAD ACT (instrumental) (Bill Walker)

RIBBON OF STEEL (L. Pouliot)

HI ROVIN' GAMBLER (instrumental) (Bill Walker)

RIBBON OF STEEL (instrumental) (L. Pouliot)

MESSAGE OF HOPE-BATTLE HYMN OF THE REPUBLIC
(instrumental) (W. Steffe & J.W. Howe. Arr: John R. Cash)

RIDIN' THE RAILS #2 (John R. Cash)

POUNDIN' OF THE RAILS (Arr: John R. Cash)

LAYIN' TRACK (instrumental) (R. McGibony-Robert Johnson)

LEGEND OF JOHN HENRY'S HAMMER
(John R. Cash-June Carter)

CATTLE DRIVE (instrumental) (Bill Walker)

NIGHTRIDERS-THE RAILROAD CORRAL #1
(Arr: & Adapted: John R. Cash-Bill Walker)

SHAVE AND A HOT BATH (John R. Cash)

NIGHTRIDERS-THE RAILROAD CORRAL #2
(Arr: & Adapted: John R. Cash-Bill Walker)

TRAIN ROBBERS (instrumental) (Bill Walker)

SATIRICAL AIRE-AFTER THE BALL (instrumental)
(C.K. Harris. Arr: Bill Walker)

RIDIN' THE RAILS #1 (instrumental) (John R. Cash)

CASEY JONES #1 (T.L. Seibert-E. Newton)

WRECK OF THE OLD 97
(Arr: John R. Cash-Norman Blake-Robert Johnson)

CASEY JONES #2 (T.L. Seibert-E. Newton)

TOM THUMB #4 (instrumental) (Bill Walker)

OVER THERE #1 (instrumental) (G.M. Cohan)

RIDIN' THE RAILS #2 (instrumental) (John R. Cash)

OVER THERE #2 (instrumental) (G.M. Cohan)

RIDIN' THE RAILS #3 (instrumental) (John R. Cash)

WAR IS OVER (instrumental) (Bill Walker)

SINGIN' BRAKEMAN (instrumental) (Bill Walker)

RAILROADS RIDIN' HIGH (instrumental) (Bill Walker)

BROTHER CAN YOU SPARE A DIME (J. Gorney-E.Y. Harburg)

CRYSTAL CHANDELIERS AND BURGUNDY (Jack W. Routh)

DOESN'T ANYBODY KNOW MY NAME (Rod McKuen)

CITY OF NEW ORLEANS (instrumental) (Steve Goodman)

CITY OF NEW ORLEANS (Steve Goodman)

THE L&N DON'T STOP HERE ANYMORE (B. Goldsboro)

THESE HANDS (instrumental) (E. Noack)

RIDIN' THE RAILS #3 (John R. Cash)

RIDIN' THE RAILS #4 (John R. Cash)

NOTE: The August 1 and 2, 1974 sessions were done for the soundtrack of the ABC TV special *"Johnny Cash Ridin' The Rails: The Great American Train Story,"* a musical history of railroading aired on November 22, 1974. Additional instruments, brass and strings, were overdubbed on October 28-29, 1974. (Information provided by House of Cash in telephone conversation July 21, 1989 and Dyann Rivkin, August 17, 1990.) Ms. Rivkin says that because this special "spanned the historical period from 1830 to the present, as part of the production and sound design of the special, no instruments were used on the soundtrack before they were historically in use, for example, only acoustic instruments were used in the soundtrack covering the earlier years of the special." This is also witnessed by the use of an upright bass by Marshall Grant. The House of Cash also listed **FIL-AH-ME-OREE-AY (DADDY WORKS ON THE RAILWAY)** and **THESE ARE MY PEOPLE** as being part of this project but no mention is made of these titles in the information furnished by Dyann Rivkin.

===

June 1975
Superior Sound Studio, Nashville, Tennessee
Oak Ridge Boys: Duane Allen, Joe Bonsall, Bill Golden, Richard Sterban, vocals; JOHNNY CASH, vocal; remaining musicians unknown. Prod. Duane Allen.

NCO-120055 **NO EARTHLY GOOD** (John R. Cash)
    B - CBS/KC-33935 *Old Fashioned, Down Home, Hand Clappin', Foot Stompin', Southern Style, Gospel Quartet Music*

NOTE: Information for this Oak Ridge Boys session was provided by CBS Records.
===

September 17, 1976 (soundtrack)
Christian Broadcasting Network
Johnny Cash, vocal; remaining musicians unknown.

RAGGED OLD FLAG (John R. Cash)
B - HOUSE TOP/HTR-702 *It's Time To Pray America*

NOTE: This is from the soundtrack of a radio-television special from the Christian Broadcasting Network (CBN) hosted by Pat Robertson. This, then, is a new master as opposed to the studio version done January 28, 1974. Cash also does a narrative introduction to the song. The soundtrack was released in 1976 on the "House Top" record label entitled *It's Time To Pray America* (HTR-702).

September 21, 1976
House of Cash Studios, Hendersonville, Tennessee
Bob Luman, vocal, guitar; JOHNNY CASH, vocal harmony, guitar -1; remaining musicians unknown. Prod. Johnny Cash.

NCO-121011 **LABOR OF LOVE** (S. Warner)
   A - EPIC/8-50297 b/w **Blond Haired Woman**
   B - EPIC/KE-34445 *Bob Luman-Alive And Well*

NCO-121012 **BLOND HAIRED WOMAN** (S. Warner)
   A - EPIC/8-50297 b/w **Labor Of Love**
   B - EPIC/KE-34445 *Bob Luman-Alive And Well*

NCO-121013 **HE'S GOT A WAY WITH WOMEN** (S. Warner)
   A - EPIC/8-50323 b/w **Where We Are Making Love Again**
   B - EPIC/KE-34445 *Bob Luman-Alive And Well*

NCO-121014 **I STILL MISS SOMEONE** -1 (John R. Cash-R. Cash, Jr)
   B - EPIC/KE-34445 *Bob Luman-Alive And Well*

NOTE: This, and the sessions for September 22, 1976 and October 5, 1976, are Bob Luman sessions and listed here because Cash produced. The singles and the album entitled *Alive And Well* (KE-34445) were released on the Epic label. The album was released in early 1977. Information for the Luman sessions was provided by CBS Records. Cash says he also appeared instrumentally on **I STILL MISS SOMEONE** and can be heard providing vocal harmony as well. (Conversation with Johnny Cash - April 1987).

September 22, 1976
House of Cash Studio, Hendersonville, Tennessee
Bob Luman, vocal, guitar; JOHNNY CASH, vocal, guitar -1; remaining musicians unknown. Prod. Johnny Cash.

NCO-121015 **GOT TO HAVE ROOM TO CHANGE MY MIND** (S. Warner)
   B - EPIC/KE-34445 *Bob Luman-Alive And Well*

NCO-121016 **SWEET DREAMS** (D. Gibson)
   B - EPIC/KE-34445 *Bob Luman-Alive And Well*

NCO-121017 **GET RHYTHM** -1 (John R. Cash)
   B - EPIC/KE-34445 *Bob Luman-Alive And Well*

NOTE: See note for session dated September 21, 1976. Cash says he also appeared instrumentally on **GET RHYTHM** and can be heard vocally as well. (Conversation with Johnny Cash - April 1987).

October 5, 1976
House of Cash Studio, Hendersonville, Tennessee

Bob Luman, vocal, guitar; JOHNNY CASH, vocal harmony, guitar -1, guitar only -2; Waylon Jennings, possible vocal harmony -3; remaining musicians unknown.   Prod. Johnny Cash.

NCO-126009 **BIG RIVER** -1,3 (John R. Cash)
   B - EPIC/KE-34445 *Bob Luman-Alive And Well*

NCO-126010 **HERE WE ARE MAKING LOVE AGAIN** (M. Schrimpf-R. Saucier)
   A - EPIC/8-50323 b/w **He's Got A Way With Women**
   B - EPIC/KE-34445 *Bob Luman-Alive And Well*

NCO-126011 **HEY PORTER** -2 (John R. Cash)
   B - EPIC/KE-34445 *Bob Luman-Alive And Well*

NOTE: See note for session dated September 21, 1976.   Cash says he appeared instrumentally on **HEY PORTER** and **BIG RIVER** and added vocal harmony to **BIG RIVER**. He was uncertain as to whether or not Waylon was on **BIG RIVER** but aural evidence would seem to indicate he was. (Conversation with Johnny Cash - April 1987.)
==
August 8, 1978
Pete's Place, Nashville, Tennessee
Ernest Tubb, vocal; JOHNNY CASH, vocal. Overdub session only. Prod. Pete Drake.

      JEALOUS LOVING HEART (Ernest Tubb-Talmadge Tubb)
   A - FIRST GENERATION/CS4-4501 b/w **Waltz Across Texas** (w/o Cash)
   B - FIRST GENERATION/FG.LP-0002 *Ernest Tubb: The Legend And The Legacy*

NOTE: This master was originally cut on March 25, 1977 (6p-9p) and used in the 1977 album release entitled *Ernest Tubb: The Living Legend* (FG-LP-001). It was then overdubbed with Cash at this session for inclusion in the above-listed album. It is not clear whether Tubb was actually at this overdub session. Musicians included from the March 25, 1977 session: Owen Bradley, piano; Wayne Hammond, guitar; Peter Michaud, lead electric guitar; Howard Lynn Owsley, steel guitar; Joe Pruneda, bass; Robert Rector, Jack Solomon, guitars. (Source for this session: Ronnie Pugh's "Ernest Tubb Discography, Part II, 1958-1982", *("Journal Of Country Music,"* vol. XI, no. 1, 1985).
==
August 8, 1978 or September 12, 1978
Pete's Place, Nashville, Tennessee
Ernest Tubb, vocal; JOHNNY CASH, vocal. Overdub session only. Prod. Pete Drake.

      SOLDIER'S LAST LETTER (Redd Stewart-Ernest Tubb)
   B - FIRST GENERATION/FG.LP-0002 *Ernest Tubb: The Legend And The Legacy*

NOTE: This master was originally cut sometime between April 5, 1977 and October 17, 1977 and included in *Ernest Tubb: The Living Legend* (FG.LP-001). While it was overdubbed with Cash as shown above and included in the two listed albums, it is not clear whether or not Tubb actually attended this present session. Musicians included from the original session were: Ronnie Blackwell, guitar; Charles Browning, drums; possibly Wayne Hammond, guitar; Peter Michaud, lead electric guitar; Howard Lynn Owsley, steel guitar; Joe Purneda, bass; Jack Solomon, guitar; Jeff Twell, piano. (Source for this session: Ronnie Pugh's "Ernest Tubb Discography, Part II, 1958-1982", (*"Journal Of Country Music,"* vol. XI, no. 1, 1985).

==

August 31, 1981
CBS Studio A or Woodland Sound Studio, Nashville, Tennessee
Rosanne Cash, vocal; Richard Bennett, acoustic guitar; Tony Brown, piano; JOHNNY CASH, vocal; Rodney Crowell, vocal harmony; Hank DeVito, steel guitar; Emory Gordy, Jr., bass, rhythm guitar; Albert Lee, electric guitar; Larrie Londin, drums; Reggie Young, electric guitar. Prod. Rodney Crowell.

NCO-129239 **THAT'S HOW I GOT TO MEMPHIS** (Tom T. Hall)
   B - CBS/FC-37570 *Somewhere In The Stars*

NOTE: This is a Rosanne Cash session, John's Daughter. She is currently pursuing a very successful career in her own right.

==

Possibly August/September 1981
Studio Location Unknown
Merle Kilgore, vocal; JOHNNY CASH, vocal; remaining musicians unknown.

MISTER GARFIELD (Jack Elliott)
   A - ELEKTRA/E-47252 b/w **I'm A One Woman Man** (w/o Cash)

NOTE: Cash is one of several "guest" performers on this Kilgore single on the Elektra Record label.

==

1983
Studio Location Unknown
Johnny Cash, vocal, guitar; Waylon Jennings, vocal, guitar; the following musicians are assumed to have been present: Earl Ball, keyboard; W.S. Holland, drums; Marty Stuart, guitar; Jimmy Tittle, electric bass; Bob Wootton, electric guitar.

WHEN I GET TO GLORY

NOTE: This is an unissued master resulting from Waylon's unplanned appearance at a Cash session. A tape of this master is in my possession and leads me to believe the above musicians were in attendance.

==

APPENDIX B

ALPHABETICAL "BILLBOARD" CHART ENTRIES

TITLE	LABEL & RLSE NO.	DATE ENTERED	WKS ON	PEAK POS.
A BELIEVER SINGS THE TRUTH (a)	CACHET/CL3-9001	Jan 19 80	6	43
A BOY NAMED SUE (s)	CBS 44944	Jul 26 69	14	1 (5)
A BOY NAMED SUE* (s)	CBS 44944	Jul 26 69	12	2 (3)
A SONG TO MAMA (s)	CBS 45428	Sep 4 71	11	37
A THING CALLED LOVE (s)	CBS 45534	Jan 29 72	16	2
A THING CALLED LOVE* (s)	CBS 45534	Feb 5 72	1	103
A THING CALLED LOVE (a)	CBS/KC-31332	Apr 29 72	24	2
A THING CALLED LOVE* (a)	CBS/KC-31332	Apr 29 72	9	112
AFTER THE BALL (s)	CBS 10623	Oct 22 77	12	32
ALL OVER AGAIN* (s)	CBS 41251	Oct 6 58	11	38
ALL OVER AGAIN++ (s)	CBS 41251	Oct 13 58	1	6
ALL OVER AGAIN (s)	CBS 41251	Oct 20 58	18	4
ALLEGHENY (s)	CBS 45929	Sep 29 73	10	69
AMERICA (a)	CBS/KC-31645	Sep 2 72	19	3
AMERICA* (a)	CBS/KC-31645	Sep 16 72	7	176
ANY OLD WIND THAT BLOWS (s)	CBS 45740	Dec 23 72	15	3
ANY OLD WIND THAT BLOWS (a)	CBS/KC-32091	Feb 3 73	14	5
ANY OLD WIND THAT BLOWS* (a)	CBS/KC-32091	Feb 24 73	4	188
AT FOLSOM PRISON (a)	CBS/CL-2839/CS-9639	Jun 15 68	89	1 (4)
AT FOLSOM PRISON* (a)	CBS/CL-2839/CS-9639	Jun 15 68	122	13
AT FOLSOM PRISON (a) (re-entry)	CBS/CL-2839/CS-9639	Apr 4 70	3	38
AT SAN QUENTIN* (a)	CBS/CS-9827	Jul 5 69	70	1 (4)
AT SAN QUENTIN (a)	CBS/CS-9827	Jul 15 69	55	1 (20)
BAD NEWS (s)	CBS 43058	Jul 25 64	15	8
BALLAD OF A TEENAGE QUEEN++ (s)	Sun 283	Jan 20 58	21	1
BALLAD OF A TEENAGE QUEEN (s)	Sun 283	Jan 27 58	23	1 (8)
BALLAD OF A TEENAGE QUEEN* (s)	Sun 283	Feb 3 58	19	16
BALLAD OF A TEENAGE QUEEN (s)	M/P-872.420.7	Feb 25 89	9	45
BALLAD OF IRA HAYES, THE (s)	CBS 43058	Jul 11 64	20	3
BARON, THE (s)	CBS 60516	Mar 21 81	15	10
BARON, THE (a)	CBS/KC-37179	Jul 4 81	12	24
BIG BATTLE, THE (s)	CBS 42301	Mar 31 62	3	24
BIG RIVER++ (s)	Sun 283	Feb 10 58	14	4
BIG RIVER (s)	Sun 283	Mar 3 58	8	1
(on w/ BALLAD OF A TEENAGE QUEEN)				
BIG RIVER (s)	SUN-1121	Dec 5 70	7	41

TITLE	LABEL & RLSE NO.	DATE ENTERED	WKS ON	PEAK POS.
BITTER TEARS* (a)	CBS/CL-2248/CS-9048	Nov 7 64	13	47
BITTER TEARS (a)	CBS/CL-2248/CS-9048	Nov 14 64	20	2
BLISTERED* (s)	CBS 45020	Nov 8 69	8	50
BLISTERED (s)	CBS 45020	Nov 22 69	13	4
BLOOD, SWEAT AND TEARS* (a)	CBS/CL-1930/CS-8730	Mar 16 63	15	80
BOA CONSTRICTOR* (s)	CBS 43763	Sep 3 66	2	107
BOA CONSTRICTOR (s)	CBS 43763	Sep 10 66	5	39
BONANZA* (s)	CBS 42512	Sep 15 62	1	94
BULL RIDER (s)	CBS 11237	Apr 19 80	5	66
BUSTED (s)	CBS 42665	Apr 6 63	3	13
CARRYIN' ON (a)	CBS/CL-2728/CS-9528	Sep 2 67	17	5
CARRYIN' ON* (a)	CBS/CL-2728/CS-9528	Oct 7 67	3	194
CHATTANOOGA CITY LIMITS SIGN (s) (on w/THE REVEREND MR. BLACK)	CBS 02669	Jan 23 82	5	71
CHICKEN IN BLACK (s)	CBS 04513	Jul 14 84	11	45
CHILDREN (s)	CBS 45786	Apr 21 73	9	30
CHRISTMAS SPIRIT, THE* (a)	CBS/CL-2117/CS-8917	Dec 13 69	1	7
CLASS OF '55 (a)	A/S-830.002.1	Jun 21 86	25	15
CLASS OF '55* (a)	A/S-830.002.1	Jun 21 86	12	87
COLD LONESOME MORNING (s)	CBS 11340	Aug 23 80	8	53
COME IN STRANGER (s) (on w/GUESS THINGS HAPPEN THAT WAY)	Sun 295	Jun 2 58	9	1
COME IN STRANGER++ (s)	Sun 295	Jun 2 58	13	6
COME IN STRANGER* (s)	Sun 295	Jun 9 58	9	66
CRY, CRY, CRY (s)	Sun 221	Nov 26 55	1	14
DADDY SANG BASS (s)	CBS 44689	Dec 7 68	20	1 (6)
DADDY SANG BASS* (s)	CBS 44689	Dec 28 68	10	42
DARK AS A DUNGEON* (s)	CBS 42964	Feb 8 64	1	119
DARK AS A DUNGEON (s)	CBS 42964	Mar 7 64	1	49
DESPERADOS (s)	CBS 05594	Sep 14 85	17	15
DON'T MAKE ME GO (s) (on w/ NEXT IN LINE)	Sun 266	Jun 17 57	9	9
DON'T TAKE YOUR GUNS TO TOWN (s)	CBS 41313	Jan 19 59	20	1 (6)
DON'T TAKE YOUR GUNS TO TOWN* (s)	CBS 41313	Jan 19 59	12	32
DOWN THE STREET TO 301* (s)	Sun 343	Jul 11 60	3	85
EVEN COWGIRLS GET THE BLUES (s)	CBS 05896	May 17 86	11	35
EVERYBODY LOVES A NUT (a)	CBS/CL-2492/CS-9292	Jun 4 66	13	5
EVERYBODY LOVES A NUT (s)	COL 43673	Jul 2 66	9	17
EVERYBODY LOVES A NUT* (s)	CBS 43673	Jul 2 66	2	96
EVERYBODY LOVES A NUT* (a)	CBS/CL-2492/CS-9292	Jul 9 66	9	88
FABULOUS JOHNNY CASH* (a)	CBS/CL-1253/CS-8122	Dec 8 58	11	19
FIVE FEET HIGH AND RISING (s)	CBS 41427	Aug 24 59	9	14
FIVE FEET HIGH AND RISING* (s)	CBS 41427	Aug 24 59	3	76
FIVE FEET HIGH AND RISING (a)	CBS/C-32951	Aug 10 74	4	33
FLESH AND BLOOD* (s)	CBS 45269	Dec 12 70	7	54
FLESH AND BLOOD (s)	CBS 45269	Dec 19 70	13	1
FOLSOM PRISON BLUES (s)	Sun 232	Feb 11 56	23	5
FOLSOM PRISON BLUES++ (s)	Sun 232	Feb 11 56	15	4
FOLSOM PRISON BLUES+ (s)	Sun 232	Mar 17 56	13	4
FOLSOM PRISON BLUES* (s) (live)	CBS 44513	May 25 68	12	32
FOLSOM PRISON BLUES (s) (live)	CBS 44513	Jun 1 68	18	1 (4)
FRANKIE'S MAN, JOHNNY* (s)	CBS 41371	Apr 27 59	7	57
FRANKIE'S MAN, JOHNNY (s)	CBS 41371	May 4 59	11	9
FROM SEA TO SHINING SEA (a)	CBS/CL-2647/CS-9447	Feb 10 68	14	9
GENERAL LEE, THE (s)	CBS 02803	Apr 17 82	12	26
GEORGIA ON A FAST TRAIN (s)	CBS 03058	Aug 7 82	8	55

TITLE	LABEL & RLSE NO.	DATE ENTERED	WKS ON	PEAK POS.
GET RHYTHM (s)	Sun 241	Jun 9 56	1	8
(on w/I WALK THE LINE)				
GET RHYTHM+ (s)	Sun 241	Jun 30 56	9	1
(on w/I WALK THE LINE+)				
GET RHYTHM (s)	SUN-1103	Oct 11 69	12	23
GET RHYTHM (a)	SUN-105	Nov 15 69	9	30
GET RHYTHM* (s)	SUN-1103	Nov 15 69	6	60
GET RHYTHM* (a)	SUN-105	Nov 29 69	6	164
GHOST RIDERS IN THE SKY (s)	CBS 10961	May 19 79	16	2
GIVE MY LOVE TO ROSE++ (s)	Sun 279	Mar 9 57	2	13
GIVE MY LOVE TO ROSE (s)	Sun 279	Oct 14 57	19	6
(on w/HOME OF THE BLUES)				
GOIN' BY THE BOOK (s)	M/P-878.292.7	Sep 22 90	4	69
GONE GIRL (s)	CBS 10817	Sep 9 78	8	44
GOODBYE LITTLE DARLING (s)	Sun 331	Nov 9 59	5	22
GOSPEL ROAD (a) (soundtrack)	CBS/KG-32253	May 5 73	14	12
GREATEST HITS #1 (a)	CBS/CL-2678/CS-9478	Jul 22 67	35	1 (3)
GREATEST HITS #1* (a)	CBS/CL-2678/CS-9478	Jul 22 67	16	83
GREATEST HITS #1* (a) (re-entry)	CBS/CL-2678/CS-9478	Aug 16 69	55	82
GREATEST HITS #2 (a)	CBS/KC-30887	Oct 23 71	30	5
GREATEST HITS #2* (a)	CBS/KC-30887	Oct 23 71	8	94
GREATEST HITS #3 (a)	CBS/KC-35637	Jan 13 79	2	49
GUESS THINGS HAPPEN THAT WAY (s)	Sun 295	May 26 58	24	1 (8)
GUESS THINGS HAPPEN THAT WAY++ (s)	Sun 295	May 26 58	20	1
GUESS THINGS HAPPEN THAT WAY* (s)	Sun 295	Jun 2 58	16	11
HAPPINESS IS YOU (a)	CBS/CL-2537/CS-9337	Nov 12 66	26	10
HAPPY TO BE WITH YOU (s)	CBS 43420	Nov 20 65	14	9
HELLO, I'M JOHNNY CASH (a)	CBS/KCS-9943	Feb 14 70	38	1 (4)
HELLO, I'M JOHNNY CASH* (a)	CBS/KCS-9943	Feb 14 70	30	6
HIGHWAYMAN (s)	CBS 04881	May 18 85	20	1
HIGHWAYMAN (a)	CBS/FC-40056	Jun 1 85	62	1
HIGHWAYMAN* (a)	CBS/FC-40056	Jun 1 85	35	92
HIGHWAYMAN (a) (re-entry)	CBS/FC-40056	Aug 25 90	3	59
HIGHWAYMAN II (a)	CBS/C-45240	Mar 17 90	46	4
HOLY LAND, THE (a)	CBS/KCS-9726	Feb 8 69	25	6
HOLY LAND, THE* (a)	CBS/KCS-9726	Feb 15 69	20	54
HOME OF THE BLUES (s)	Sun 279	Sep 16 57	23	5
HOME OF THE BLUES++ (s)	Sun 279	Sep 16 57	20	3
HOME OF THE BLUES* (s)	Sun 279	Oct 14 57	4	88
HONKY TONK GIRL* (s)	CBS 41707	Jul 25 60	1	92
I GOT STRIPES* (s)	CBS 41427	Aug 3 59	11	43
I GOT STRIPES (s)	CBS 41427	Aug 10 59	20	4
I JUST THOUGHT YOU'D LIKE TO KNOW* (s)	Sun 309	Dec 15 58	1	85
I LOVE YOU BECAUSE (s)	Sun 334	Mar 7 60	2	20
I WALK THE LINE (s)	Sun 241	Jun 9 56	43	2
I WALK THE LINE+ (s)	Sun 241	Jun 30 56	37	1
I WALK THE LINE* (s)	Sun 241	Sep 15 56	22	19
I WALK THE LINE (a)	CBS/CL-2190/CS-8990	Jul 11 64	25	1 (4)
I WALK THE LINE* (a)	CBS/CL-2190/CS-8990	Jul 25 64	17	53
I WALK THE LINE* (a) (soundtrack)	CBS/S-30397	Dec 12 70	6	176
I WALK THE LINE (a) (soundtrack)	CBS/S-30397	Dec 19 70	17	9
I WILL ROCK AND ROLL WITH YOU (s)	CBS 10888	Jan 13 79	13	21
I WISH I WAS CRAZY AGAIN (s)	CBS 10742	Nov 17 79	12	22
I WOULD LIKE TO SEE YOU AGAIN (s)	CBS 10681	Feb 11 78	13	12
I WOULD LIKE TO SEE YOU AGAIN (a)	CBS/KC-35313	May 13 78	14	23

TITLE	LABEL & RLSE NO.	DATE ENTERED	WKS ON	PEAK POS.
I'LL SAY IT'S TRUE (s)	CBS 11103	Oct 20 79	7	42
I'M RAGGED BUT I'M RIGHT (s)	CBS 04060	Sep 24 83	4	75
IF I HAD A HAMMER (s)	CBS 45631	Jul 15 72	7	29
IF I WERE A CARPENTER (s)	CBS 45064	Jan 24 70	15	3
IF I WERE A CARPENTER* (s)	CBS 45064	Jan 24 70	8	36
IN THE JAILHOUSE NOW (s)	CBS 42425	Jul 14 62	10	8
IT AIN'T ME, BABE* (s)	CBS 43145	Oct 31 64	8	58
IT AIN'T ME, BABE (s)	CBS 43145	Nov 7 64	22	4
IT'LL BE HER (s)	CBS 10855	Dec 9 78	2	89
IT'S ALL OVER (s)	CBS 10424	Oct 23 76	8	41
IT'S JUST ABOUT TIME* (s)	Sun 309	Dec 15 58	7	47
IT'S JUST ABOUT TIME (s)	Sun 309	Jan 19 59	1	30
JACKSON (s)	CBS 44011	Mar 4 67	17	2
JOHNNY CASH* (a)	CBS/HS-11342	Oct 11 69	2	186
JOHNNY CASH AND HIS WOMAN (a)	CBS/KC-32443	Sep 29 73	15	32
JOHNNY CASH IS COMING TO TOWN (a)	M/P-832.031.1	May 16 87	26	36
JOHNNY CASH SHOW, THE (a)	CBS/KC-30100	Nov 14 70	32	1 (2)
JOHNNY CASH SHOW, THE* (a)	CBS/KC-30100	Nov 14 70	18	44
JOHNNY CASH SONGBOOK, THE (a)	CBS/KH-31602	Nov 11 72	2	43
JUNKIE & THE JUICEHEAD MINUS ME (a)	CBS/KC-33086	Nov 9 74	4	48
KATE (s)	CBS 45590	May 6 72	12	2
KATE* (s)	CBS 45590	May 13 72	7	75
KATY TOO* (s)	Sun 321	Jul 13 59	8	66
KATY TOO (s)	Sun 321	Jul 21 59	11	11
LADY (s)	CBS 10587	Aug 6 77	9	46
LADY CAME FROM BALTIMORE, THE (s)	CBS 10066	Dec 14 74	12	14
LAST GUNFIGHTER BALLAD, THE (s)	CBS 10483	Feb 26 77	9	38
LAST GUNFIGHTER BALLAD, THE (a)	CBS/KC-34314	Mar 5 77	7	29
LAST TIME, THE (s)	CBS 11399	Nov 29 80	4	85
LITTLE DRUMMER BOY, THE* (s)	CBS 41481	Dec 21 59	3	63
LITTLE DRUMMER BOY, THE (s)	CBS 41481	Jan 4 60	1	24
LONG LEGGED GUITAR PICKING MAN (s)	CBS 44158	Jun 24 67	17	6
LOOK AT THEM BEANS (s)	CBS 10177	Jul 26 75	12	17
LOOK AT THEM BEANS (a)	CBS/KC-33814	Oct 11 75	9	38
LOVIN' GIFT, THE (s)	CBS 45758	Jan 20 73	10	27
LUTHER PLAYED THE BOOGIE (s)	Sun 316	Mar 30 59	13	8
MAN IN BLACK* (s)	CBS 45339	Mar 20 71	6	58
MAN IN BLACK (s)	CBS 45339	Mar 27 71	13	3
MAN IN BLACK (a)	CBS/C-30550	Jun 19 71	29	1 (2)
MAN IN BLACK* (a)	CBS/C-30500	Jun 26 71	12	56
MATADOR, THE* (s)	CBS 42880	Oct 26 63	7	44
MATADOR, THE (s)	CBS 42880	Nov 9 63	16	2
MEAN AS HELL (a)	CBS/CL-2446/CS-9246	Apr 2 66	18	4
MEAN EYED CAT (s)	Sun 347	Dec 26 60	1	30
MOBILE BAY (s)	CBS 02189	Jul 25 81	5	60
MR. GARFIELD (s)	CBS 43313	Jul 10 65	13	15
MY OLD KENTUCKY HOME (s)	CBS 10116	Apr 12 75	9	42
NEXT IN LINE (s)	Sun 266	May 27 57	15	9
NEXT IN LINE++ (s)	Sun 266	May 27 57	12	9
NEXT IN LINE* (s)	Sun 266	Jul 1 57	2	99
NIGHT H. WILLIAMS CAME TO TOWN (s)	M/P-888.459.7	Mar 28 87	11	43
NO NEED TO WORRY (s)	CBS 45431	Sep 11 71	13	15
OH, LONESOME ME* (s)	Sun 355	Dec 31 60	2	93
OH, LONESOME ME (s)	Sun 355	Feb 6 61	9	13
OLD TIME FEELING (s)	CBS 10436	Nov 20 76	11	26
ONE ON THE RIGHT IS ON THE LEFT (s)	CBS 43496	Feb 12 66	18	2

TITLE	LABEL & RLSE NO.	DATE ENTERED	WKS ON	PEAK POS.
ONE ON THE RIGHT IS ON THE LEFT* (s)	CBS 43496	Feb 26 66	6	46
ONE PIECE AT A TIME (s)	CBS 10321	Apr 10 76	15	1 (2)
ONE PIECE AT A TIME* (s)	CBS 10321	Apr 17 76	10	29
ONE PIECE AT A TIME (a)	CBS/KC-34193	Jun 12 76	15	2
ONE PIECE AT A TIME* (a)	CBS/KC-34193	Jul 17 76	2	185
ONEY (s)	CBS 45660	Aug 26 72	15	2
ONEY* (s)	CBS 45660	Sep 9 72	4	103
ORANGE BLOSSOM SPECIAL* (s)	CBS 43206	Feb 13 65	6	80
ORANGE BLOSSOM SPECIAL (s)	CBS 43206	Feb 20 65	16	3
ORANGE BLOSSOM SPECIAL (a)	CBS/CL-2309/CS-9109	Mar 20 65	14	3
ORANGE BLOSSOM SPECIAL* (a)	CBS/CL-2309/CS-9109	Mar 20 65	13	49
ORIGINAL GOLDEN HITS #1 (a)	SUN-100	Sep 27 69	20	4
ORIGINAL GOLDEN HITS #1* (a)	SUN-100	Sep 27 69	13	95
ORIGINAL GOLDEN HITS #2 (a)	SUN-101	Sep 27 69	33	3
ORIGINAL GOLDEN HITS #2* (a)	SUN-101	Sep 27 69	8	98
ORLEANS PARISH PRISON (s)	CBS 45997	Feb 23 74	8	52
PAPA WAS A GOOD MAN (s)	CBS 45460	Oct 16 71	11	16
PAPA WAS A GOOD MAN* (s)	CBS 45460	Oct 23 71	3	104
PICK THE WILDWOOD FLOWER (s)	CBS 45938	Nov 17 73	10	34
PRAISE THE LORD AND PASS THE SOUP (s)	CBS 45890	Aug 4 73	7	57
RAGGED OLD FLAG (s)	CBS 46028	Apr 27 74	13	31
RAGGED OLD FLAG (a)	CBS/KC-32917	Jun 15 74	11	16
RAMBLER, THE (a)	CBS/KC-34833	Jul 30 77	8	31
REBEL-JOHNNY YUMA, THE* (s)	CBS 41995	May 29 61	2	108
REBEL-JOHNNY YUMA, THE (s)	CBS 41995	Jun 12 61	2	24
REVEREND MR. BLACK, THE (s)	CBS 02669	Jan 23 82	5	71
RING OF FIRE* (s)	CBS 42788	Jun 1 63	13	17
RING OF FIRE (s)	CBS 42788	Jun 8 63	26	1 (7)
RING OF FIRE* (a)	CBS/CL-2053/CS-8853	Jul 27 63	68	26
RING OF FIRE (a)	CBS/CL-2053/CS-8853	Jan 11 64	31	1 (14)
ROCK ISLAND LINE (s)	SUN-1111	Feb 28 70	7	35
ROCK ISLAND LINE* (s)	SUN-1111	Feb 28 70	1	93
ROSANNA'S GOING WILD (s)	CBS 44373	Dec 23 67	15	2
ROSANNA'S GOING WILD* (s)	CBS 44373	Jan 27 68	2	91
SEASONS OF MY HEART (s)	CBS 41618	Apr 25 60	15	10
SECOND HONEYMOON* (s)	CBS 41707	Jul 4 60	4	79
SECOND HONEYMOON (s)	CBS 41707	Aug 22 60	7	15
SEE RUBY FALL (s) (on w/BLISTERED)	CBS 45020	Nov 8 69	15	4
SEE RUBY FALL* (s) (on w/BLISTERED*)	CBS 45020	Nov 29 69	3	50
SHOWTIME (a)	SUN-106	Nov 29 69	19	14
SHOWTIME* (a)	SUN-106	Dec 27 69	4	181
SILVER (a)	CBS/JC-36086	Sep 8 79	10	28
SILVER STALLION (s)	CBS 73233	Mar 3 90	14	25
SINGING IN VIET NAM TALKING BLUES* (s)	CBS 45393	Jun 19 71	3	124
SINGING IN VIET NAM TALKING BLUES (s)	CBS 45393	Jun 26 71	10	18
SINGING STORY TELLER, THE (a)	SUN-115	May 9 70	2	45
SINGING STORY TELLER, THE* (a)	SUN-115	May 16 70	3	186
SMILING BILL McCALL (s)	CBS 41618	May 9 60	8	13
SMILING BILL McCALL* (s)	CBS 41618	?	?	110
SO DOGGONE LONESOME (s) (on w/FOLSOM PRISON BLUES)	Sun 232	Feb 11 56	23	5
SO DOGGONE LONESOME++ (s)	Sun 232	Feb 18 56	13	6
SO DOGGONE LONESOME+ (s) (on w/FOLSOM PRISON BLUES+)	Sun 232	Mar 17 56	14	4
SOLD OUT OF FLAGPOLES (s)	CBS 10381	Jul 24 76	8	29
SONG OF THE PATRIOT (s)	CBS 11283	Jun 7 80	8	54

TITLE	LABEL & RLSE NO.	DATE ENTERED	WKS ON	PEAK POS.
SONS OF KATIE ELDER, THE* (s)	CBS 43342	Aug 28 65	5	119
SONS OF KATIE ELDER, THE (s)	CBS 43342	Sep 4 65	9	10
STORY SONGS OF TRAINS AND RIVERS (a)	SUN-104	Dec 13 69	24	2
STORY SONGS OF TRAINS AND RIVERS* (a)	SUN-104	Dec 27 69	2	197
STRAIGHT A's IN LOVE (s)	Sun 334	Feb 15 60	10	16
STRAIGHT A's IN LOVE* (s)	Sun 334	Mar 14 60	2	84
STRAWBERRY CAKE (s)	CBS 10279	Feb 7 76	7	54
STRAWBERRY CAKE (a)	CBS/KC-34088	Apr 3 76	8	33
SUNDAY MORNING COMING DOWN* (s)	CBS 45211	Aug 29 70	7	46
SUNDAY MORNING COMING DOWN (s)	CBS 45211	Sep 5 70	15	1 (2)
SUNDAY MORNING COMING DOWN (a)	CBS/C-32240	Oct 6 73	9	35
SURVIVORS, THE (a)	CBS/FC-37961	Apr 24 82	13	21
TENNESSEE FLAT TOP BOX* (s)	CBS 42147	Nov 6 61	7	84
TENNESSEE FLAT TOP BOX (s)	CBS 42147	Dec 18 61	14	11
TEXAS '47 (s)	CBS 10237	Nov 15 75	12	35
THANKS A LOT (s)	Sun 316	Mar 30 59	9	12
THAT OLD WHEEL (s)	M/P-870.688.7	Sep 24 88	19	21
THAT'S THE TRUTH (s)	CBS 04428	May 12 84	5	84
THERE AIN'T NO GOOD CHAIN GANG (s)	CBS 10742	May 20 78	13	2
THERE YOU GO (s)	Sun 258	Dec 22 56	27	2
THERE YOU GO++ (s)	Sun 258	Dec 29 56	22	2
THERE YOU GO+ (s)	Sun 258	Jan 8 57	20	1
TRAIN OF LOVE (s) (on w/THERE YOU GO)	Sun 258	Dec 22 56	23	7
TRAIN OF LOVE++ (s)	Sun 258	Jan 12 57	12	2
TRAIN OF LOVE+ (s)	Sun 258	Feb 9 57	13	1
UNDERSTAND YOUR MAN* (s)	CBS 42964	Feb 15 64	8	35
UNDERSTAND YOUR MAN (s)	CBS 42964	Feb 22 64	22	1 (6)
W. LEE O'DANIEL (AND THE LIGHT CRUST DOUGHBOYS) (s)	M/P-870.010.7	Dec 12 87	5	72
WATER FROM THE WELLS OF HOME (a)	M/P-834.778.1	Dec 17 88	21	48
WAYS OF A WOMAN IN LOVE (s)	Sun 302	Aug 25 58	16	2
WAYS OF A WOMAN IN LOVE* (s)	Sun 302	Aug 25 58	11	24
WAYS OF A WOMAN IN LOVE++ (s)	Sun 302	Aug 25 58	7	2
WE MUST BELIEVE IN MAGIC (s)	CBS 03524	Feb 26 83	2	84
WHAT DO I CARE (s)	CBS 41251	Oct 13 58	15	7
WHAT DO I CARE++ (s)	CBS 41251	Oct 13 58	1	11
WHAT DO I CARE* (s)	CBS 41251	Oct 20 58	8	52
WHAT IS TRUTH* (s)	CBS 45134	Apr 11 70	8	19
WHAT IS TRUTH (s)	CBS 45134	Apr 18 70	14	3
WIND CHANGES, THE (s)	CBS 44288	Oct 28 67	6	60
WITHOUT LOVE (s)	CBS 11424	Jan 24 81	5	78
WORLD NEEDS A MELODY, THE (s)	CBS 45679	Sep 23 72	8	35
WORLD OF JOHNNY CASH, THE (a)	CBS/GP-29	Jun 6 70	38	2
WORLD OF JOHNNY CASH, THE* (a)	CBS/GP-29	Jun 6 70	34	54
YOU BEAT ALL I EVER SAW (s)	CBS 43921	Dec 24 66	13	20
YOU DREAMER YOU (s)	CBS 41371	May 11 59	11	13
YOU'RE THE NEAREST THING TO HEAVEN++ (s)	Sun 302	Sep 1 58	7	5
YOU'RE THE NEAREST THING TO HEAVEN (s)	Sun 302	Oct 20 58	9	5

BIBLIOGRAPHY

Cash, Johnny. *Man in Black.* Zondervan Publishing House. Grand Rapids, Michigan. 1975.

Dickerson, Jim. *Sun Record Reunion: Together Again in Memphis.* Nine-O-One Publications. Memphis, Tennessee. 1986.

Escott, Colin and Martin Hawkins. *Sun Records: The Discography.* Bear Family Publications. Vollersode, Germany. 1987.

Johnny Cash: A Man and His Music. Cherry Lane Music Company. Port Chester, New York (Distributed by Hal Leonard Publishing Corporation). 1993.

Krogsgaard, Michael. *Positively Bob Dylan.* Popular Culture, Ink Press. Ann Arbor, Michigan. 1991.

Pugh, Ronnie. "Ernest Tubb Discography," *Journal of Country Music* XI:1 (1985) Country Music Foundation. Nashville, Tennessee.

Smith, John L. *The Johnny Cash Discography.* Greenwood Publishing Group. Westport, Connecticut. 1985.

_____ . *One Step over the Line: The Authorized Waylon Jennings Recording History.* Popular Culture, Ink Press. Ann Arbor, Michigan. Spring 1994.

SESSIONS INDEX

115
Wittaker, John (*see*: Twenty-first
   Century Singers)
WIZARD ON THE HILL: (I) 107-08,
   112, 112n
WO IST ZU HAUSE MAMA (FIVE
   FEET HIGH AND RISING): (I) 17
Wolfe, Danny: (I) (composer): 12, 14
Wolfe, Pam: (II) (composer): 55
Wolfe, Rusty: (II) (composer): 55
Womack, Casey (*see*: One Bad Pig)
W-O-M-A-N: (I) 104-05, 105n, 108,
   109n
Wonderful World Of Disney: (II) 47n
Wood, Bobby: (I) 28, 57, 69, 110-11,
   113-14, 123; (II) 2-3, 3n, 4, 4n, 5,
   5n, 7, 7n, 8-9, 9n, 10, 41-44, 47-49, 57
Wood, Del: (I) 36, 36n, 37
Wood, R.: (I) (composer): 15
WOODCARVER, THE: (II) 55
Woodland Studio: (I) 111-12; (II)
   3, 15, 12, 165
Wooley, Sheb: (I) (composer): 24, 30
Woolfe, Stephanie: (I) 44-46, 53, 61-62,
   66, 76, 80, 85, 106, 114
Wootton, Bob: (I) 41n, 42, 42n, 43-53,
   55-68, 68n, 70-74, 76-101, 103-105,
   105n, 108, 108n, 111-12, 115-22,
   122n; (II) 10, 17-18, 25-26, 28, 30,
   36, 47, 160, 166
Word Records: (II) 13n
Worf, Glenn: (II) 57-58, 60-61
WORLD NEEDS A MELODY, THE: (I)
   50
WORLD'S GONNA FALL ON YOU,
   THE: (I) 47
Worley, Paul: (II) 7
WORRIED MAN BLUES: (I) 26; (II)
   16, 16n
WOULD YOU RECOGNIZE JESUS: (I)
   77
Wray, Robert: (I) 111, 113-14, 120, 123;
   (II) 2-3, 44
WRECK OF THE OLD '97: (I) 8, 28, 43,
   45, 74-75, 77, 87-88, 112; (II) 162
Wren, Christopher: (I) (composer): 45,
   50-53, 71
Wright, G.E.: (I) (composer): 21

Wright, William: (I) 46, 109-10
WRINKLED, CRINKLED, WADDED
   DOLLAR BILL: (I) 44
Wyatt, Cynthia: (II) 43

YABBA DABBA DOO: (II) 48
Yandell, Paul: (I) 82
YANKEE DOODLE (*see*: COLLAGE
   OF YESTERDAY)
Yates, JoAnne Cash: (II) 29, 29n, 45,
   46n
YOU AND ME: (I) 88
YOU AND TENNESSEE: (I) 38
YOU ARE MY FLOWER: (I) 64; (II) 14
YOU ARE MY SUNSHINE: (I) 43
YOU BEAT ALL I EVER SAW: (I) 37,
   115; (II) 9
YOU COMB HER HAIR: (I) 35, 35n
YOU DREAMER YOU: (I) 14n, 16 (*see
   also*: OH WHAT A DREAM)
YOU GIVE ME MUSIC: (II) 2-3
YOU JUST CAN'T BEAT JESUS
   CHRIST: (I) 107
YOU MUST BELIEVE IN MAGIC: (I)
   113 (*see also*: WE MUST BELIEVE
   IN MAGIC)
YOU REMEMBERED ME: (I) 22, 66
YOU TELL ME: (I) 10-11
YOU WILD COLORADO: (I) 31, 31n
YOU WIN AGAIN: (I) 11, 11n
YOU WON'T HAVE FAR TO GO: (I)
   22
YOU'LL BE ALL RIGHT: (I) 39
YOU'LL GET YOURS AND I'LL GET
   MINE: (I) 91-92, 96, 96n, 99
Young, Chip: (I) 50, 50n, 57
Young, Jimmy: (I) 58
Young, Neil: (II) 69, 69n
Young, Reggie: (I) 66-68; (II): 4-5,
   7-10, 13, 47-49, 51, 51n, 52-55, 165
Young, Steve: (II) (composer): 17n
Young'un Sound Studio: (I) 120
YOUR LOVE IS MY REFUGE: (I) 80
YOU'RE A PART OF ME: (I) 89
YOU'RE DRIFTIN' AWAY: (I) 121
YOU'VE GOT A NEW LIGHT
   SHINING IN YOUR EYES: (I) 49
YOU'RE MY BABY: (I) 3, 3n, 5n

About the Compiler

JOHN L. SMITH is an independent discographer, retired after 30 years with American Telephone & Telegraph. His interests include anthropology, with specific attention to the culture of the Native Americans of the Plains. He is the compiler of *The Johnny Cash Discography* (Greenwood, 1985) and *I Ain't No Ordinary Dude—A Bio-Discography of Waylon Jennings*. His articles have appeared in *Journal of Country Music, Plains Anthropologist,* and *Powwow Trails.*